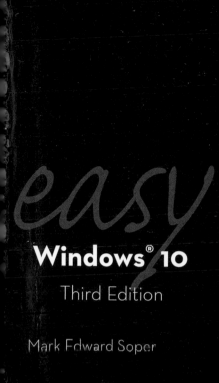

easy

Windows® 10

Third Edition

Mark Edward Soper

que®

800 East 96th Street
Indianapolis, Indiana 46240

ONLINE CONTENT
Additional tasks are available to you at informit.com/title/9780789759795. Click the Downloads tab to access the links to download the PDF file.

CONTENTS

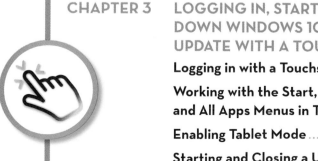
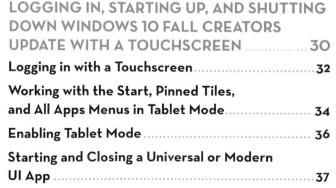

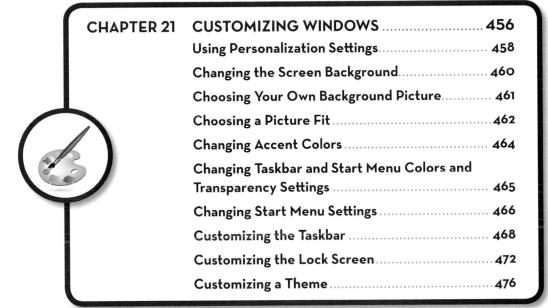

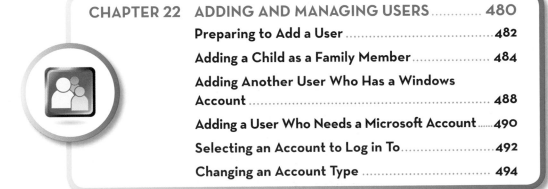

ONLINE CONTENT

Additional tasks are available to you at informit.com/title/9780789759795. Click the Downloads tab to access the links to download the PDF file.

EASY WINDOWS® 10

ISBN-13: 978-0-7897-5979-5
ISBN-10: 0-7897-5979-9

Library of Congress Control Number: 2017960305

1 18

TRADEMARKS

WARNING AND DISCLAIMER

SPECIAL SALES

For information about buying this title in bulk quantities, or for special sales opportunities (which may include electronic versions; custom cover designs; and content particular to your business, training goals, marketing focus, or branding interests), please contact our corporate sales department at corpsales@pearsoned.com or (800) 382-3419.

For government sales inquiries, please contact governmentsales@pearsoned.com.

For questions about sales outside the U.S., please contact intlcs@pearson.com.

Editor-in-Chief
Greg Wiegand

Senior Acquisitions Editor
Laura Norman

Development Editor
The Wordsmithery LLC

Managing Editor
Sandra Schroeder

Senior Project Editor
Lori Lyons

Indexer
Ken Johnson

Proofreader
Gill Editorial Services

Technical Editor
Vince Avarello

Editorial Assistant
Cindy Teeters

Cover Designer
Chuti Prasertsith

Compositor
Bronkella Publishing

ABOUT THE AUTHOR

Mark Edward Soper has been using Microsoft Windows since version 1.0, and since 1992 he has taught thousands of computer troubleshooting and network students across the country how to use Windows as part of their work and everyday lives. Mark is the author of *Easy Windows 10, Easy Windows 8.1, Easy Windows 8, Easy Microsoft Windows 7, Teach Yourself Windows 7 in 10 Minutes,* and *Using Microsoft Windows Live.* Mark also has contributed to Que's *Special Edition Using* series on Windows Me, Windows XP, and Windows Vista, as well as *Easy Windows Vista* and *Windows 7 In Depth.* In addition, he has written two books about Windows Vista: *Maximum PC Microsoft Windows Vista Exposed* and *Unleashing Microsoft Windows Vista Media Center.*

When he's not teaching, learning, or writing about Microsoft Windows, Mark stays busy with many other technology-related activities. He has written three books on computer troubleshooting, including *The PC and Gadget Help Desk: A Do-It-Yourself Guide to Troubleshooting and Repairing.* He is a longtime contributor to *Upgrading and Repairing PCs,* working on the 11th through 18th, 20th, and subsequent editions. Mark has co-authored *Upgrading and Repairing Networks,* Fifth Edition, written several books on CompTIA A+ Certification (including two titles covering the 2016 exams), a guest column on certification for Computerworld.com, and two books about digital photography: *Easy Digital Cameras* and *The Shot Doctor: The Amateur's Guide to Taking Great Digital Photos.* Mark also has become a video content provider for Que Publishing and InformIT and has posted many blog entries and articles at InformIT.com, MaximumPC.com, and other websites. In addition, Mark has taught digital photography, digital imaging, and Microsoft Office for Ivy Tech Corporate College's southwest Indiana campus in Evansville, Indiana, and Windows and Microsoft Office for the University of Southern Indiana's continuing education department.

DEDICATION

To Cheryl, as we continue our journey together.

ACKNOWLEDGMENTS

This book might have my name on the cover, but plenty of people behind the scenes make it possible and provide the encouragement needed to create a useful and enjoyable work. Thank you for reading this book. Here are some of the people who helped make it possible.

First of all, I humbly thank God for His blessings, including this wonderful world, the many peoples in it, and the gift of eternal life He offers through His Son, Jesus. It's amazing to me that people all around the world can read my books, but God's love is even more amazing.

My wife, Cheryl, is the reason I am a technology writer. Her encouragement has helped me every moment since we first met. We celebrate 41 years of marriage this year, and more than that as a team. She is truly a gift from God.

I have used Microsoft Windows since it was first used as the home for a simple paint program and a simple word-processing program that needed MS-DOS to work. Windows has come a long way, and here are some of the people who gave me the opportunity to learn about it.

Thanks go to Jim Peck and Mayer Rubin, for whom I taught thousands of students how to troubleshoot systems running Windows 3.1, 95, and 98; magazine editors Edie Rockwood and Ron Kobler, for assigning me to dig deeper into Windows; Ed Bott, who provided my first opportunity to contribute to a major Windows book; Scott Mueller, who asked me to help with *Upgrading and Repairing Windows*; Ivy Tech Corporate College and the University of Southern Indiana, for teaching opportunities; Bob Cowart and Brian Knittel, for helping continue my real-world Windows education. And, of course, the Microsoft family.

Thanks also to my family, both for their encouragement over the years and for the opportunity to explain various Windows features and fix things that go wrong.

I also want to thank the editorial and design team that Que put together for this book.

Many thanks to Greg Wiegand and Laura Norman for the opportunity to write another *Easy* series book, and thanks to Charlotte Kughen, Vince Averello, and Lori Lyons. Thanks also to Cindy Teeters for keeping track of invoices and making sure payments were timely. Finally, thanks to Ken, Tricia, and Karen.

I have worked with Que Publishing and Pearson since 1999, and I'm looking forward to many more years—and books—together!

READER SERVICES

Register your copy of *Easy Windows 10* at informit. com for convenient access to downloads, updates, and corrections as they become available. To start the registration process, go to informit.com/register and log in or create an account*. Enter the product ISBN, 9780789759795, and click Submit. When the process is complete, you will find any available bonus content under Registered Products.

*Be sure to check the box that you would like to hear from us to receive exclusive discounts on future editions of this product.

INTRODUCTION

WHY THIS BOOK WAS WRITTEN

Que Publishing's *Easy* series is famous for providing accurate, simple, step-by-step instructions for popular software and operating systems. Windows 10 Fall Creators Update (or FCU for short) is the latest major update to Windows 10. FCU provides better system protection, photo editing and organizing, new integration with Spotify for digital music fans, easier use of online storage, and much more. Whether you use a mouse or touchpad and keyboard, prefer a touchscreen, or use a tablet, *Easy Windows 10*, Third Edition, is written to help you use Windows 10 FCU's new and improved features the way you prefer.

Whether you're a veteran Windows user or new to Windows and computers, there's a lot to learn. *Easy Windows 10*, Third Edition, gives you a painless and enjoyable way to discover the essential features of Windows. I spent months with Windows 10 FCU to discover its new and improved features and learn the best ways to show you what it does, and you get the benefit: an easy-to-read visual guide that gets you familiar with the latest Microsoft product in a hurry.

Your time is valuable, so this book concentrates on features you're likely to use every day. The objective: to help you use Windows to make your computing life better, more productive, and even more fun.

HOW TO READ *EASY WINDOWS 10*, THIRD EDITION

So, what's the best way to read this book?

You have a few options, based on what you know about computers and Windows. Try one of these:

- Start at Chapter 1, "What's New and Improved in Windows 10 Fall Creators Update," and work your way through.

- Go straight to the chapters that look the most interesting.
- Hit the table of contents or the index and go directly to the sections that tell you stuff you don't know already.

Any of these methods will work—and to help you get a better feel for what's inside, here's a closer look at what's in each chapter.

BEYOND THE TABLE OF CONTENTS—WHAT'S INSIDE

Chapter 1, "What's New and Improved in Windows 10 Fall Creators Update," provides a quick overview of the most important new and improved features in Windows 10 FCU, including new photo- and video-editing features in Photos, People's new Timeline and pinning features, OneDrive Files on Demand, combining 3D objects with your device's camera with the Mixed Reality Viewer, game broadcasting with the Mixer service, more powerful voice interaction with Cortana, Paint 3D for combining 3D objects with traditional 2D graphics, Windows Defender Security Center, more uses for Windows Ink, and tab previews in the Edge browser. If you're reading this book mainly to brush up on what's new and different, start here and follow the references to the chapters with more information.

Chapter 2, "Upgrading to Windows 10 Fall Creators Update," is designed for users of Windows 7 or Windows 8.1 who are upgrading to Windows 10 FCU and for existing Windows 10 users who want to get Fall Creators Update right away rather than waiting for Windows Update. This chapter covers the updating process and helps you make the best choices along the way.

Chapter 3, "Logging In, Starting Up, and Shutting Down Windows 10 Fall Creators Update with a Touchscreen," shows you how to log in to Windows 10 FCU, how to use Tablet mode, how to find and launch programs from the Start or All Apps menu, how to use the touch keyboard or handwriting interface, how to add emojis, how to use voice recognition, how to lock and unlock your computer, and how to shut it down or put it into Sleep mode.

Chapter 4, "Logging In to Windows 10 Fall Creators Update and Customizing the Start Menu," helps you understand how to use both panes of the Start menu, customize it, use keyboard shortcuts, lock and unlock your system from the keyboard, and shut it down or put it into sleep mode.

Chapter 5, "Using Cortana Search," provides step-by-step instructions on how to use Cortana in Desktop or Tablet modes, enable and use voice search, create and edit voice reminders, start apps by voice, add Cortana to iOS or Android mobile devices, use the new "Pick up where I left off" feature, and turn off Cortana's digital assistant features.

Chapter 6, "Running Apps," shows you how to search for, run, switch between, change window size, and close desktop and Modern UI apps. You also learn how to snap windows, use Windows Peek to hide open windows, open files within apps, add apps to the Taskbar, and use jump lists.

Chapter 7, "Web Browsing with Microsoft Edge," helps you use new and improved features such as importing and exporting favorites, cookies, and settings; working with tab previews; adding tabs to the taskbar; switching to/from full-screen views; using Zoom; using Reading View; reading EPUB books and PDFs; using Web Notes; finding more browser extensions; and adjusting privacy settings.

Chapter 8, "Groove Music," shows you how to manage your digital music collection with Groove Music with new features such as an enhanced playlist feature. You also learn how to enjoy free streaming music with Spotify for Windows 10.

Chapter 9, "Taking, Editing, and Sharing Photos and Videos," is your guide to the Camera and Photos apps. You'll discover how to capture videos and photos with your device's built-in webcam or backward-facing camera and learn new ways to enjoy your

photos and videos with Photos features including Collections, Creations, Video Remix, enhancements, trimming videos, and adding slow motion to videos.

Chapter 10, "Enjoying Videos, TV, and Movies," shows you how to manage and add to your digital video, TV, and movie collection using Movies & TV. New features covered include support for 360-degree video, an improved interface, casting video to devices such as set-top streaming video boxes, and easier access to video files on media servers on your network.

Chapter 11, "Connecting with Friends," shows you how to use the new and improved People, Facebook, Mail, Calendar, and Skype apps in Windows 10 FCU to stay in touch with friends and family.

Chapter 12, "News, Weather, Sports, Maps, and Money," introduces you to key features in the News, Weather, Sports, Maps, and Money apps.

Chapter 13, "Using Windows Ink," introduces you to the improved Windows Ink Workspace and its pen-enabled apps. Create notes, reminders, and simple drawings you can store and share, and learn how to look for and use Ink in other apps.

Chapter 14, "Storing and Finding Your Files," helps you manage files, folders, and drives, copy/move files safely, avoid data loss with Recycle Bin and filename conflict management, and use the new OneDrive Files on Demand cloud/local storage feature.

Chapter 15, "Discovering and Using Windows 10 FCU's Tools and Accessories," helps you locate Windows tools and accessories and use Alarms & Clock, Calculator's new date calculator feature, and new 3D apps (Paint 3D, Mixed Reality Viewer, and Print 3D).

Chapter 16, "Using the Microsoft Store," takes you on a tour of the preferred way to get free and commercial apps for your device. Learn how to search for apps, download free apps, buy new apps, review apps, and uninstall apps.

Chapter 17, "Gaming," shows you how to customize the new Microsoft Solitaire Collection, enjoy a new version of Minesweeper, shop for games in the

Microsoft Store, use the Game bar to optimize your system for gaming, capture game screens and videos, use the new broadcast games feature, create and use an Xbox Live account, connect to your Xbox One, stream your games to your Windows 10 device, and use the new Xbox Smart Glass app to configure your Xbox.

Chapter 18, "Printing and Scanning," shows you how to use your printer or multifunction device to print documents and photos on plain or photo paper, and how to scan documents and photos with your scanner or multifunction device.

Chapter 19, "Managing Windows 10 Fall Creators Update," helps you master Windows 10 FCU's improved Settings features, such as individual volume controls for specific apps, streamlined Display dialogs, improved Battery Saver, Storage Sense, system health, streamlined Bluetooth dialogs, enhanced touchpad configuration, connections to Android or iOS smartphones, repairing malfunctioning apps, new video playback settings, game features, and privacy settings.

Chapter 20, "Networking Your Home," shows you how to connect to wireless networks, create a mobile hotspot, and use the HomeGroup feature to set up and manage a network with Windows 7, Windows 8/8.1, and Windows 10 computers.

Chapter 21, "Customizing Windows," helps you make Windows look the way you want by tweaking the Start menu, desktop background, screen saver, taskbar, and mouse pointers.

Chapter 22, "Adding and Managing Users," introduces you to different ways to set up a Windows login for users, how to add additional users, and how to create Child accounts for use with Microsoft Family parental controls.

Chapter 23, "Protecting Your System," shows you how to keep Windows 10 FCU updated, protect and recover your files with File History backups, and use the new Windows Defender Security Center.

Chapter 24, "System Maintenance and Performance," helps you improve system speed and battery life, check disk capacity, solve disk errors, learn more about what Windows is doing by using Task Manager, and learn to use Reset and Troubleshooters to solve problems that can prevent your system from running properly.

Baffled by PC and Windows terminology? Check out the Glossary, available online!

There's so much to say about Windows 10 that some book content is online. Be sure to go to informit.com/register to get every bit of *Easy Windows 10* goodness.

Enjoy!

WHAT'S NEW AND IMPROVED IN WINDOWS 10 FALL CREATORS UPDATE

Windows 10 Fall Creators Update, or FCU for short, brings more new features for all kinds of users. Whether you like to create stories with photos, need easier access to cloud storage, or want to learn more about creating and using 3D imagery, FCU brings you these and many more new and improved features.

Creating a 3D scene with Paint 3D

Setting up game broadcasting

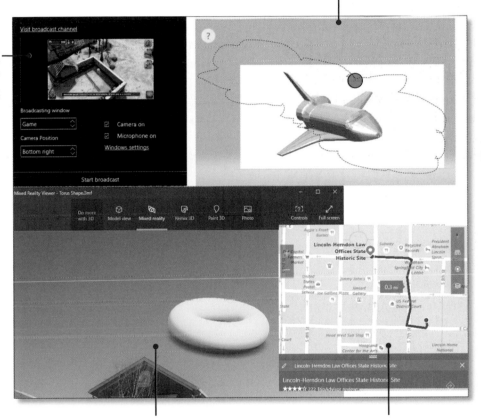

Combining a live photo with a 3D object with Mixed Reality Viewer

Using Windows Ink in Maps to calculate walking distances

DO MORE WITH PICTURES AND VIDEOS IN PHOTOS

Photos is more than storage for your favorite pictures. It now creates collections from the photos you took on a particular day, provides more powerful effects (including Windows Ink support), adds slow motion to videos, and makes adding music to slideshows easier than ever before.

Start

1 Slideshow timings are automatically synchronized to music.

2 Plenty of creative filters enable you to transform an ordinary photo.

Continued

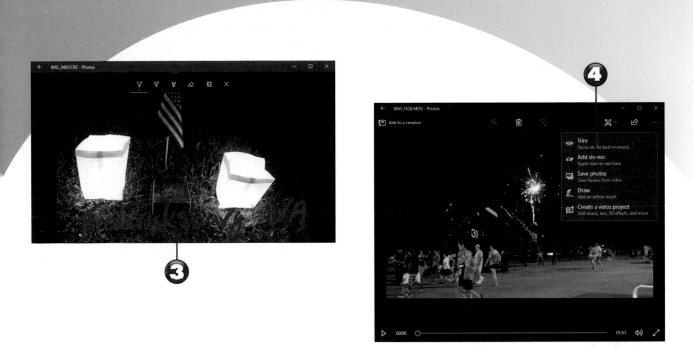

3 Add Windows Ink to your favorite photos and videos for captions, callouts, and more.

4 Add slow-motion effects, trim unwanted footage, and create a project from your favorite video captures.

End

NOTE

Learn More About Photos and Windows Ink   Discover more features of Photos in Chapter 9, "Taking, Editing, and Sharing Photos and Videos." See Chapter 13, "Using Windows Ink," to learn more about using Windows Ink. ∎

PICK UP WHERE I LEFT OFF

You can now link your iOS or Android smartphones with Windows 10 FCU, which enables you to start a task on your smartphone and finish it on Windows 10.

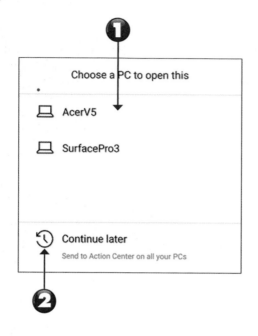

 Start

1 After you have linked your smartphone to your Windows account, use an app's Share feature to share to a particular PC running Windows 10 FCU for immediate action.

2 Share to the Action Center on all your PCs to continue later.

3 Open the Action Center to see a share from your smartphone. Click or tap it, and the task continues immediately.

End

NOTE

See Settings for Phone Linking and More Settings now supports more devices with more features. Learn all about it in Chapter 19, "Managing Windows Fall Creators Update." ■

PEOPLE TIMELINE AND PINNING

The People app makes managing personal and business contacts easier than ever before. New Timeline and pinning options help you track activity and have one-click access to your best friends and closest family members.

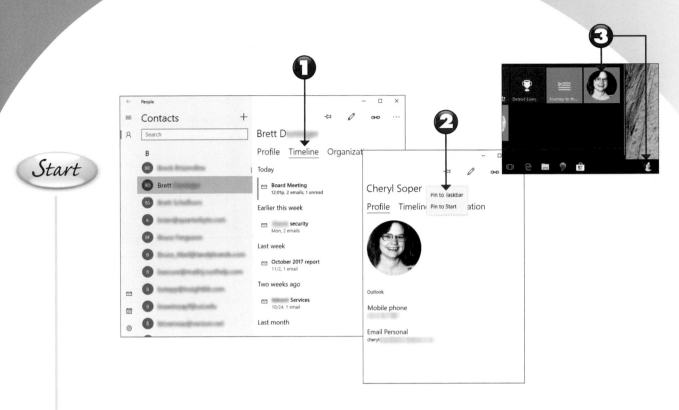

Start

① After you select a contact in People, click or tap **Timeline** for a history of emails or other connections.

② You can pin your contacts to the Taskbar or Start menu.

③ Click or tap a pinned contact to go directly to that person's Profile tab.

End

NOTE

Staying in Touch   See Chapter 11, "Connecting with Friends," to learn more about People, Facebook, Mail, and Skype. ■

MANAGE FILES WITH ONE DRIVE FILES ON DEMAND

With more and more users running tablets, laptops, or convertible 2-in-1 devices with SSD or flash storage, Microsoft's new OneDrive Files on Demand helps you use your cloud-based data as easily as you use locally stored files.

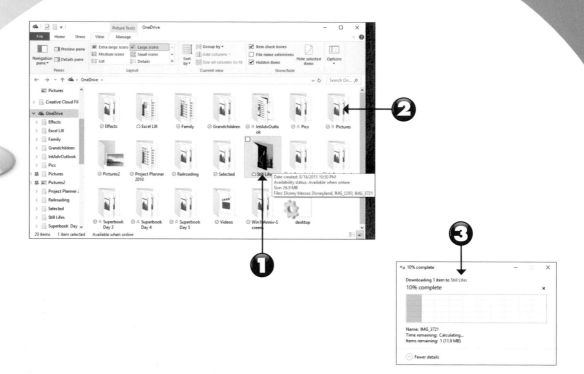

Start

1 This folder is stored on OneDrive.

2 This folder is stored locally and on OneDrive.

3 When you open a file stored on OneDrive, it is quickly downloaded to your system.

End

NOTE

Discovering More OneDrive Features See Chapter 14, "Storing and Finding Your Files," to learn more about using OneDrive and local storage in Windows 10 FCU. ■

EXPERIENCE MIXED REALITY

Windows 10 FCU includes new support for mixed-reality, which enables computer-generated images to be combined with real-life scenery. You can buy mixed-reality goggles made for Windows 10 FCU, but you can also experience mixed reality by using your device's webcam with the new Mixed Reality Viewer.

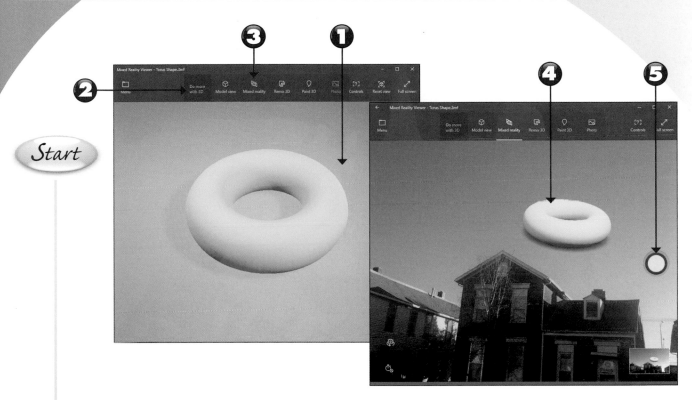

Start

1. Open a 3D object in Mixed Reality Viewer.

2. Open the **Do more with 3D** menu.

3. Select **Mixed reality**.

4. After the viewer starts your device's webcam, position and adjust the size of the object against the background captured by the webcam.

5. Take a picture when you're satisfied.

End

NOTE

Immerse Yourself in 3D   You can learn more about Windows 10 FCU's new and improved 3D features in Chapter 15, "Discovering and Using Windows 10 FCU's Tools and Accessories." ▪

GAME BROADCASTING

Windows 10 FCU brings many new and improved gaming features to your PC, including the ability to broadcast your gameplay live on Mixer.

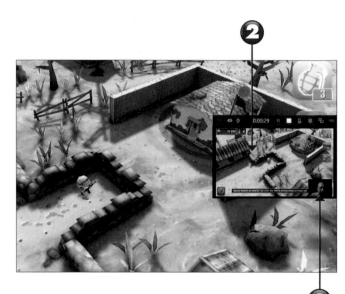

Start

1 After you start your game, use the Game bar to set up and start broadcasting.

2 Keep an eye on your broadcast while you continue to play.

3 You can provide live audio or live audio and video commentary.

End

NOTE

Get Your Game On   See Chapter 17, "Gaming," to learn more about the new gaming features, including the return of Minesweeper! ▪

EXPLORE CORTANA'S NEW POWERS

Cortana can now respond to a wide range of questions and supports Cortana-enabled speakers. It also provides more help than ever to keep your life organized.

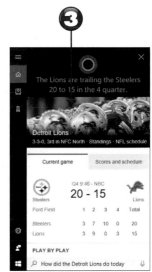

1 You can now create monthly reminders with Cortana.

2 Connected home and connected services are just two of the new ways that Cortana works harder for you.

3 Ask for news, weather, or sports, and Cortana has the information you need.

NOTE

More Cortana to Discover See Chapter 5, "Using Cortana Search," to learn more about using Cortana. ■

GET CREATIVE WITH PAINT 3D

Windows 10 FCU now includes Paint 3D as the replacement for the venerable Paint (which is still available free from the Microsoft Store). Paint 3D lets you combine existing and new 2D and 3D objects into new projects that can be saved as 3D or 2D files.

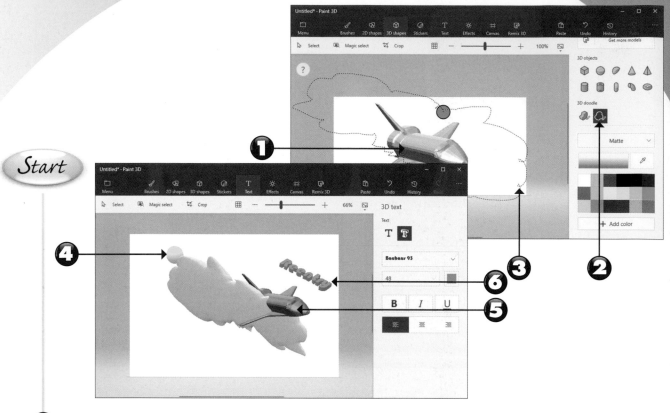

Start

1 Open a 3D object supplied with Paint 3D or download one.

2 Add 3D objects or doodles.

3 Position the 3D objects or doodles.

4 Add additional objects.

5 Change the color of objects as desired.

6 Add 3D text effects.

End

NOTE

More 3D Elsewhere See Chapter 15 to learn more about using Paint 3D and other new 3D apps. ■

STAY SAFE WITH WINDOWS DEFENDER SECURITY CENTER

Windows Defender is now more than an antivirus app. It's part of the new Windows Defender Security Center.

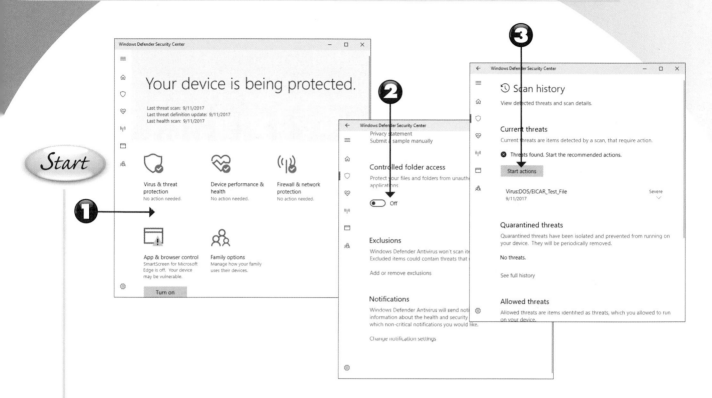

1 It provides real-time monitoring of virus protection, device performance and health, firewall and network protection, and app and browser control.

2 Enable the new **Controlled folder access** option for protection against ransomware.

3 Removing detected threats is a click or tap away.

NOTE

More Protection   See Chapter 23, "Protecting Your System," to learn more about using Windows Defender Security Center and other system protection features. ■

USE WINDOWS INK WITH MAPS

Plan a walking tour, a flight, or a Sunday drive by using Windows Ink along with Maps.

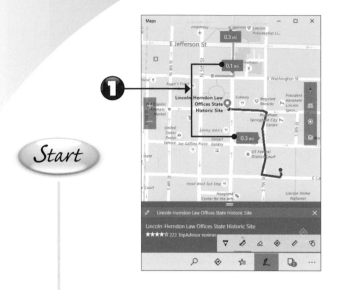

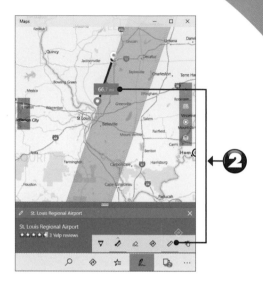

① Use Ink along city streets to figure out how far to walk to the next tourist attraction.

② Use Ink's ruler tool to get the straight-line distance between airports.

NOTE

More Maps Plus Ink See Chapter 12, "News, Weather, Sports, Maps, and Money," to learn more about using Maps, and see Chapter 13 to learn more about using Windows Ink.

EDGE TAB PREVIEW BAR

The Edge browser now offers tab previews, so you know exactly what's lurking behind each tab. No more surprises!

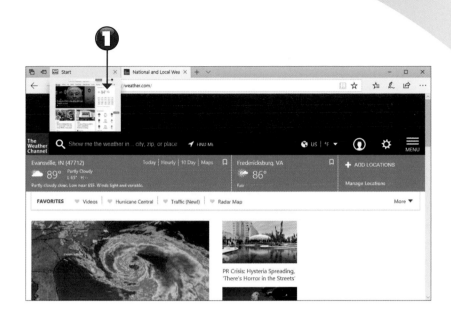

 Start

 Hover your mouse over a tab that is not active to see the contents of that tab.

End

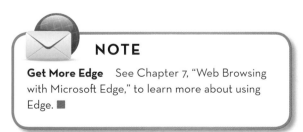

NOTE

Get More Edge See Chapter 7, "Web Browsing with Microsoft Edge," to learn more about using Edge. ∎

UPGRADING TO WINDOWS 10 FALL CREATORS UPDATE

You can install Windows 10 Fall Creators Update (FCU) as an upgrade to either Windows 7 or Windows 8.1, retaining your existing apps, settings, and personal data. You can purchase the software license and upgrade from Microsoft or from third-party vendors in two forms: a downloadable file or a USB flash drive that contains the upgrade files. If you don't want to wait for your current Windows 10 installation to be upgraded to Windows 10 FCU via Windows Update, you can start the upgrade process manually. This chapter covers the process of upgrading to Windows 10 FCU using the media creation tool to help you download the upgrade.

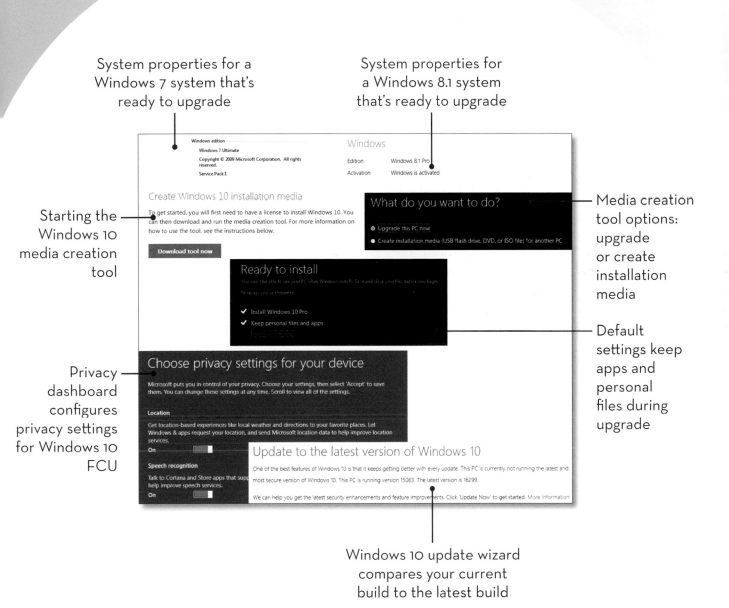

System properties for a Windows 7 system that's ready to upgrade

System properties for a Windows 8.1 system that's ready to upgrade

Starting the Windows 10 media creation tool

Media creation tool options: upgrade or create installation media

Default settings keep apps and personal files during upgrade

Privacy dashboard configures privacy settings for Windows 10 FCU

Windows 10 update wizard compares your current build to the latest build

Windows edition

Windows 7 Ultimate

Copyright © 2009 Microsoft Corporation. All rights reserved.

Service Pack 1

Windows

Edition   Windows 8.1 Pro

Activation   Windows is activated

Create Windows 10 installation media

To get started, you will first need to have a license to install Windows 10. You can then download and run the media creation tool. For more information on how to use the tool, see the instructions below.

Download tool now

What do you want to do?

○ Upgrade this PC now

○ Create installation media (USB flash drive, DVD, or ISO file) for another PC

Ready to install

You won't be able to use your PC while Windows installs. Save and close your files before you begin.

To recap, you've chosen to:

✓ Install Windows 10 Pro

✓ Keep personal files and apps

Choose privacy settings for your device

Microsoft puts you in control of your privacy. Choose your settings, then select 'Accept' to save them. You can change these settings at any time. Scroll to view all of the settings.

Location

Get location-based experiences like local weather and directions to your favorite places. Let Windows & apps request your location, and send Microsoft location data to help improve location services.

On

Speech recognition

Talk to Cortana and Store apps that support help improve speech services.

On

Update to the latest version of Windows 10

One of the best features of Windows 10 is that it keeps getting better with every update. This PC is currently not running the latest and most secure version of Windows 10. This PC is running version 15063. The latest version is 16299.

We can help you get the latest security enhancements and feature improvements. Click 'Update Now' to get started. More information

DETERMINING THE UPGRADE YOU NEED IN WINDOWS 7

Windows 10 FCU is available in two versions: Windows 10 Home and Windows 10 Pro. Follow this procedure in Windows 7 to make sure you order the correct upgrade.

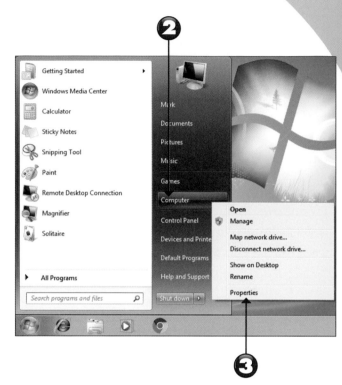

1 Click or tap **Start**.

2 Right-click or press and hold **Computer**.

3 Click or tap **Properties**.

Continued

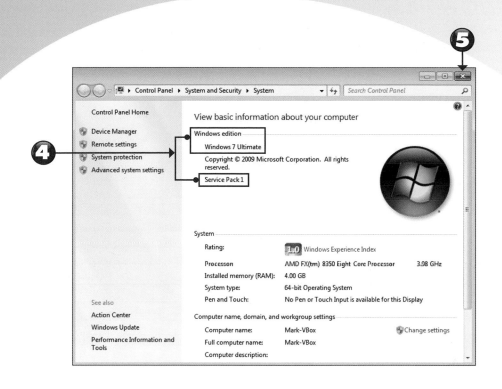

4 This system is running Windows 7 Ultimate with Service Pack 1.

5 Click **Close** to exit.

End

TIP

Which Windows 10 FCU Version to Order? If your version is Windows 7 Ultimate or Professional, order Windows 10 Pro. If it is Windows 7 Home Premium or Home Basic, order Windows 10 Home. If it is Windows 7 Enterprise, upgrades are provided by the organization that supports the computer. ■

DETERMINING THE UPGRADE YOU NEED WITH WINDOWS 8.1

Windows 10 FCU is available in two versions: Windows 10 Home and Windows 10 Pro. Follow this procedure in Windows 8.1 to make sure you order the correct upgrade.

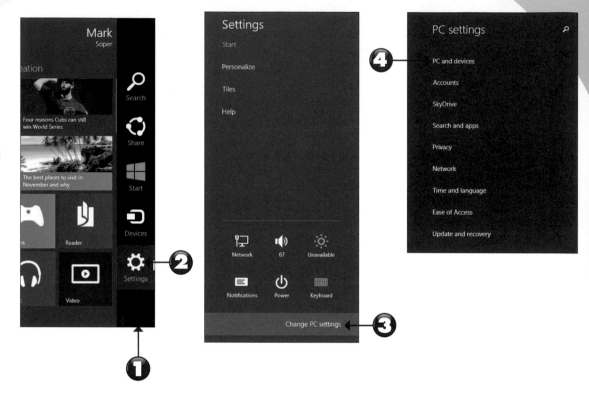

1 From the Start screen, point to the lower-right corner (mouse) or flick the right edge of the screen (touchscreen).

2 Click or tap **Settings**.

3 Click or tap **Change PC settings**.

4 Click or tap **PC and devices**.

Continued

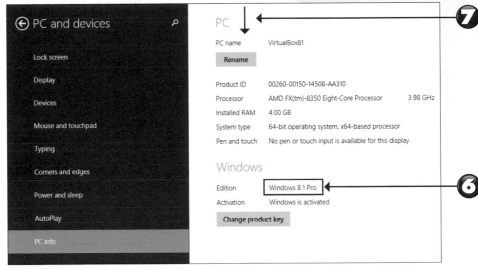

5 Click or tap **PC info**.

6 This computer is running Windows 8.1 Pro.

7 To close this window, click or press and drag at the top of the window and drag it down to the bottom of the screen until it disappears.

End

TIP

Which Windows 10 FCU Version to Order?   If your Windows 8.1 version is Windows 8.1 Pro, order Windows 10 Pro. If it is Windows 8.1 Home Premium or Home Basic, order Windows 10 Home. If you are still running Windows 8 Home or Pro, get the free upgrade to Windows 8.1 from the Microsoft Store before upgrading to Windows 10. If it is Windows 8 or 8.1 Enterprise, upgrades are provided by the organization that provides the computer. ■

INSTALLING THE UPGRADE WITH THE MEDIA CREATION TOOL

To start the upgrade, use the Download Windows 10 web page to perform the upgrade process. If you choose custom setup options later in the process, some steps will be different from those shown here.

Start

Continued

1 Open your web browser and go to https://www.microsoft.com/software-download/windows10.

2 Click or tap **Download tool now**.

3 Click or tap **Run** when prompted.

4 Click or tap **Yes** in the User Account Control dialog box.

NOTE

Creating Install Media When you reach step 6, you can choose to create installation media (USB flash drive or DVD) for another computer. Choose this option if you don't want to install Windows 10 FCU on this computer right now. ■

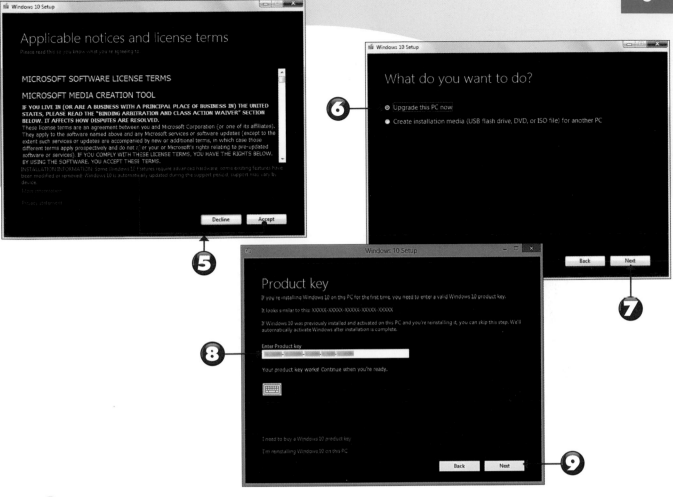

5 Review the agreement, and then click or tap **Accept**.

6 Click or tap **Upgrade this PC now**.

7 Click or tap **Next** to continue. If you are not prompted for a license key, continue with step 10.

8 After Windows 10 is downloaded, you might be prompted to provide the license key you received when you purchased Windows. Enter it.

9 Click or tap **Next** to continue.

Continued

NOTE

Reinstalling Windows 10   When you reach step 8, if you have already installed and activated Windows 10 on this computer, choose **I am reinstalling Windows 10 on this PC**. You can continue without entering your product key again. ■

NOTE

Forgot to Buy a Key?   If you don't yet have a valid product key when you reach step 8, you can click or tap **I need to buy a Windows 10 product key**, and you will be directed to the Microsoft website for ordering. ■

10 Default settings for the upgrade.

11 Click or tap here to change what to keep.

12 Click or tap **Install** to continue.

13 The Privacy dashboard opens. To disable any feature, drag a slider to **Off**.

14 Scroll down to see all settings.

Continued

(15) After reviewing and making any changes, click or tap **Accept**.

(16) To skip setting up Cortana now, click or tap **Not now**.

(17) To use Cortana, click or tap **Use Cortana**.

Continued

NOTE

Cortana Now or Later? If you don't set up Cortana when you install Windows 10, some search features are limited. We recommend enabling it during installation. ■

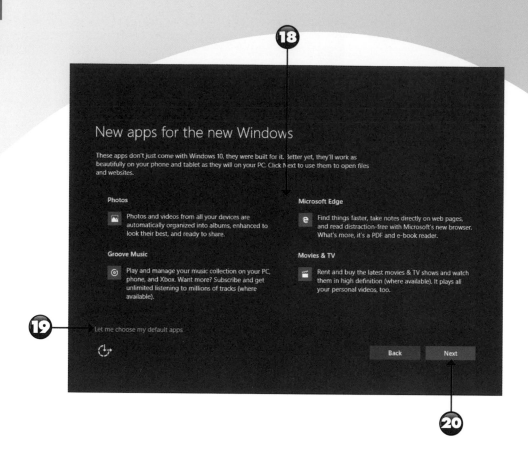

18 The default Windows 10 FCU apps for photos, web browsing, music, and movies & TV are listed here.

19 If you want to choose your own default apps, click or tap **Let me choose my default apps**.

20 To use the default apps, click or tap **Next**.

Continued

Mark E. Soper

21 The Windows 10 FCU Lock screen. Begin the login process here. After you log in for the first time, the Edge browser displays a welcome message.

End

NOTE

Logging in with a Touchscreen If your device uses a touchscreen, go to Chapter 3, "Logging In, Starting Up, and Shutting Down Windows 10 Fall Creators Update with a Touchscreen."

NOTE

Logging in with a Mouse and Keyboard If your device uses a mouse and keyboard, go to Chapter 4, "Logging In to Windows 10 Fall Creators Update and Customizing the Start Menu."

UPDATING WINDOWS 10 TO THE FALL CREATORS UPDATE

If you are willing to wait, Microsoft will eventually deliver the Fall Creators Update (also known as build 16299) to your Windows 10 computer or tablet via Windows Update, a process that could take months. But why wait? Microsoft makes it easy to get Fall Creators Update on *your* schedule. After all, Fall Creators Update is what this book is all about. Here's what to do.

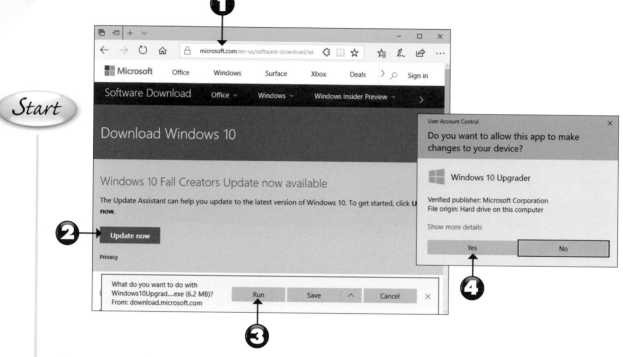

Start

1 Open your web browser and go to https://www.microsoft.com/software-download/windows10.

2 Click or tap **Update now**.

3 Click or tap **Run** when prompted.

4 Click or tap **Yes** in the User Account Control dialog box.

Continued

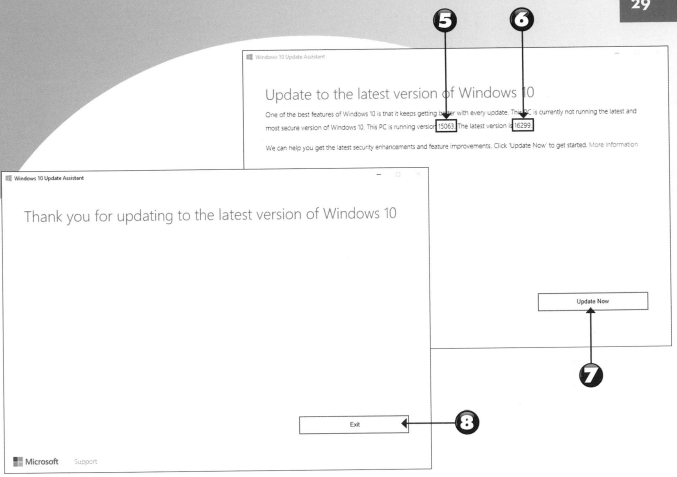

5 Note the current version you're running.

6 Note the new version (16299 or greater).

7 Click or tap **Update Now** and follow the onscreen prompts. Your system may need to reboot to finish the process.

8 At the end of the process, click or tap **Exit**. You can start using the latest Windows 10 edition.

End

Chapter 3

LOGGING IN, STARTING UP, AND SHUTTING DOWN WINDOWS 10 FALL CREATORS UPDATE WITH A TOUCHSCREEN

Whether you're upgrading from Windows 7, switching to a new PC after running older versions of Windows, or upgrading from Windows 8/8.1, Windows 10 Fall Creators Update (FCU) is designed to work the way you're accustomed to working. In this chapter, you find out how to use a touchscreen (such as those found on tablets, convertible 2-in-1 devices, or some all-in-one desktops) to log in to Windows, move around the Windows menus, and lock, sleep, or shut down your system. You also learn how to use a touch keyboard and voice recognition for text in this chapter. If you use a mouse and keyboard instead of a touchscreen, skip ahead to Chapter 4, "Logging In to Windows Fall Creators Update and Customizing the Start Menu."

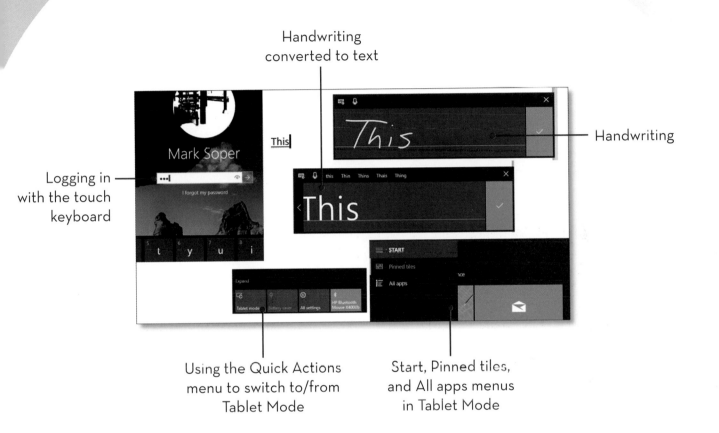

Handwriting
converted to text

Handwriting

Logging in
with the touch
keyboard

Using the Quick Actions
menu to switch to/from
Tablet Mode

Start, Pinned tiles,
and All apps menus
in Tablet Mode

LOGGING IN WITH A TOUCHSCREEN

To log in to Windows 10 Fall Creators Update, you must know the username and password (if any) set up for your account. If you installed Windows 10 FCU yourself, be sure to make note of this information when you are prompted to provide it during the installation process. You also log in to Windows 10 FCU when you are waking up the computer from sleep, unlocking it, or restarting it.

Wireless network signal strength

Battery charge level/AC power

1 Tap your touchscreen and drag it upward when the Lock screen appears.

2 Tap the password field.

3 The alphabetic keyboard appears first.

4 Tap each letter in your password.

5 Tap to switch to the symbols and numbers keyboard.

Continued

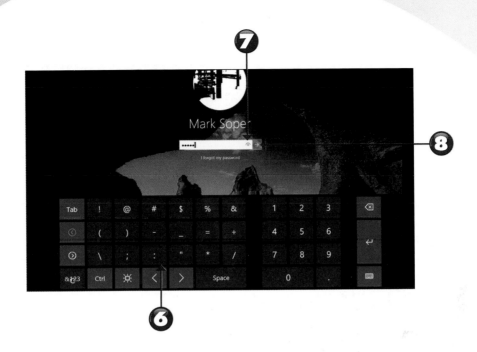

6 Tap symbols and numbers in your password.

7 To see your password as you enter it, hold down the eye symbol (visible after you enter at least one character of your password).

8 Tap to start Windows.

End

NOTE

Touch Keyboards and Handwriting Recognition The touch keyboard works with any app that uses the keyboard and is also used to start the handwriting recognition feature. See "Using Handwriting Recognition," p. 42, this chapter, for details. ▨

NOTE

Logins for Multiple Users If you have more than one user set up on your computer, there are additional steps to follow. See the section "Selecting an Account to Log In To," in Chapter 22, "Adding and Managing Users," for details. ▨

WORKING WITH THE START, PINNED TILES, AND ALL APPS MENUS IN TABLET MODE

Devices that do not have a physical keyboard (or have the keyboard detached or folded away) typically start Windows 10 Fall Creators Update in Tablet Mode. In this lesson, you learn the major features of Tablet Mode.

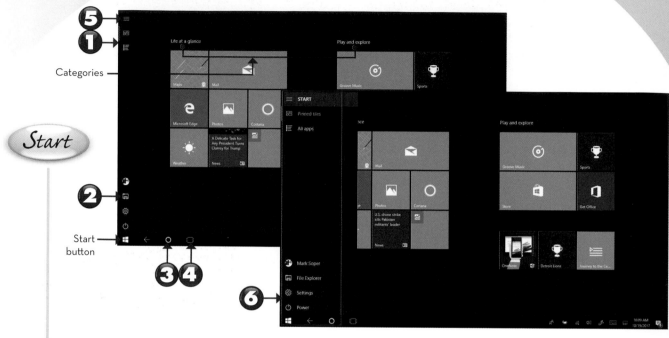

Categories

Start

Start button

1 The Pinned Tiles menu opens by default.

2 Tap to open File Manager.

3 Tap to open the Cortana Search box.

4 Tap to open Task Switcher.

5 Tap to expand the Start menu.

6 Expanded Start menu.

Continued

TIP

Opening the Start Menu To open the Start menu while another app is running in Tablet mode, tap or click the Start button. ■

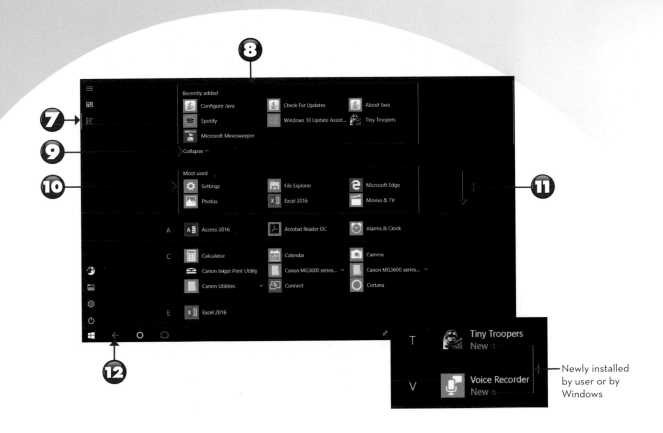

7 Tap to open the All apps menu.

8 Recently added apps.

9 Click to expand/collapse list of recently added apps.

10 Most-used apps.

11 Scroll down or flick up to see apps in alphanumeric order.

12 Click or tap to return to the previous view.

End

NOTE

More About New Apps Windows 10 FCU places the word "New" next to apps you installed or apps that have been recently updated by Windows. ■

ENABLING TABLET MODE

As you have seen in the previous lessons, Tablet Mode is designed to be touch-friendly. If you use a convertible or two-in-one (tablet plus laptop) device, Tablet Mode might not be configured to start automatically. If Tablet Mode did not start automatically when you started Windows, you can start it from the Notifications menu. Here's how.

Start

End

1 Click or tap the **Notifications/Quick actions** button.

2 Tap to toggle **Tablet Mode** off or on. (Tablet Mode is off in this example.)

3 Tap an empty area of the screen to close Notifications.

4 The system has switched to Tablet Mode.

NOTE

Learning More about Tablet Mode   You can configure Tablet Mode by using the Tablet Mode menu in the Settings dialog box's System menu. See Chapter 19, "Managing Windows 10 Fall Creators Update," for details. ■

STARTING AND CLOSING A UNIVERSAL OR MODERN UI APP

Modern UI apps and Universal apps (which work on any Windows device, including Windows 10 Mobile) are optimized for touchscreens. Although they are started the same way in either regular or Tablet Mode, Tablet Mode uses a different way to close them. In this example, I start and close Calculator from the All Apps menu.

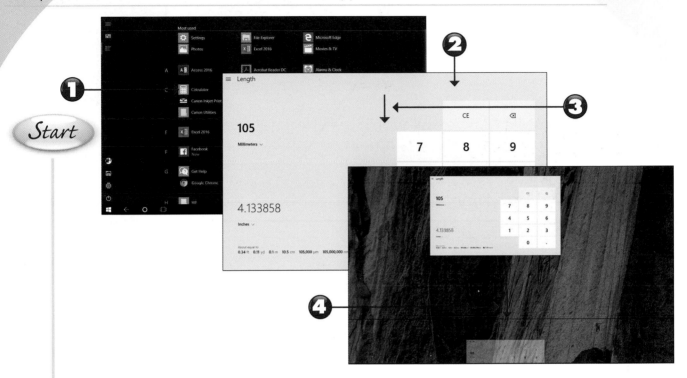

1 Tap a Modern UI or Universal app to start it.

2 When you are finished using the app, press and hold the top edge of the screen.

3 Drag the app downward.

4 Continue to drag the app window down until it disappears. The Tablet Mode Start menu appears immediately afterward.

NOTE

Pinning Files and Apps To learn more about pinning files and apps to the Start menu or the taskbar, see Chapter 6, "Running Apps."

LOCKING YOUR PC

If you have a password on your account, you can lock your PC when you leave it and unlock it when you return. On laptop and desktop computers, you typically lock your system with the Windows key+L combination. However, you can also lock it with a touchscreen. Here's how.

Start

1 Tap your icon or username.

2 Tap **Lock**.

End

NOTE

Logging Back In to Your System To log back in to your system, follow the procedure given earlier in this chapter in "Logging In with a Touchscreen." ■

NOTE

Other Options To sign out, tap **Sign out** from the menu. To view and change account settings, tap **Change account settings**. For details about account settings, see Chapter 22, "Adding and Managing Users." ■

CHOOSING SLEEP, SHUT DOWN, OR RESTART

When it's time to put away the computer, Windows 10 Fall Creators Update makes it easy. Want to go back to work (or play) right where you left off? Choose Sleep. Want to "put away" your PC and start fresh next time? Choose Shut Down. In this lesson, you learn how to perform these tasks using the Start menu's Power button. These same tasks can also be performed from the login screen shown earlier in this chapter.

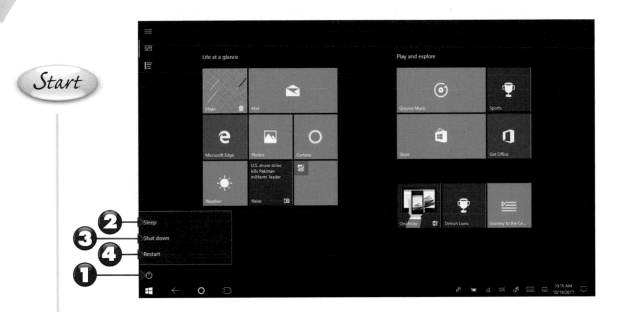

1 Tap the **Power** button.

2 Tap **Sleep** to put the device into low-power mode.

3 Tap **Shut down** to shut down the device.

4 Tap **Restart** to close Windows FCU and restart it.

CAUTION

Power Options from the Login Screen The Power button is also available from the login screen and works the same way as from the Start menu. However, if you select **Shut down** or **Restart** when you or other users are logged in to the system, you are warned that shutting down or restarting can cause data loss. Be sure that any logged-in users have saved their work and closed their apps before you shut down or restart Windows 10 FCU. ■

SWITCHING TO A TOUCH KEYBOARD AND ENTERING EMOJIS

Windows 10 FCU introduces improved touch (on-screen) keyboard layouts. In this lesson, you learn how to choose the touch keyboard you prefer and use it to enter text and emojis into WordPad (found in the Windows Accessory folder in All Apps).

Full keyboard layout with number/symbol keys

One-hand type keyboard

Default keyboard layout

Start

Keyboard locked to bottom edge

Keyboard floats in window

1 Tap the touch keyboard button.

2 The Windows 10 default keyboard layout appears in its default bottom-of-screen position.

3 For other options, tap the keyboard layout button.

4 Choose a different layout if desired.

5 Use the default keyboard layout at the bottom of the screen.

Continued

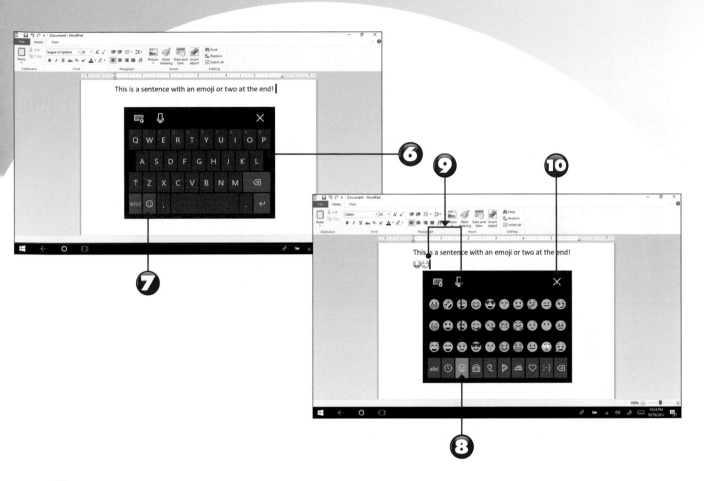

6 Note the one-hand keyboard layout in the floating window.

7 Tap to display emoji keys.

8 Tap an emoji character group.

9 Tap an emoji to place it in the document.

10 Click to close the touch keyboard.

End

NOTE

Emoji Access You can also access the emoji library from the default Windows 10 keyboard shown in step 2. ▪

USING HANDWRITING RECOGNITION

On tablets and laptops with touchscreens, the touch keyboard can also be used for text input using handwriting recognition. And if you have a touchpad with a stylus, you can also use handwriting recognition. Here's how to use handwriting recognition using WordPad.

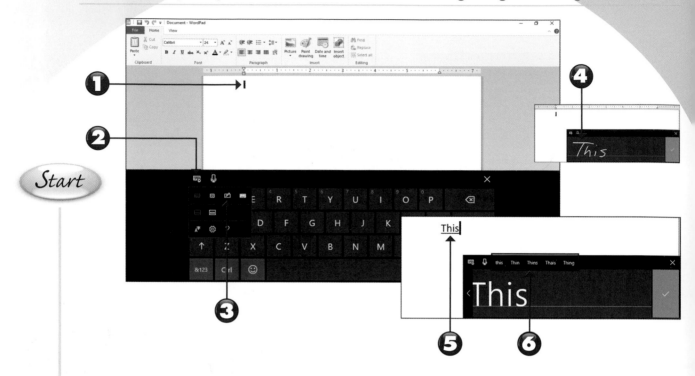

Start

1 Tap the text input window or screen.

2 When the touch keyboard appears, tap the keyboard button.

3 Tap the **stylus** button.

4 Print the text you want to insert with your finger or stylus.

5 The text is automatically inserted into your text input area as it is recognized.

6 The word prediction logic can help you write faster by displaying possible matches as you begin writing. Tap a word to use it.

Continued

NOTE

Improved Editing Handwriting recognition now recognizes spaces between handwritten words. You can highlight and delete handwritten text or correct misspelled words from within the handwriting window. ■

USING VOICE RECOGNITION

The touch keyboard and stylus input tools now support voice recognition. In addition to using voice recognition in a word processing window, you can also use it to enter a search phrase into a web browser, as in this example using Microsoft Edge.

Start

1 Tap the text input window (web address window in this example).

2 After opening the touch keyboard or stylus, tap the microphone button on the stylus (shown) or touch keyboard.

3 Make sure the microphone is "listening."

4 Speak the phrase ("cnn"), and it is placed into the text input window.

5 Tap the best match.

End

Chapter 4

LOGGING IN TO WINDOWS 10 FALL CREATORS UPDATE AND CUSTOMIZING THE START MENU

This chapter shows you how to log in to Windows 10 Fall Creators Update (FCU) and navigate the standard Windows desktop and Start menu with a mouse and a keyboard. Whether you use a mouse/keyboard or touchscreen, you also find out how to customize the Start menu's contents.

Moving a tile on
the Start menu

Logging in

Resizing a tile on
the Start menu

The Windows
(Win) key on a
typical keyboard

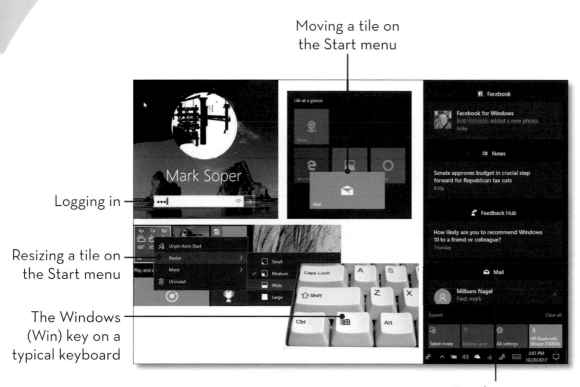

Quick actions
(Windows key+A)

LOGGING IN TO WINDOWS 10 FALL CREATORS UPDATE

To log in to Windows 10 FCU, you must know the password (if any) to the account you want to log in to. If you installed Windows 10 FCU yourself, be sure to make note of this information when you are prompted to provide it during the installation process. You also log in to Windows 10 FCU when you are waking up the computer from sleep, unlocking it, or restarting it.

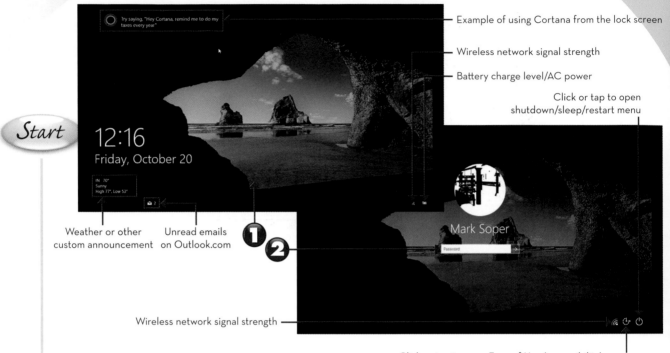

Try saying, "Hey Cortana, remind me to do my taxes every year"

Example of using Cortana from the lock screen

Wireless network signal strength

Battery charge level/AC power

Click or tap to open shutdown/sleep/restart menu

12:16
Friday, October 20

IN 70°
Sunny
High 77°, Low 53°

Mark Soper

Password

Weather or other custom announcement

Unread emails on Outlook.com

Wireless network signal strength

Click or tap to open Ease of Use (accessibility) menu

Start

1 Press the spacebar, click your mouse, or tap your touchpad when the Lock screen appears.

2 Type your password.

Continued

3 To see your password as you type it, click or press and hold the eye icon. (You must type at least one character to see this icon.)

4 Password characters are visible when you click or press the eye icon.

5 Press **Enter** or click the arrow when the password is entered. The Windows desktop appears.

End

NOTE

Logins for Multiple Users   If you have more than one user set up on your computer, there are additional steps to follow. See the section "Selecting an Account to Log In To," in Chapter 22, "Adding and Managing Users," for details. ■

USING THE START MENU

In this exercise, you learn how to open the Windows 10 Start menu (Desktop mode). You use the left button on your mouse, the lower-left corner of your device's integrated touchpad, or the Windows key on the keyboard or tablet.

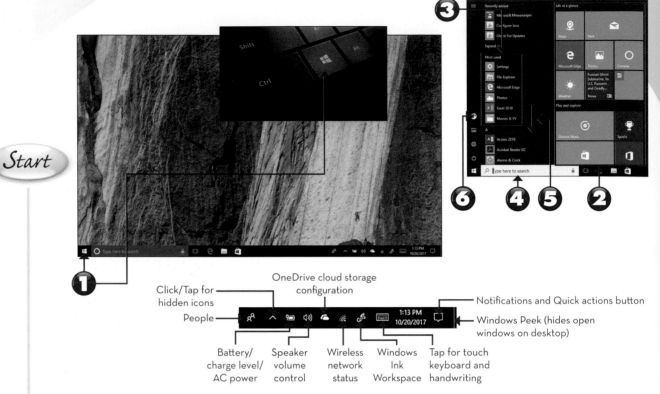

Start

Click/Tap for hidden icons

People

OneDrive cloud storage configuration

Notifications and Quick actions button

Windows Peek (hides open windows on desktop)

Battery/ charge level/ AC power

Speaker volume control

Wireless network status

Windows Ink Workspace

Tap for touch keyboard and handwriting

1 Click or tap the **Start** button in the lower-left corner of the desktop, or press the Windows key on the keyboard.

2 Links to Universal and Modern UI apps and other apps are pinned to the Start menu.

3 Shortcuts to frequently used apps are grouped here.

4 Use the Cortana Search window to find what you're looking for.

5 Scroll down to see all apps.

6 Click or tap to change account settings, log out, or lock the system.

End

NOTE

Click or Tap to Start an App Start apps from either the left or the right menus by clicking or tapping the app icon once. ▪

USING KEYBOARD SHORTCUTS

This lesson illustrates a few of the dozens of Windows 10 FCU shortcuts that use the Windows key.

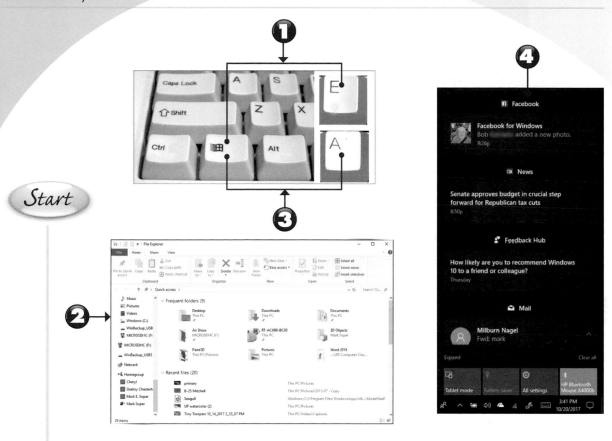

Start

1 Press **Windows key+E**.

2 The Quick access view of File Explorer opens on the Windows desktop.

3 Press **Windows key+A**.

4 The Notifications pane (Action Center and Quick actions) is displayed at the right of the Windows desktop.

End

NOTE

More Keyboard Shortcuts   Some keyboard shortcuts used in Windows 7 and 8.1 also work in Windows 10 FCU. For Microsoft's official list of keyboard shortcuts for Windows and apps, go to http://windows.microsoft.com/en-us/windows/keyboard-shortcuts and select the version of Windows you use. ■

RESIZING TILES ON THE START MENU

You can change the size of app tiles on the Start menu in either Desktop mode or Tablet mode to help make them easier to use, smaller, or larger. In the example shown here, the Weather tile is resized, showing how it can display more or less information as its size changes.

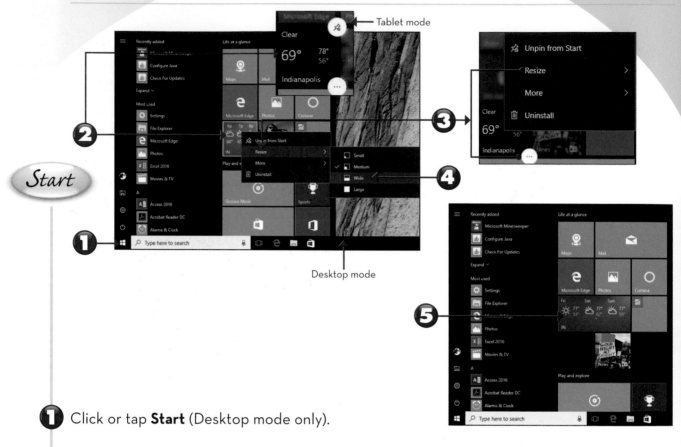

Tablet mode

Desktop mode

1 Click or tap **Start** (Desktop mode only).

2 Right-click (Desktop mode) or press and hold (Tablet mode) the tile to resize.

3 Click **Resize** (Desktop mode) or tap the three-dot icon, **Resize** (Tablet mode).

4 Select the size desired (Wide in this example).

5 The tile is resized.

End

TIP

Turning On/Off Live Updates   In this example, the Weather tile is set as a live tile, displaying updates. To turn on live tiles, click or tap **More** (after step 2 in Desktop mode or step 3 in Tablet mode) and click or tap **Turn Live Tile on**. To turn off a live tile, click or tap **Turn Live Tile off**. To turn off live updates (tiles such as Weather, Photos, Calendar, and others), right-click or press and hold the tile, click or tap the three-dot button, click or tap **More**, and click or tap **Turn Live Tile off**. ▪

CHANGING TILE POSITIONS ON THE START MENU

Moving a tile to a new location is a simple drag-and-drop process, as this tutorial demonstrates.

Start

1 Click and hold or press and hold the tile to move it.

2 Drag it to the new location.

3 Release the tile when it is in the correct position.

4 The tile is in its new position.

End

REMOVING AN APP FROM THE START MENU

You can remove an app from the Most used list on the left side of the Start menu or pinned app tiles from the right side of the Start menu. You can still run an app from All Apps, so use these methods for apps you don't use frequently.

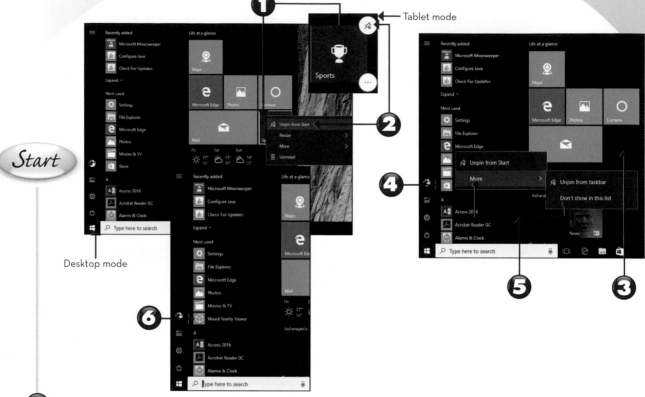

Tablet mode

Desktop mode

Start

1 Right-click (Desktop mode) or press and hold (Tablet mode) the tile you want to remove.

2 Click or tap **Unpin from Start** (Desktop mode) or the pushpin icon (Tablet mode).

3 The tile is removed from the Start menu.

4 Right-click or press and hold an app you want to remove from the Most used list.

5 Select **More**, and then click or tap **Don't show in this list**.

6 Another frequently used app takes the place of the one you removed in step 5.

End

TIP

Other Options If you use an app frequently, you might prefer to put its shortcut on the taskbar. Choose **Pin to Taskbar** in step 5. If the app is already pinned to the taskbar, you see "Unpin from taskbar" as shown in Step 5. ■

LOCKING YOUR SYSTEM

You can lock your system by clicking your name/icon in the Start menu. (For details, see Chapter 3, "Logging In, Starting Up, and Shutting Down Windows 10 Fall Creators Update with a Touchscreen.") However, you might prefer to use the keyboard, as shown in this lesson.

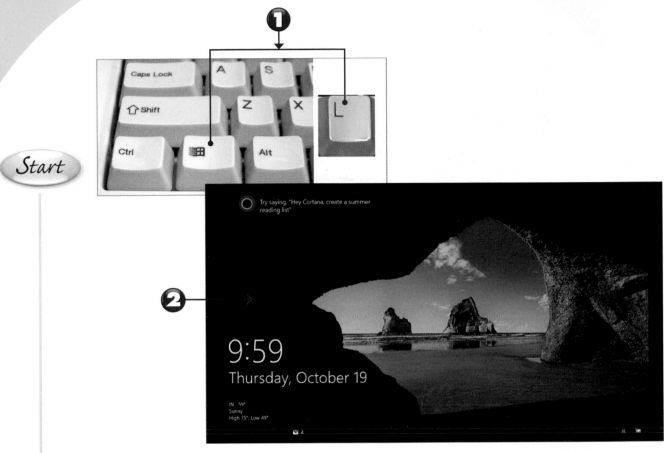

Start

1 Press the **Windows key+L** key on your keyboard.

2 The Lock screen appears.

End

NOTE

Logging Back In To log back in, see "Logging In to Windows 10 Fall Creators Update," this chapter, p. 46. ■

CHOOSING SLEEP, SHUT DOWN, OR RESTART

When it's time to put away the computer, Windows 10 FCU makes it easy. Want to go back to work (or play) right where you left off? Choose Sleep. Want to start from scratch the next time you start up Windows, or need to put away your PC for more than a few hours? Choose Shut Down. Need to restart the computer? Choose Restart. In this lesson, you learn how to perform these tasks using the Start menu's Power button. These same tasks can also be performed from the login screen shown earlier in this chapter.

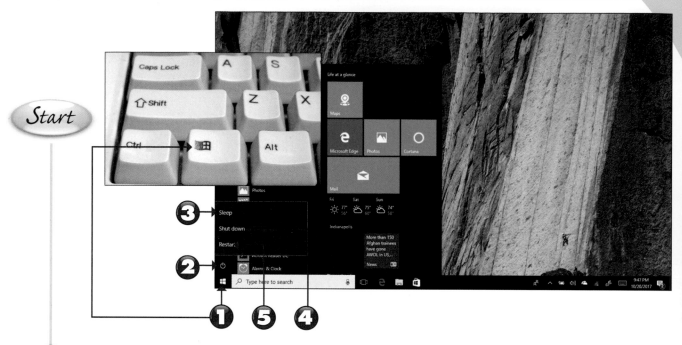

Start

1 Click or tap the **Start** button or press the **Windows key** on your keyboard.

2 Click or tap the **Power** button.

3 Tap **Sleep** to put the device into low-power mode.

4 Tap **Shut down** to shut down the device.

5 Tap **Restart** to close Windows and restart it.

End

 CAUTION

Power Options from the Login Screen   The Power button is also available from the login screen and works the same way as from the Start menu. However, if you select **Shut down** or **Restart** when you or other users are logged in to the system, you are warned that shutting down or restarting can cause data loss. Be sure that any logged-in users have saved their work and closed their apps before you shut down or restart Windows. ■

Chapter 5

USING CORTANA SEARCH

Windows 10 Fall Creators Update's Search is powered by an improved version of Cortana. For any user with a Microsoft account, Cortana provides voice-activated or text search of both the Web and your device. Cortana can send you reminders and works hard to discover what you like so you get better search results. If you sign out of Cortana or use a local account, basic search is still available. Whichever you prefer, this chapter shows you how to get the most from the enhanced search tools in Windows 10 FCU.

Asking Cortana to display weather anywhere you specify

Launching an app with Cortana

You can add Cortana to your iOS or Android smartphone

Searching for content by type and keyword

Asking Cortana about your favorite team's current game

Creating a monthly reminder

FIRST-TIME SETUP

The first time you use Cortana Search in Windows 10 FCU, there are a few steps you might want to take to make sure it works as well for you as possible. Here's what to expect.

Click or tap to expand menu.

Devices tab; click or tap to buy or set up a Cortana-enabled speaker.

Home tab

Notebook tab

Start

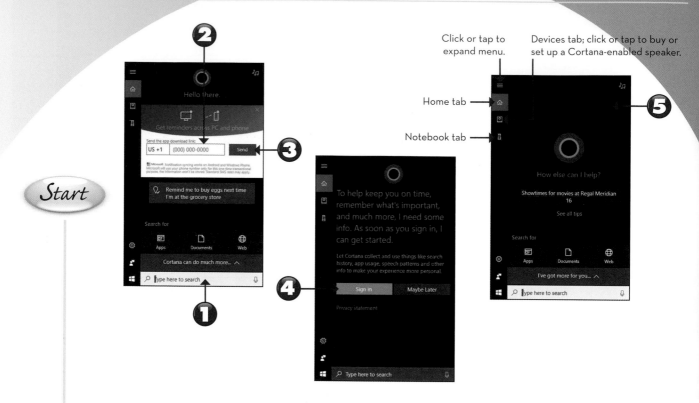

Start

1 Click or tap the **Search** box.

2 If you want Cortana reminders on your Android or iOS smartphone, enter your smartphone's area code and number.

3 Click or tap **Send** to send a link to your smartphone.

4 Click or tap **Sign in** to use Cortana's reminders and other deluxe features.

5 Cortana is now ready to help you with searches, reminders, and news.

End

SEARCHING WITH CORTANA

Cortana enables you to search by typing or by using your voice. Cortana can bring you web results quickly, as you see in this example.

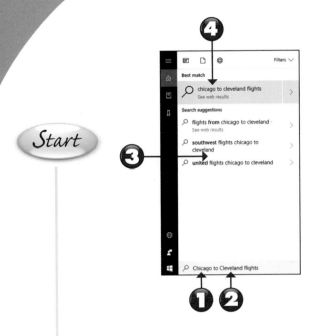

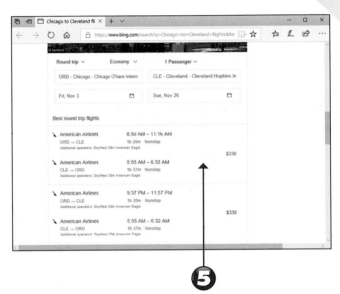

Start

① Click or tap the **Search** box.

② Type your search terms.

③ Cortana displays the search results.

④ Click or tap a link for more information.

⑤ A Microsoft Edge browser window containing detailed information opens.

End

VOICE SEARCHES WITH CORTANA

Have a Windows tablet? Want to give your keyboard a rest? Here's how to perform a voice-driven web search using Cortana.

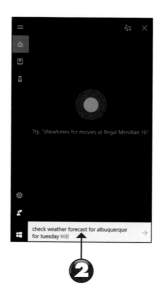

Start

1 To search by voice, click or tap the microphone.

2 Speak your search terms.

3 Some search results may be displayed (and spoken) in the Cortana search window. Otherwise, Cortana opens an Edge browser window to display results.

4 Use sliders or clickable areas in the results windows to learn more.

End

STARTING APPS WITH CORTANA

Cortana can also start installed apps for you. Here's how.

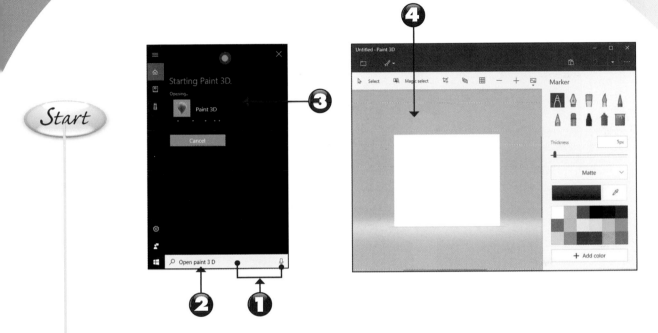

Start

1 Click or tap the microphone or search box.

2 Speak or type **open *name of app*** (in this example, *Paint 3D*).

3 Cortana checks the names of installed apps and selects the matching app.

4 The app opens.

End

NOTE

Start Any App with Cortana   You can start built-in apps, apps from the Microsoft Store, or apps you install yourself from downloads, USB drives, or optical drives using Cortana. ■

DISCOVERING MORE CORTANA SEARCHES

In addition to searching your system and launching apps, Cortana knows how to find many different types of information. Here's an easy way to discover Cortana's talents.

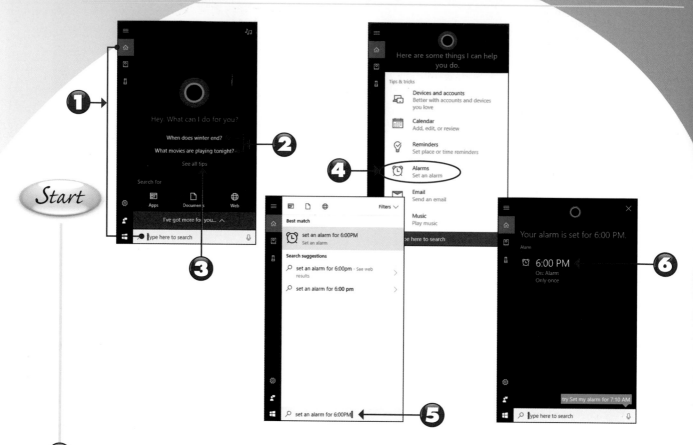

1 Click or tap the **Cortana/Search** box, and the Home tab opens.

2 Click or tap a suggested search. The results open in a browser window.

3 To see more suggestions, click or tap **See all tips**.

4 Review the list of suggestions.

5 Click or tap the search box or microphone and type/say **set an alarm for 6:00PM**.

6 Cortana sets an alarm for you using the Alarms & Clock app.

Continued.

7 Scroll down for more suggestions.

8 You can use natural-language searches to find what you're looking for (for example, **How did *name of team* do today**).

9 Cortana says the results and provides more detail.

10 Scroll down for more suggestions.

11 Enter text and language for translation.

12 Cortana displays the results and source. Click or tap the Speaker icon to hear the word or phrase pronounced.

End

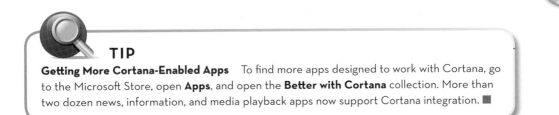

TIP

Getting More Cortana-Enabled Apps To find more apps designed to work with Cortana, go to the Microsoft Store, open **Apps**, and open the **Better with Cortana** collection. More than two dozen news, information, and media playback apps now support Cortana integration. ■

SEARCHING FOR FILES, APPS, AND SETTINGS

When you search (with or without Cortana running), you can specify what to search for. In this exercise, you learn how this feature provides a wider variety of search results.

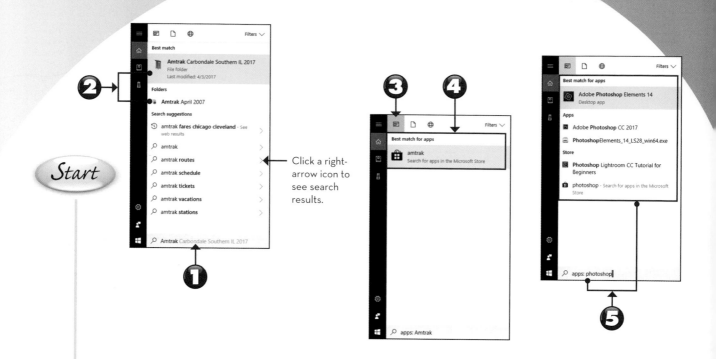

Click a right-arrow icon to see search results.

Start

1. Click or tap the **Cortana/Search** window and type your search word or phrase.

2. The best matches on your system (if any) are shown along with search suggestions.

3. Click or tap the **Apps** icon.

4. If no matching apps are found, a Microsoft Store search is offered.

5. A different app search (**photoshop**) reveals installed apps and matches from the Microsoft Store.

Continued

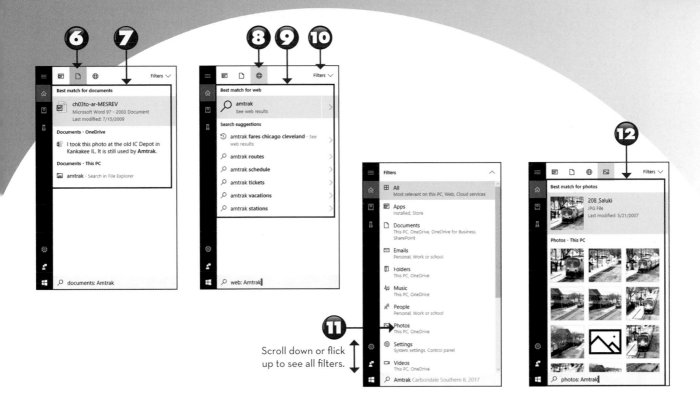

Scroll down or flick up to see all filters.

6 Click or tap the **Documents** icon.

7 Notice the documents stored on This PC as well as on OneDrive.

8 Click or tap the **Web** icon.

9 Choose a web search.

10 Click or tap **Filters** to search for other types of matches.

11 Click or tap a filter to see more matches.

12 Matches for **photos: Amtrak** on the author's PC (scroll down for OneDrive matches).

End

USING "PICK UP WHERE I LEFT OFF"

Cortana also powers Windows 10 FCU's "Pick up where I left off" feature. Here's how to make sure it's turned on so you can use it to continue apps that were running before you (or Windows Update) restarted your computer.

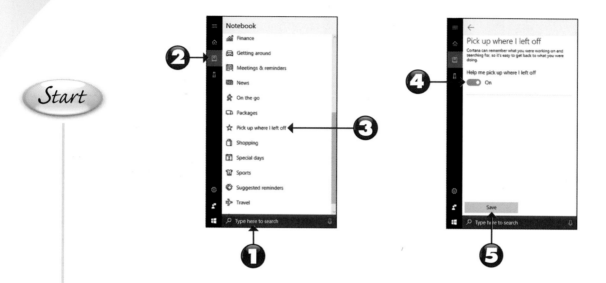

Start

1 Click or tap the Cortana window.

2 Click or tap the **Notebook** tab.

3 Click or tap **Pick up where I left off**.

4 If the feature is turned off, click and drag or press and drag to **On**.

5 Click or tap **Save**.

Continued

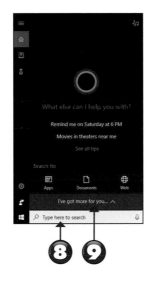

6 After you restart your computer (or it is restarted by Windows Update), click or tap **Notifications**.

7 Click or tap the **Here's what you had going** message to go directly to the list (step 10).

8 To go to the list later, click or tap the **Search** box.

9 Click or tap **I've got more for you**.

10 Click or tap the app(s) you want to continue to use.

11 Click or tap **See more** to see additional apps you can continue to use.

End

CUSTOMIZING TALK TO CORTANA

You can make voice searches easier by turning on "Hey Cortana," which enables you to use Cortana as a voice-activated personal assistant. To customize "Hey Cortana" to respond only to you, to set up a keyboard shortcut for talking to Cortana, or to use Cortana from the Lock Screen, open the Talk to Cortana page, available either from Cortana or from Settings. (See Chapter 19 for more about Settings.)

1 After opening Cortana, click or tap **Settings** (the gear icon).

2 To enable anyone to say "Hey Cortana" to start voice searches, click or press and drag the **Hey Cortana** toggle to **On**.

3 To enable you to press Windows key + C to start voice searches, click or press and drag the **Keyboard shortcut** toggle to **On**.

4 To enable Cortana to work from the Lock screen, click or tap and drag the **Use Cortana** toggle to **On**.

5 To enable Cortana to use your calendar and other listed data from the lock screen, click or tap the empty **Let Cortana access my calendar, email, messages, and Power BI data when my device is locked** check box.

Continued

Clear this check box if you want your
computer to sleep when plugged in
and not listen for 'Hey Cortana.'

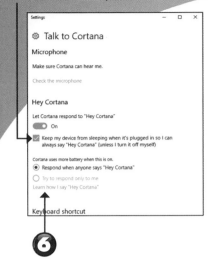

6 The default is for Cortana to respond to anyone. If you cannot select **Try to respond only to me**, click or tap **Learn how I say "Hey Cortana."**

7 Read the instructions and then click or tap **Start**.

8 Speak each phrase Cortana displays. Cortana displays the next one after it recognizes the current phrase.

9 When you see this, Cortana has learned your voice.

10 Say, "Hey Cortana," followed by your search or command.

11 Cortana responds.

End

USING CORTANA NOTEBOOK

To help Cortana provide more customized search results, open its Notebook tab and customize the categories that apply to you. This example demonstrates customizing the **Eat & drink** category.

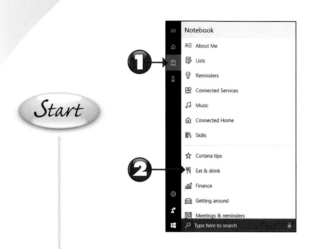

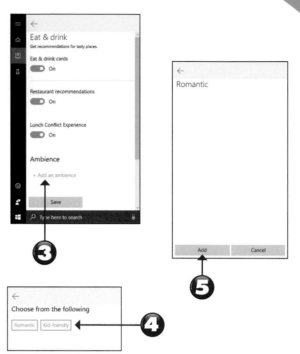

Start

1. Click or tap **Notebook**.

2. Click or tap **Eat & drink**.

3. Click or tap **Add an ambiance**.

4. Click or tap an option.

5. Click or tap **Add**.

Continued

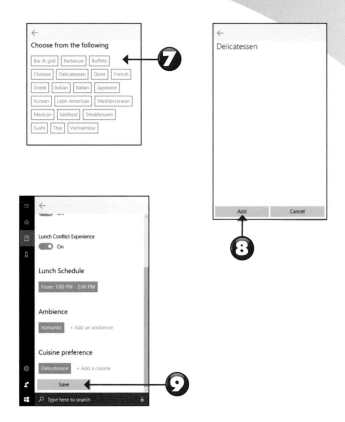

6 Click or tap **Add a cuisine**.

7 Click or tap an option.

8 Click or tap **Add**.

9 Click or tap **Save** to save your changes.

End

CREATING A REMINDER

You can create a reminder by using the Notebook's Reminder's button or by voice. Here's how to use your mouse and keyboard to have Cortana remind you of a task or event. In this example, we will use Cortana's new support for monthly reminders.

1 Click or tap **Notebook**.

2 Click or tap **Reminders**.

3 Click or tap the plus (+) sign to add a new reminder.

4 Click or tap **Remember to** and type what you want to be reminded about.

5 Click or tap **Time** to select when you want to be reminded.

6 Click or tap **Another time**.

Continued

7 Scroll to select the month, day, and year.

8 Click or tap the check box when finished.

9 To change the time, click or tap the time box.

10 Scroll to select hour, minute, AM, or PM.

11 Click or tap the check box when finished.

Continued

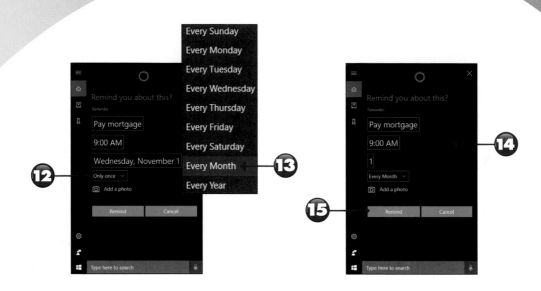

12 Click or tap **Only once**.

13 Click or tap **Every Month**.

14 Review the reminder. Click or tap any element you need to edit.

15 Click or tap **Remind** when you are satisfied.

Continued

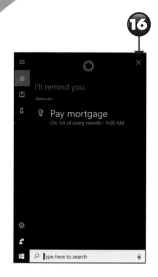

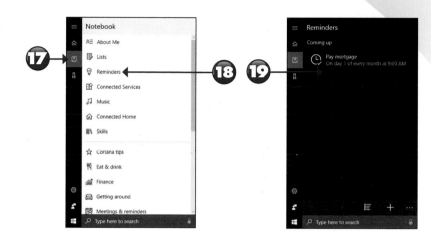

16 Click or tap **X** to close the confirmation message.

17 To review reminders, click or tap **Notebook**.

18 Click or tap **Reminders**.

19 Upcoming reminders are listed.

End

NOTE

Reminder Popups When a reminder is triggered, it appears in the Notifications pane at the right end of the taskbar. You can snooze or dismiss the reminder. ■

DISABLING CORTANA'S DIGITAL ASSISTANT FEATURES

In Windows 10 FCU, you can't turn off Cortana completely. However, by signing out of Cortana, you can disable voice-enabled digital assistant features, online storage of your search history, and reminders and appointments. If you prefer to use Cortana mainly for searching and launching apps, here's what to do.

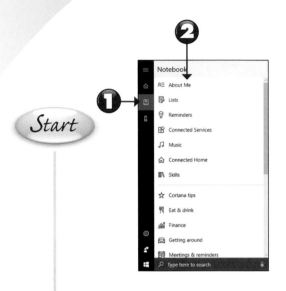

Start

1 Click or tap **Notebook**.

2 Click or tap **About Me**.

3 Click or tap your account.

4 Click or tap **Sign out**.

End

TIP

Removing Cortana's Stored Information   To remove the information that Cortana maintains for you in the cloud, go to https://privacy.microsoft.com and open the **Privacy Dashboard**. Change settings for Cortana's Notebook, voice activity, search history, and browsing history as desired. To change what Cortana can do on your device, open the Privacy and Permissions page in Settings (see Chapter 19). ■

Chapter 6

RUNNING APPS

Windows 10 FCU includes desktop apps (the same types of apps found in Windows 8.1 and earlier versions that run from the Windows desktop) and Modern UI and Universal apps, which are optimized for touchscreens. All types of apps are run from the Start menu. This chapter shows you how to locate the app you want and how to switch between running apps. You also learn how to run apps in full-screen or windowed modes, how to adjust the window size, how to add apps to the taskbar, and how to close an app when you're finished.

A live preview from
the Taskbar

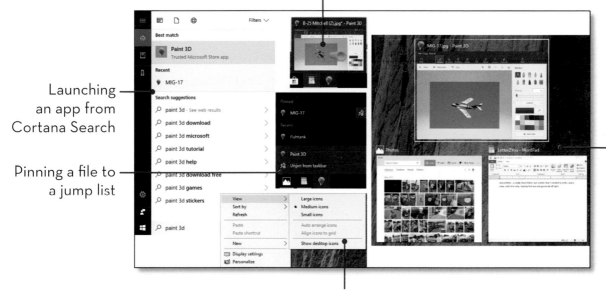

Launching
an app from
Cortana Search

Pinning a file to
a jump list

Selecting desktop
icon settings

Selecting
an app to
snap to one
side of the
desktop

FINDING APPS ON THE START MENU (DESKTOP MODE)

Windows 10 FCU has a two-pane start menu in Desktop mode. The Start menu's left pane includes two automatically generated lists: Recently added and Most used. You can also find many Universal apps on the right side of the menu (tiles). Scroll down to find both Universal/Modern UI and Win32 (classic Windows) apps. Whether they are installed as part of Windows, installed from the Microsoft Store (app store), downloaded by the user, or installed from media, they are listed alphabetically. Here's how to locate an app.

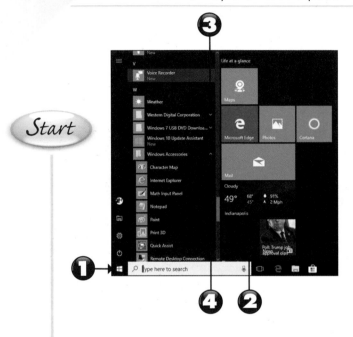

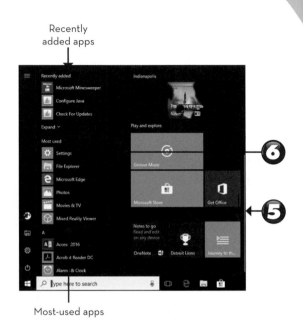

Recently added apps

Most-used apps

Start

1 Click or tap **Start**.

2 Scroll down the list of apps (left side).

3 To view the contents of a folder, click or tap the down-arrow icon.

4 Note the expanded folder.

5 Scroll down the tiled menu (right side).

6 To return to the original Start menu view, scroll both panes back to the top.

End

FINDING APPS IN TABLET MODE

In Tablet mode, Windows 10 FCU's Start menu is a full-width tiled view. To find apps not listed on the tiled menu, open the All apps menu.

Recently added apps

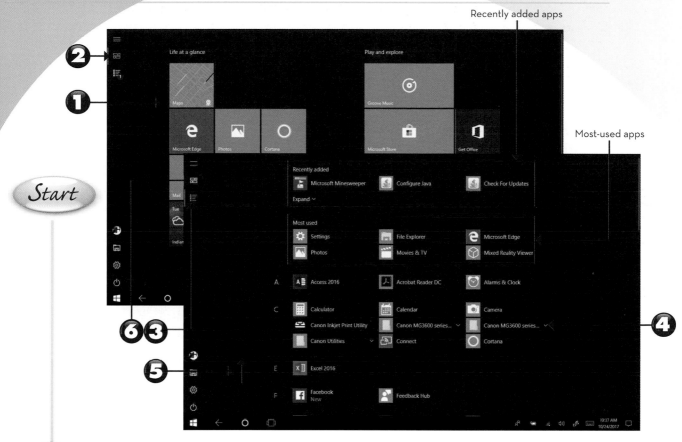

Most-used apps

Start

1. The default Pinned tiles menu appears whenever apps are not running.

2. The active menu view is highlighted in a contrasting color.

3. Tap **All apps** to see all installed apps.

4. Tap to expand the folder.

5. Flick up to see the remainder of apps.

6. Tap to return to the default Pinned apps menu.

End

STARTING AN APP IN DESKTOP MODE

Starting apps from the Start menu is simple. Here's how, using two popular apps (Alarms & Clock and Notepad) as examples.

Start

1 Click or tap **Start**.

2 Scroll to and click or tap **Alarms & Clock**.

3 Click or tap **Start**.

4 Click or tap **Windows Accessories** and then **Notepad**.

Continued

Both types of apps can be run in
a window (as here), minimized,
or maximized in desktop mode.

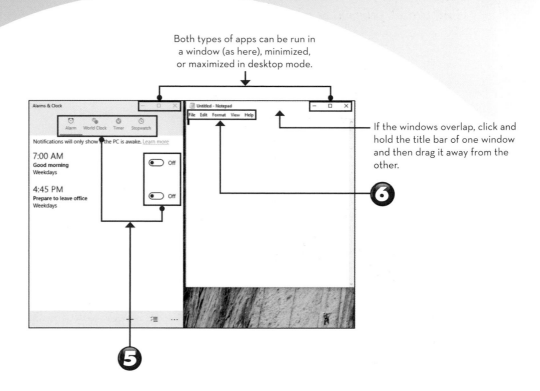

If the windows overlap, click and
hold the title bar of one window
and then drag it away from the
other.

5 Alarms & Clock is a Modern UI/Universal app. It features large menu icons and other touch-friendly options, such as slider controls.

6 Notepad is a Win32 app. It uses a text-based menu (some apps also use icons) that is designed for use with a mouse.

End

NOTE

Maximizing, Minimizing, and Windowed Modes A maximized app uses the entire active display (except for the taskbar). A minimized app does not have a visible window but is still running. Its icon is visible on the taskbar. A windowed app runs in a window that occupies part of the display and can be dragged around that display or to a different display. See "Maximizing and Restoring an App Window," this chapter, p. 87, for more information. ■

STARTING AN APP IN TABLET MODE

If you use Tablet mode, the process of starting an app and the app window appearance are different. In this example, we will open the same apps (Alarms & Clock and Notepad) as in the previous lesson.

Modern UI/Universal apps cannot run in a window in Tablet mode, so there are no window controls.

1 Tap the **Start** button (if the menu isn't visible).

2 If the app you want isn't visible, tap **All apps**.

3 Tap **Alarms & Clock**.

4 Modern UI/Universal apps run full-screen.

Continued

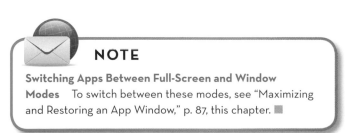

NOTE

Switching Apps Between Full-Screen and Window Modes   To switch between these modes, see "Maximizing and Restoring an App Window," p. 87, this chapter. ■

All apps run in full-screen in Tablet mode. Win32 apps have window controls, so they can be run in a window (except on some tablets with screens under 10 inches), maximized (as shown here), or minimized.

5 Tap **Start**.

6 Tap **All apps**.

7 Scroll to **Windows Accessories** and tap it.

8 Tap **Notepad**.

9 Tap to minimize the app to the taskbar.

10 Tap to run the app in a window.

11 Tap to close the app.

End

OPENING A FILE FROM WITHIN AN APP

This exercise explains how to open a file after starting an app using the WordPad app as an illustration. The WordPad app is a typical example of a traditional desktop app (also called a Win32 app), which is how Microsoft refers to apps that work the same way as in Windows 7 and earlier versions. The File menu works in a similar fashion in other desktop apps in Windows, such as Notepad.

If the file you want to open is shown in the Recent menu, click or tap it.

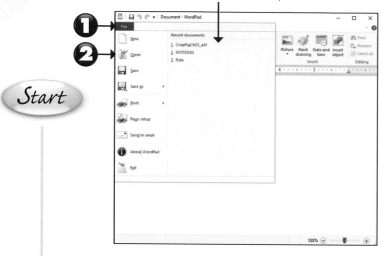

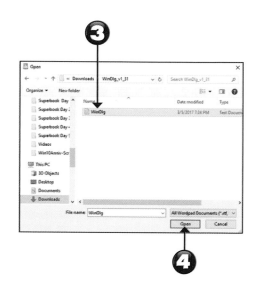

Start

End

1 Click or tap the **File** tab.

2 Click or tap **Open**.

3 Click or tap a file.

4 Click or tap **Open**.

NOTE

Supported File Formats WordPad can work with Rich Text (.rtf), Office Open XML Document (.docx), OpenDocument Text (*.odt), and plain text documents (.txt). ■

MAXIMIZING AND RESTORING AN APP WINDOW

Some apps start in full-screen view (maximized), whereas others start in a window. If you prefer to have an app use the entire screen in Desktop mode, you can maximize it. Here's how.

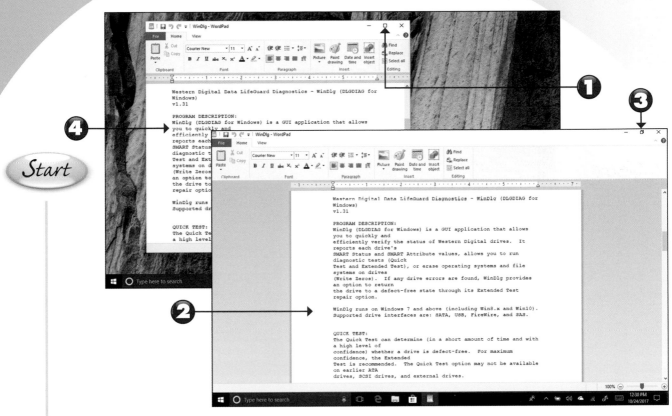

1 Click or tap the **Maximize** (box) icon.

2 The app window expands to fill the screen.

3 Click or tap the **Restore** (double-box) icon.

4 The app returns to a window.

Start

End

NOTE

Minimized Apps Are Still Running A minimized app does not have a visible window but is still running. Its icon is visible on the taskbar. To interact with a minimized app, click or tap its taskbar icon. It returns to the desktop. ■

STARTING AN APP FROM SEARCH

As an alternative to scrolling through the Start menu for an app you use occasionally, you can search for the app. This example demonstrates how to search for Windows 10 FCU's new graphics app, Paint 3D.

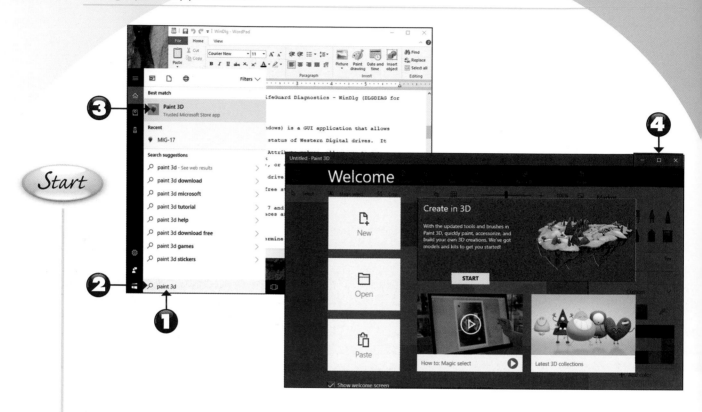

Start

Click or tap the **Search/Cortana** window.

Type **paint 3d**.

Click or tap **Paint 3D**.

The Paint 3D window opens. Note the controls for maximizing and minimizing the app.

End

SWITCHING BETWEEN APPS WITH THE TASKBAR (DESKTOP MODE)

Windows 10 FCU can run two or more apps at the same time. In this lesson, you learn how to switch between apps in desktop mode by using the taskbar.

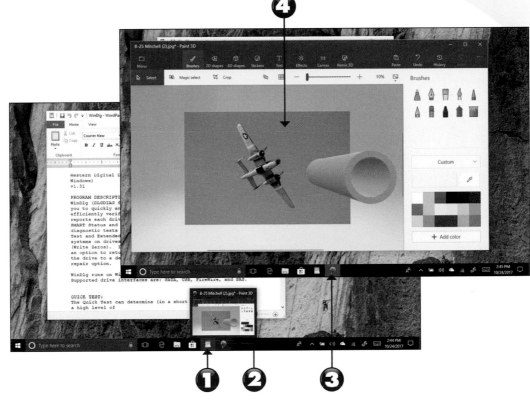

Start

1 Click or tap the WordPad icon to make it the active app.

2 Float the mouse over the Paint 3D icon. A live preview appears.

3 Click the Paint 3D icon in the taskbar.

4 Now Paint 3D is the active app.

End

NOTE

What's the Active App?   Running apps have a colored line below the taskbar app icon; however, the active app is the app you are working with (entering text, drawing, painting, entering numbers, and so on). When you see multiple windows onscreen, the active app is the one with the highlighted taskbar icon. (Compare the WordPad icon in step 1 to the Paint 3D icon in step 4.) ■

SWITCHING BETWEEN APPS WITH A TOUCHSCREEN

If you use a touchscreen device, you can swipe in from the left to switch between apps. Here's how to use this feature in either desktop mode (shown) or tablet mode.

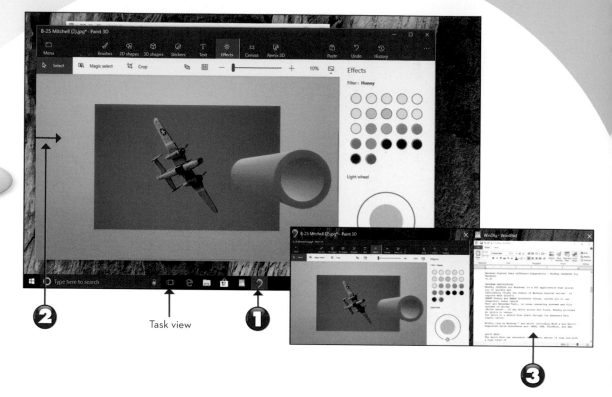

Start

Task view

1 Paint 3D is the active app.

2 Swipe from the left.

3 Tap an app preview to make it active.

End

NOTE

Active App in App Preview Window The active app is at the left end of the app previews. If there is more than one row, it is at the top left. ■

NOTE

Using the Task View Button Instead of swiping, you can click or tap the **Task View** icon on the taskbar in either mode to display active apps to choose from. ■

SWITCHING BETWEEN APPS WITH THE KEYBOARD

If you'd rather use the keyboard to switch between apps, you can do it with Windows 10 FCU. Here's how.

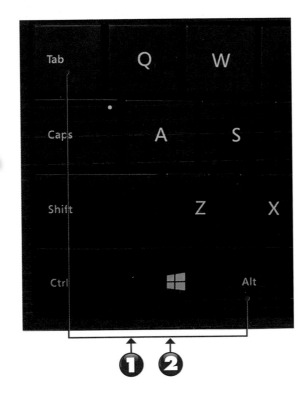

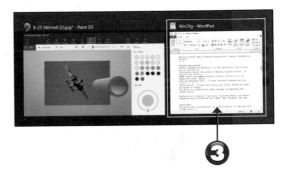

1 Press **Alt+Tab** on the keyboard.

2 Repeat step 1 until the app you want is highlighted.

3 Release the keys to make this app active.

End

 NOTE

Windows+Tab and Arrow Keys You can also use Windows+Tab to see currently open apps. Use the left- and right-arrow keys to highlight the app you want to use. ■

SAVING YOUR FILE

After you create or change a file, or if you want to save a file as a different type, you must save the new file. This lesson explains how to save a file with a new name. If you are saving a new version of an existing file, this keeps the original version intact.

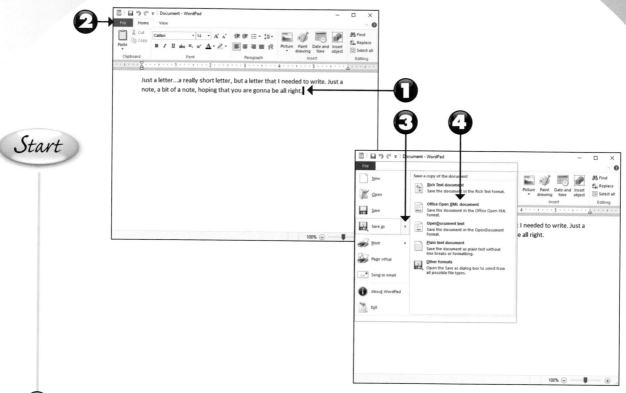

Start

1 Select WordPad as the active app and write some text.

2 Click or tap **File**.

3 Click or tap to open the **Save as** menu.

4 Choose the desired file type (Office Open XML [.docx] document in this example).

Continued

NOTE

Save As Versus Save   If you choose Save (step 3), you replace your original version with the changed version. ■

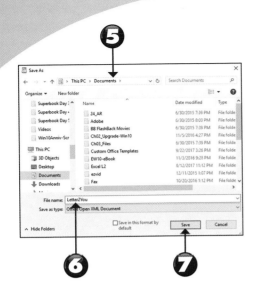

5 Navigate to the location desired.

6 Enter a new name.

7 Click or tap **Save** to save the edited document.

8 The app window shows the new filename.

End

RESIZING AN APP WINDOW

When you run an app in a window, the normal window size might not be what you want. You can easily resize it. If you use a mouse on a laptop or desktop PC that does not have a touchscreen, use this method to resize the window of a desktop app. This example demonstrates resizing the Photos app window.

Start

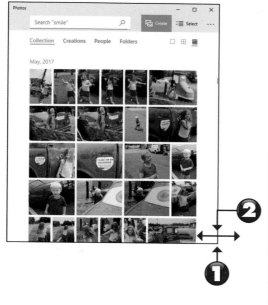

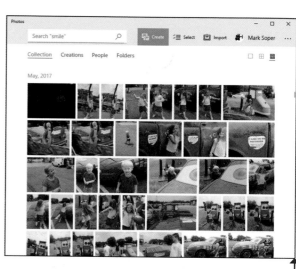

1 Move the mouse pointer over a corner or edge of a window.

2 When the mouse pointer changes to a double-headed arrow, click and drag the window corner or edge.

3 Drag the window to the size and shape you want, and release it.

End

NOTE

Resizing a Window with a Touchscreen   To resize a window using a touchscreen, press and hold on the corner of a window and drag it to the position you want. ◼

MAKING THE DESKTOP VISIBLE WITH WINDOWS PEEK

Many apps offer to create a desktop icon, also called a shortcut, during installation. If you prefer to open apps from the desktop, you might need an easy way to make open windows and maximized apps "disappear" from view without actually closing them so you can easily activate a desktop icon. The Windows Peek feature of Windows 10 FCU makes it easy to hide open apps when needed.

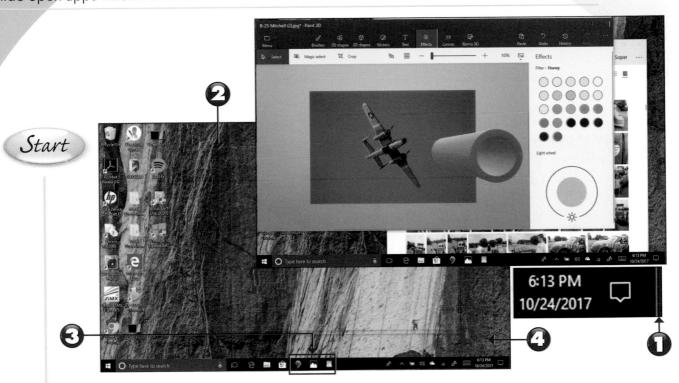

Start

1. Move your mouse to the bottom-right corner of the taskbar onto the small vertical rectangle.

2. All app windows are hidden.

3. The apps continue to run.

4. Move your mouse away from the corner to make all app windows visible.

End

TIP

Another Option for Windows Peek   If you prefer, you can click or tap the small rectangle on the taskbar as step 1. The desktop windows stay hidden until you click the small rectangle again as step 4. ■

USING DESKTOP SHORTCUTS

Most Windows desktops include shortcuts (icons) for some installed apps. If these shortcuts are not visible, here's how to make them visible and use them to open apps.

Start

1 Right-click or press and hold an empty spot on the desktop.

2 Click or tap **View**.

3 Choose the size desired.

4 Click or tap **Show desktop icons**.

Continued

NOTE

Changing Icon Sizes Windows 10 FCU normally uses medium desktop icons. To use larger or smaller icons, select the size desired in step 3. See the inset for a comparison of the icons. ■

Small icon   Medium icon (default)   Large icon

5 Double-click an icon to start the app.

End

ADDING AN APP TO THE TASKBAR

The Windows 10 FCU taskbar is a fast way to start an app. Here's how to add your favorite app to the taskbar. With this example, you pin the Paint 3D app to the taskbar.

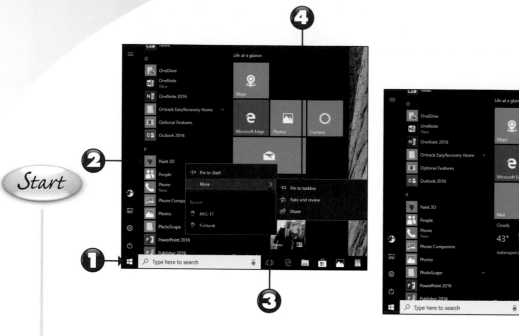

Start

1 Click or tap **Start**.

2 Right-click or press and hold an app's icon.

3 Click or tap **More**.

4 Click or tap **Pin to taskbar**.

5 The app is added to the taskbar.

6 To start the app, click or tap the icon on the taskbar.

End

TIP

Pinning a Running App to the Taskbar   To pin an app that is already running to the taskbar, right-click or press and hold the app's icon and select **Pin to taskbar**. See "Working with Taskbar Jump Lists" on the next page for an illustration. ■

WORKING WITH TASKBAR JUMP LISTS

Most icons on the taskbar, whether pinned or for a running app, also include a jump list, which includes recent files opened or common actions. In this tutorial, you learn how to use the jump list for easy access to files you've opened with a particular app and want to use again with the same app. This example uses the Paint 3D app that we started earlier in this chapter, but you can use any app that you've used to open files (such as Photos, WordPad, Microsoft Office apps, and others) that is pinned or is currently running.

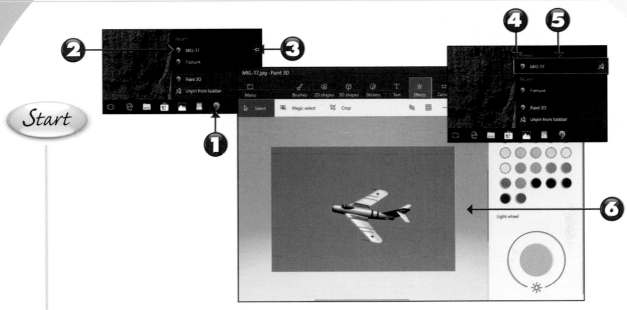

1 Right-click or press and hold the **Paint 3D** icon in the taskbar.

2 Hover your mouse over a file you want to pin. With a touchscreen, press and hold the file-name.

3 When the pushpin appears, click or tap it.

4 The file is pinned to the jump list.

5 Click or tap a file on the list to open it.

6 Paint 3D opens the file from the jump list.

TIP

Opening and Unpinning a File   You can open any file on the jump list. More recently opened files replace older files on the jump list. To remove a file from the jump list, right-click or press and hold the file, and then click or tap **Remove from this list**. Pin files you want to use frequently, because pinned files stay on the list until you remove them. To unpin a file, right-click or press and hold the file, and then click or tap **Unpin from this list**. ■

SNAPPING AND CLOSING AN APP WINDOW

You can change the position and size of the active app window directly from the keyboard by using a Windows 10 FCU feature called *snapping*. This example uses the Microsoft Edge browser app included in Windows 10 FCU.

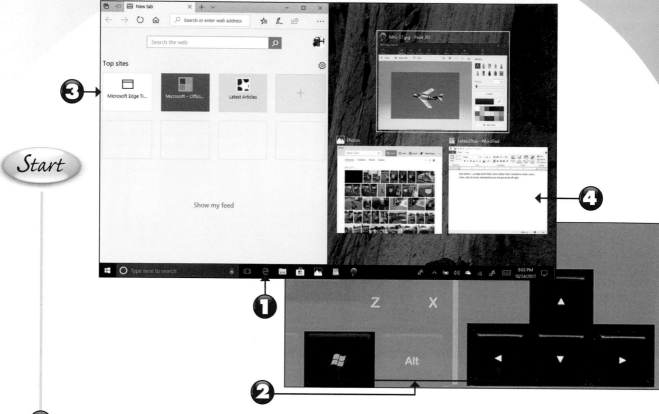

Start

1 Start **Microsoft Edge** from the taskbar or Start menu.

2 Press **Windows key+left arrow**.

3 The active app (Microsoft Edge) snaps to the left edge of the current display.

4 To snap an open app into the other half of the desktop, click or tap it.

Continued

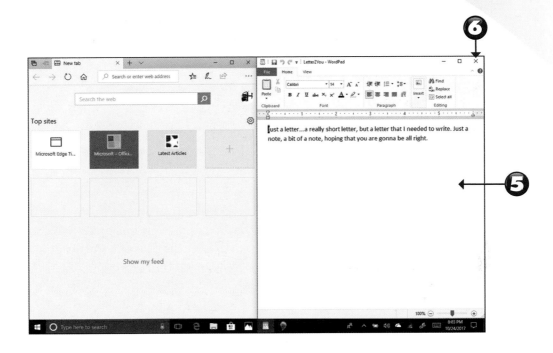

5 The selected app snaps into the right half of the desktop.

6 Click or tap to close the app.

End

TIP

More Snapping Tips Press **Windows key+right arrow** to snap the active app to the right side of the screen. Press **Windows key+up arrow** to maximize the active app. If you drag a program window to the top of the screen, it snaps to full screen. Press **Windows key+down arrow** to minimize the active app. To remove the other app windows from the left or right side of the desktop, press the **Esc** (Escape) key on the keyboard. ■

WEB BROWSING WITH MICROSOFT EDGE

Windows 10 FCU uses Microsoft Edge as its default browser. In the Fall Creators Update, Edge adds new features that make it even easier to use than previous versions for both touch and mouse/keyboard users. In this chapter, you learn how to use Microsoft Edge for all your web browsing.

Opening the
Facebook app
from Edge

Viewing
a live tab
preview

Importing
information
from another
browser

Using
Cortana to
research a
web link

Creating a note
on a web page

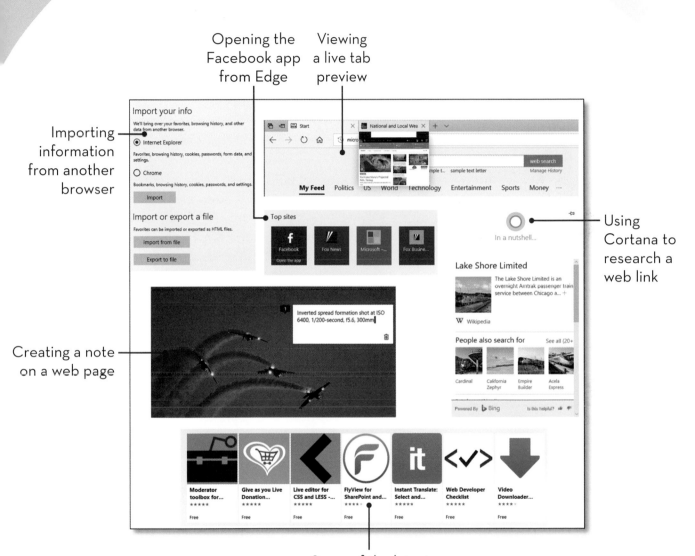

Some of the latest
Edge browser
extensions

STARTING MICROSOFT EDGE

Microsoft Edge might be on your system's taskbar. If not, you can launch it from the Start menu. Here's how.

Tablet mode

Desktop mode

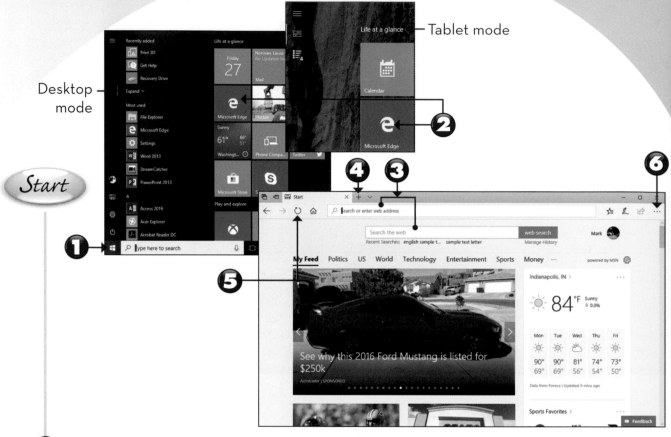

Start

End

1 Click or tap **Start** (desktop mode).

2 Click or tap **Microsoft Edge** (desktop or tablet mode).

3 Use the Microsoft Edge address bar or search box to enter web addresses to visit.

4 Click or tap the **+** to create a new tab.

5 Refresh the page.

6 Click or tap **Settings and more** for settings and more menu items.

ENTERING A WEBSITE ADDRESS (URL)

You can enter a web address, or URL, in the browser's Search box. Edge displays more than just the address when you type in a site you've previously visited. This feature makes it easier to go back to a specific address, even if you have visited several pages in the same domain.

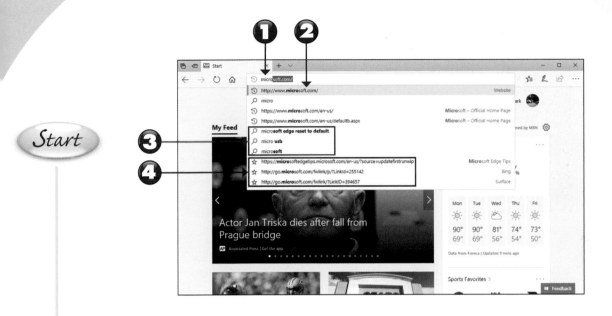

① With Microsoft Edge open, begin typing the name of a website in the address bar. You do not need to add the "www."

② Potential matches are listed with the closest site match at the top of the list.

③ Search suggestions are marked with the search icon.

④ Starred websites are from your favorites list.

TIP

Selecting a Website or Search Use your mouse, touchpad, or touchscreen to select the website or search suggestion you want to open. You can also use the down arrow to highlight the page you want to load and then press **Enter**. ▪

CAUTION

Making Sure Edge Has You Protected Before going to unfamiliar websites, make sure Edge's Smart-Screen Filter is enabled. Learn more in "Setting Browser Privacy, Services, and Platform Controls," this chapter, p. 134. ▪

WORKING WITH TABS

Microsoft Edge includes tabbed browsing, which lets you browse multiple pages in a single window. In this tutorial, you learn how to open and work with new tabs in Microsoft Edge.

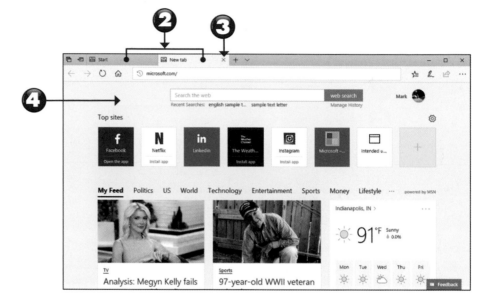

Start

1 Click or tap to open a new tab.

2 Click or tap a tab to switch to that tab.

3 Click the X to close a tab.

4 A New tab page lists top websites for easy access.

End

TIP

Changing New Tab Contents   If you prefer other content displayed when you open a new tab, change your browser settings. To learn more, see "Configuring the New Tab Page," this chapter, p. 111. ■

USING TAB PREVIEWS

Microsoft Edge now includes tab previews, so you can see the contents of a tab without clicking the tab. Here's how it works.

Start

1 Open a website in a new tab.

2 Hover the mouse over another tab that has a website loaded.

3 Edge displays a preview of that tab's contents.

4 Click that tab.

5 Hover the mouse over the original tab.

6 Edge displays a preview of that tab's contents.

End

ADDING TABS TO THE TASKBAR

Want a faster way to get to your favorite websites? In Microsoft Edge, you can now add a website URL directly to the taskbar. Here's what to do.

1 Open the website you want to add to the taskbar.

2 Click or tap the **Settings and more** icon.

3 Click or tap **Pin this page to the taskbar**.

4 Click or tap the website's icon on the taskbar to open the website in Edge.

End

TIP

Adding the Current Page to the Start Menu   To create a shortcut to the current page, click or tap **Pin this page to Start** in step 3. ■

OPENING A LINK

You can open a link to another website in one of three ways: as a replacement for the current page (default), as a new tab in the same window, or in a new window. When you click or tap on a link, the link could open in the same window or in a new window. To specifically open the link in a new tab or window, use the methods shown in this tutorial.

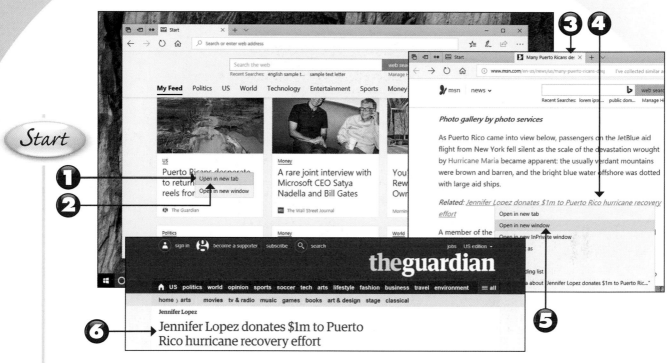

Start

1 Right-click or press and hold the link to display the options menu.

2 Click or tap **Open in new tab**.

3 Click or tap the new tab.

4 Right-click or press and hold a link.

5 Select **Open in new window**.

6 A new window opens to display the link.

End

TIP

Using InPrivate Opening a page in an InPrivate window (step 5) prevents that website from leaving tracking cookies on your system or from showing up in your browser's website history pages. ■

SETTING YOUR HOME PAGE

You can change your Microsoft Edge home page (also known as a Start page) whenever you want. Edge provides you with several options. Here's how to open Edge (or a new tab) with the options you prefer.

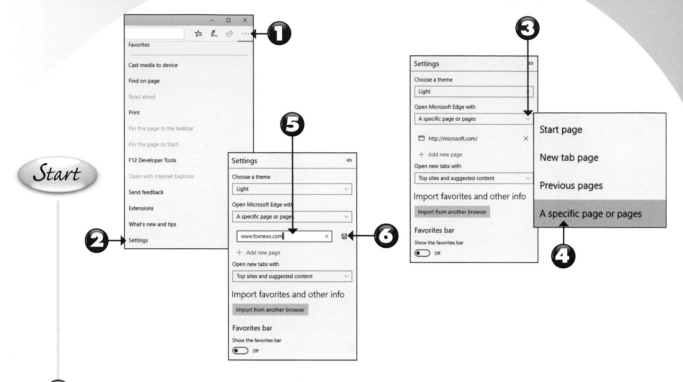

Start

1 Click or tap the **Settings and more** (three-dot) icon.

2 Click or tap **Settings**.

3 Click or tap the **Open Microsoft Edge with** drop-down menu.

4 Click or tap **A specific page or pages**.

5 Enter the URL of the page you want as your home page into the **Enter a web address** box.

6 Click the **Save** button to save your changes. After you close and reopen your browser, the new website will be used as the home page.

End

NOTE

Removing or Adding a Page   If you want to open multiple pages when you start Edge, click the **Add new page** link shown in step 3 and add a page. If you want to remove a page that's set to open automatically, click the X next to the page name (step 3). ■

CONFIGURING THE NEW TAB PAGE

The New tab page is the page that appears whenever you open a new tab. In this lesson, you learn how to customize it to show the information you want.

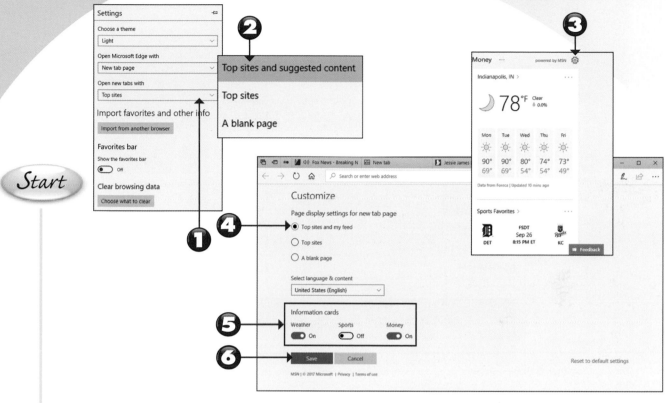

1 With the Settings menu displayed from the previous task, click or tap the **Open new tabs with** drop-down menu.

2 Click or tap **Top sites and suggested content**.

3 Open a new tab and click or tap the **Settings** (gear) button.

4 Click or tap **Top sites and my feed**.

5 Choose the information cards to display on the right side of the browser window.

6 Click the **Save** button to save your changes.

End

TIP

Weather, Sports, and Money When these information cards are enabled, the specific information displayed is configured through the Weather, Sports, and Money apps. See Chapter 12 for details. ■

SWITCHING TO/FROM FULL SCREEN VIEW

Edge can now switch between normal and full-screen views with the press of a single key or key combination. Here's what to expect.

Start

Press F11 to exit full screen.

1 Open a website.

2 Press the F11 key or Fn+F11 keys to switch to full-screen view.

3 Edge switches to full-screen view.

4 To close this reminder, click the X.

5 Press the F11 key or Fn+F11 keys to return to normal view.

End

NOTE

F11 or Fn+F11   Many laptop and some desktop keyboards assign the F11 key to a different function by default (in this example, PgUp). To use the F11 key as in this exercise, you must press and hold the Fn key while also pressing F11. ■

SWIPING BACKWARD AND FORWARD

If your Windows 10 device has a touchscreen, you can flick your way back to previous Edge screens and then forward again.

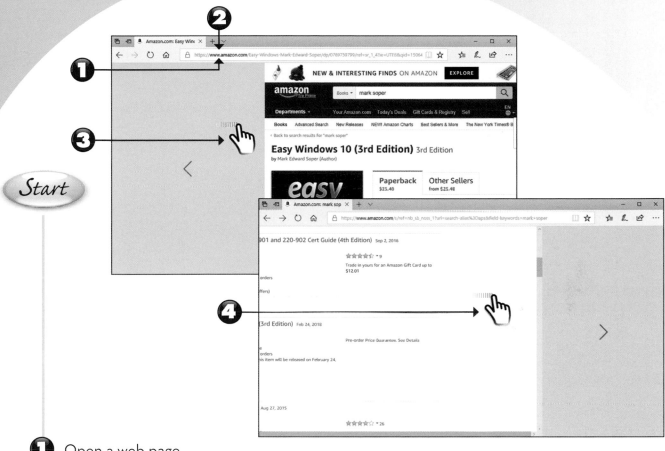

Start

1 Open a web page.

2 Go to another page.

3 Flick to the right to go back to the previous screen.

4 Flick to the left to go to the next screen.

End

USING CORTANA IN MICROSOFT EDGE

Cortana is the powerful search and information technology included in Windows 10 FCU. You can use Cortana in Microsoft Edge to get more information about a link, highlighted text, or a picture on a web page. Here's an example of how Cortana can help you learn more about what you see in a web page.

Start

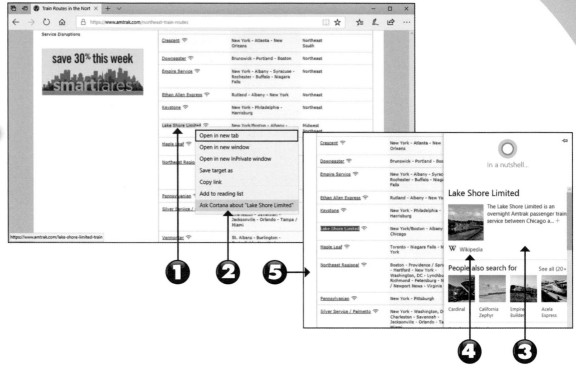

1 Highlight and right-click/press and hold text, or right-click or press and hold a picture or link.

2 Click or tap **Ask Cortana about**.

3 Cortana opens a pane in your browser with the information requested. If you select a picture, Cortana tries to identify the subject and provides a link to a full-size version if available.

4 Click or tap a link to learn more.

5 Click or tap an empty area of the browser window to close the Cortana pane.

End

NOTE

How to Highlight Text   To highlight text with your mouse or touchpad, click and hold the beginning of the text, move to the right until the text is highlighted, and then release. To highlight text with your touchscreen, press and hold a word in the text until a highlight appears. Press and drag one of the circle markers at each end of the word until all the text desired is highlighted. ■

COPYING AND PASTING A LINK

You can use the same right-click menu you use to open links or access Cortana to copy links to paste into other apps. Here's how to use this feature with Windows 10 FCU's built-in text editor, Notepad. You can also use this technique with Microsoft Word and other word-processing programs.

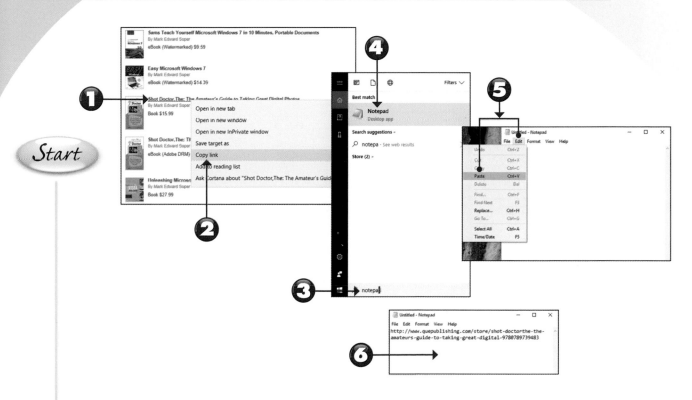

Start

End

① Right-click or press and hold a link.

② Click or tap **Copy link**.

③ Click or tap the Cortana **Search** box and type **notepad**.

④ Click or tap **Notepad**.

⑤ Click or tap **Edit** and select **Paste**.

⑥ The link is pasted into Notepad.

USING ZOOM

Zoom enables you to increase or decrease the size of text and graphics on a web page. By increasing the size, you make pages easier to read, and by reducing the size, you enable page viewing without horizontal scrolling.

1 Click or tap the **Settings and more** (three-dot) menu.

2 The current zoom setting is listed here (the default is 100%).

3 Click or tap the plus (+) sign to increase the zoom level.

4 The page is zoomed to 150%.

5 Note the large graphics.

6 Click or tap the minus (–) sign to decrease the zoom level.

Continued

NOTE

Zoom Rates Each time you tap the plus (+) sign, you increase the zoom ratio by 25% (for example, 100% to 125%). Each time you tap the minus (–) sign, you decrease the zoom ratio by 25% (for example, 100% to 75%).

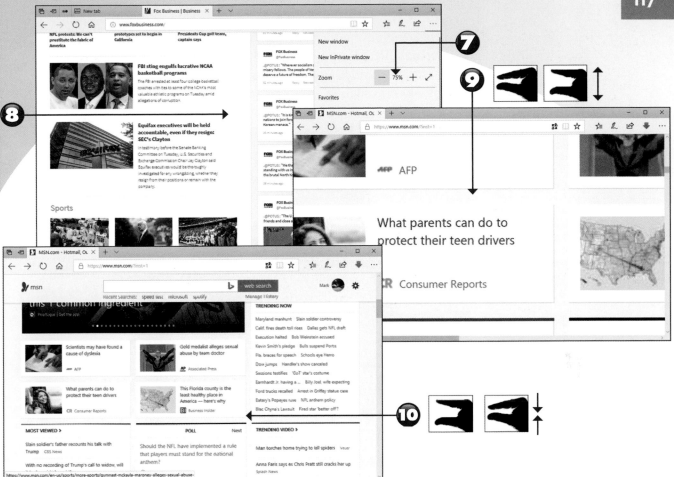

7 The page is zoomed to 75%.

8 More of the page is visible, but the text and photos are smaller.

9 To zoom in (enlarge page) with a touchscreen, touch two fingers to the screen and pinch outward.

10 To zoom out (reduce page) with a touchscreen, touch two fingers to the screen and pinch inward.

End

NOTE

When to Zoom The 150% view shown in step 5 makes the text and pictures on a web page easier to see, but you must scroll left and right as well as up and down to see the entire page. Use zoom settings smaller than 100% if you want to see more of the page without scrolling. These settings do not affect how the page prints.

USING READING VIEW

You can read a lot of terrific articles in your browser, but most commercial sites litter articles with ads and other visual distractions. The Reading view in Microsoft Edge shows you only the main contents of the current URL without the clutter. Although not all pages support it, here's how to use it when available.

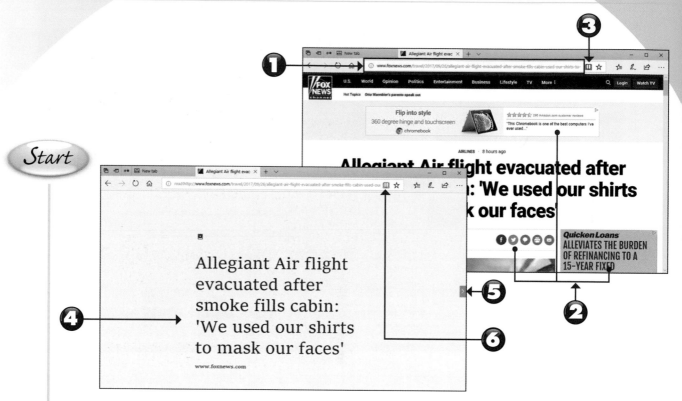

Start

1 Open the web page you want to read.

2 Note the ads and other visual distractions.

3 Click or tap **Reading view**.

4 Microsoft Edge displays the web page without the clutter.

5 Click the right arrow or swipe left to continue reading.

6 Click or tap to return to normal view.

End

PRINTING OR CREATING A PDF OF A WEB PAGE

Microsoft Edge enables you to preview and print web pages or turn them into PDFs. I recommend you switch to Reading view first (see the preceding exercise, "Using Reading View," for details) to avoid ads and other onscreen clutter, and then print your page as shown in this exercise.

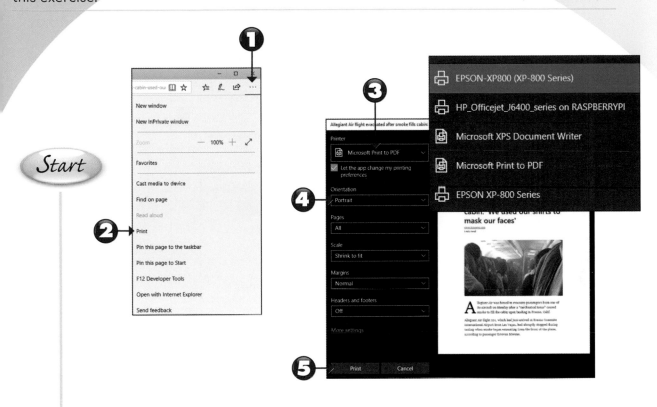

Start

1 Click or tap the **Settings and more** (three-dot) menu.

2 Click or tap **Print**.

3 Click or tap if you need to change printers. (To create a PDF file, select **Microsoft Print to PDF** from the drop-down menu.)

4 Click or tap to change page orientation.

5 Click or tap to print the page.

End

NOTE

Changing Paper Size, Type, and Other Settings   The default paper size is usually letter or A4. To change paper size, paper type (plain paper, photo paper, and so on), and other settings, click or tap **More settings**. ■

ADDING A WEB PAGE AS A FAVORITE

When you make a web page a favorite (also known as bookmarking a page), you can go to it quickly whenever you want. Microsoft Edge stores your favorites in the Favorites folder unless you specify otherwise. Here's how to save a favorite page.

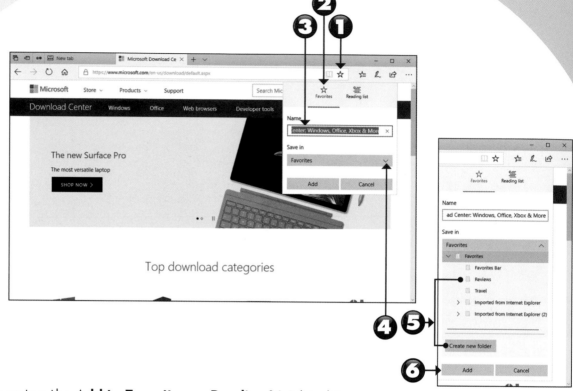

Start

1 Click or tap the **Add to Favorites or Reading List** (star) icon.

2 Click or tap **Favorites**.

3 Accept or edit the name of the page in the **Name** box.

4 If you want to store your pages in a folder other than Favorites, click or tap to open the **Save in** menu.

5 Choose an existing folder, or click **Create new folder**.

6 Click or tap **Add** to save the favorite in the selected folder.

End

NOTE

Confirming the Favorite Was Created   The outline star icon you tap or click in step 1 turns a solid gold color after you add the page as a favorite. ■

VIEWING AND OPENING FAVORITES

You can reopen a favorite web page in just a few clicks or taps, as you learn in this exercise.

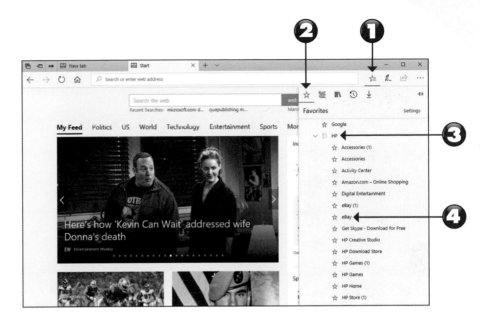

Start

1 Click or tap the **Hub** icon.

2 Click or tap the **Favorites** (star) icon.

3 Click or tap a folder to view the website links it contains.

4 Click or tap a favorite to open it.

End

TIP

Removing Favorites If a favorite becomes outdated or no longer needed, you can discard it. From the Favorites list, right-click or press and hold the favorite. Click or tap **Delete** to remove it. ■

READING EPUB EBOOKS

EPUB is a popular ebook format, and Edge can now read EPUB files without a separate app. Here's how easy it is to do it.

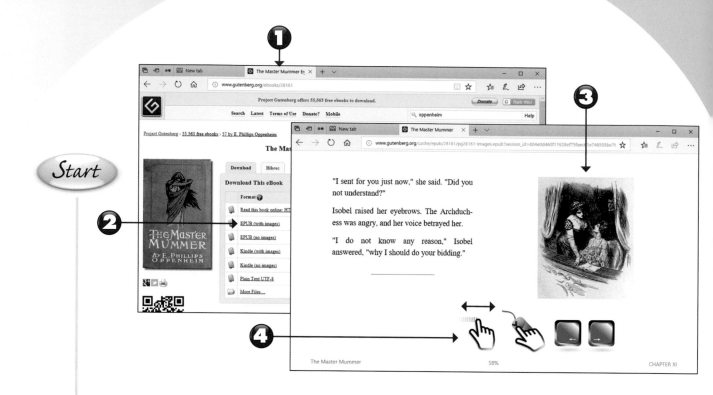

Start

End

1 Open a web page that includes a link to an EPUB ebook.

2 Click or tap the EPUB link.

3 Edge opens the file.

4 Use the left and right arrow keys on your keyboard, use the scroll wheel on your mouse, or flick with your touchpad to move through the book.

READING PDFS

PDF, like EPUB, is a popular ebook format, and Edge can now read PDF files without a separate app. Here's what to do.

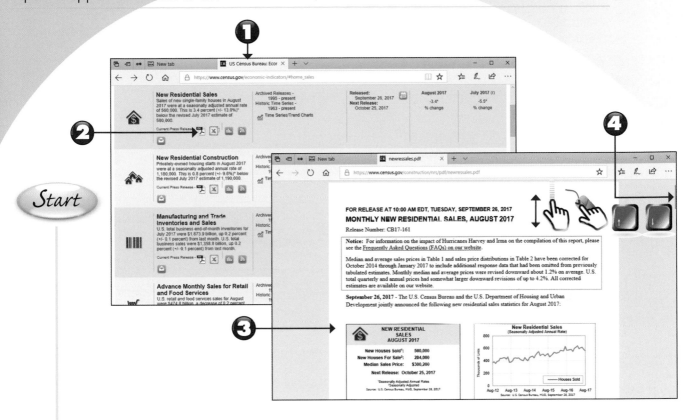

Start

1 Open a web page that includes a link to a PDF.

2 Click or tap the PDF link.

3 Edge opens the file.

4 Use the scroll bar on the right, arrow keys, or scroll mouse wheel or flick between pages to move through the document.

End

ADDING TABS TO FAVORITES FROM THE RIGHT-CLICK MENU

Edge now makes it easier than ever before to add a tab to your Favorites menu. Here's the shortcut.

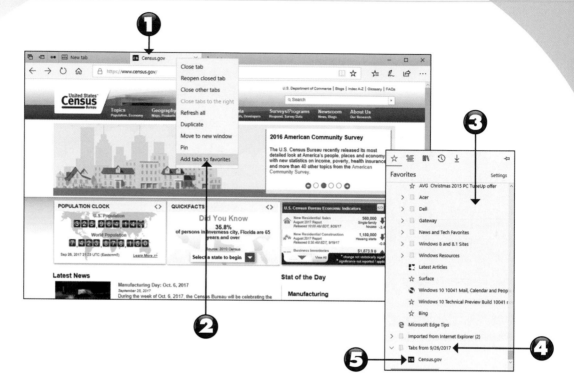

Start

1 Right-click or press and hold the browser tab.

2 Click or tap **Add tabs to favorites**.

3 The Favorites menu opens.

4 Click the **Tabs from (date)** folder to see the page(s) you saved on the date listed.

5 Note the favorite saved in step 2.

End

NOTE

Automatic Favorites Storage If you save more than one tab as a favorite on the same day, they are all stored in that day's Favorites folder. Each day you add at least one tab to favorites with the right-click menu, a new folder for that day is created in Favorites. ■

OPENING APPS FROM EDGE

Many social network services, such as Facebook, now have apps available from the Microsoft Store. These apps often provide more features than the website version. You can now use Edge to open the app instead of the website. Here's how.

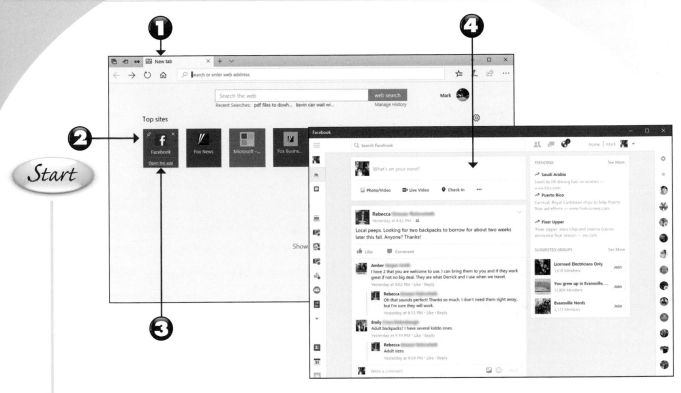

1. After you install an app that also uses a website, open a new tab with Edge.

2. If you have **Top sites** enabled, the newly added app is listed as a website or app.

3. Click or tap **Open the app**.

4. The app opens.

End

TIP
Pinning and Removing Top Sites   Some sites on your top sites list (step 2) may drop off the list if you don't use them. To keep a site on the list, hover the mouse over the icon and click the pin button (upper-left corner of the icon). To remove a site from the list, click or tap the X (remove) icon in the upper-right corner. See the Facebook icon for an example. ■

TIP
More About Apps for Websites   In some cases, you can install a website's companion app directly from an Install app link on the website without using the Store app. To decide which websites can be opened by an app, go to Edge's Advanced Settings, turn on **Open sites in apps**, and choose from the apps listed. ■

INSTALLING BROWSER EXTENSIONS IN EDGE

Edge supports an increasing number of browser extensions. A browser extension adds new features to a browser. For example, browser extensions for Edge can manage passwords, clip web content for use with Evernote and One Note information managers, block ads, translate web pages, make video playback easier, and more. Extensions for Edge are available from the Microsoft Store, and this tutorial shows you how to find and install the ones you need.

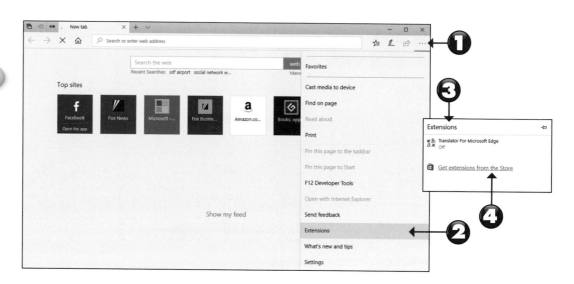

1 Click or tap the **Settings and more** (three-dot) menu.

2 Click or tap **Extensions**.

3 If you have any installed extensions, they are listed here.

4 Click or tap **Get extensions from the Store** to install new extensions.

Continued

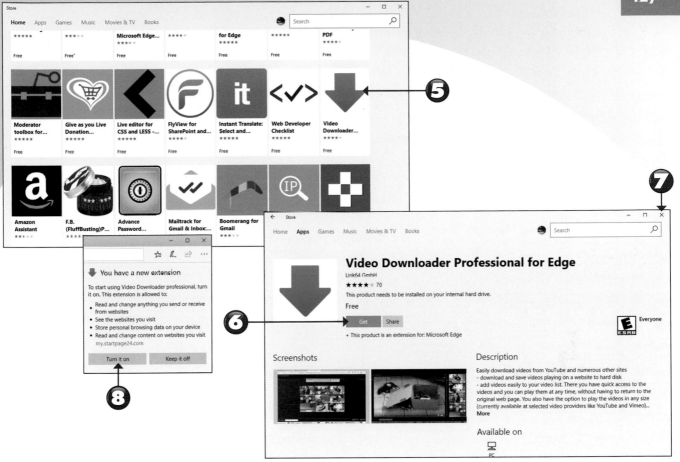

5 Each extension is rated in the Microsoft Store, and its price (or Free) is listed. Tap an extension to learn more.

6 Click or tap **Get** to start the installation process.

7 After the app is installed, close the Store window.

8 In the Edge window, click or tap **Turn it on** to start using the extension.

End

MANAGING BROWSER EXTENSIONS IN EDGE

After you install one or more extensions in Edge, use the Extensions panel to manage them. Here's what you can do, using the Translator for Microsoft Edge as an example.

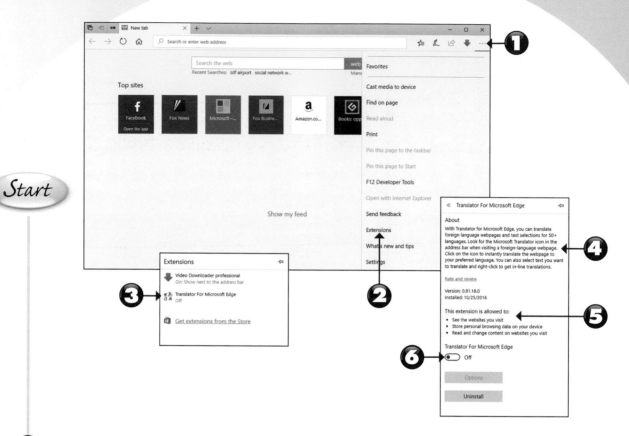

Start

1 Click or tap the **Settings and more** (three-dot) menu.

2 Click or tap **Extensions**. Click or tap an installed extension.

3 Click or tap an installed extension.

4 Read what the extension does.

5 Extension permissions are listed here.

6 Click or tap and drag to turn it on. If prompted, you can also enable **Show button next to the address bar**.

Continued

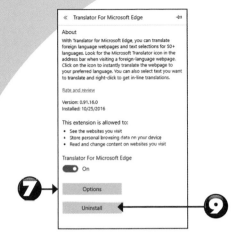

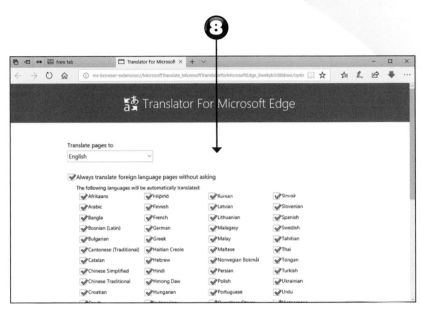

7 Click or tap to configure options.

8 Edge opens a tab with the options for the extension.

9 Click or tap to uninstall this extension.

End

USING THE WEB NOTES TEXT TOOL

In Microsoft Edge, the powerful Windows Ink tools are called Web Notes. In addition to the markup features discussed in Chapter 13, you can add a text note to a web page.

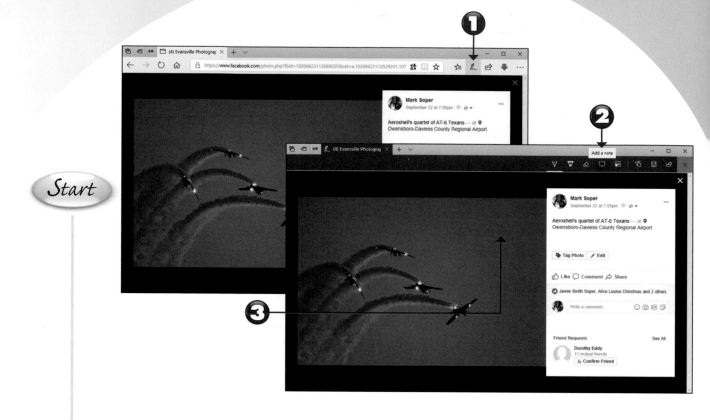

Start

1 Click or tap the Web Notes tool.

2 Click or tap **Add a note**.

3 Click or tap the location where you want to place the note.

Continued

4 Enter the note text.

5 Click or tap the note number to close the text window.

6 Click or tap to save the web page as a favorite.

7 Change the name if desired.

8 Choose the folder in Favorites to use.

9 Click or tap to save the web page as a favorite.

End

TIP

Retrieving the Note To retrieve the note, open the Favorites menu and click the link. The page is reloaded with the note. You can hide the note or go to the original page. ▪

TIP

Deleting a Web Note To delete a web note, open it and click the trash can icon. ▪

USING DOWNLOADS

Although Windows 10 FCU encourages users to get apps from the Microsoft Store, there are still many types of apps, utilities, and driver files that must be downloaded from vendor websites. Microsoft Edge makes it easy to see what you've downloaded and to get to your downloads. Here's how to use this feature. (Be sure to download at least one file first.)

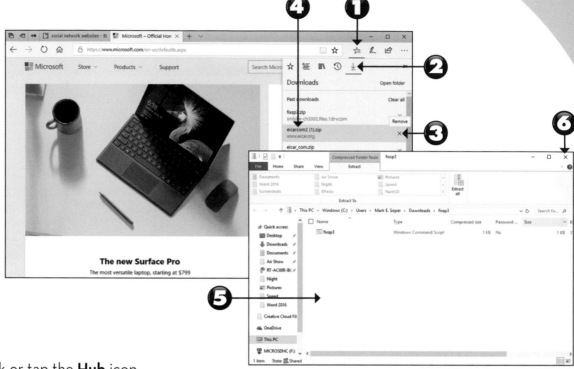

Start

1 Click or tap the **Hub** icon.

2 Click or tap the **Downloads** icon.

3 Click the X to remove a download from the list.

4 Click or tap a download to open it.

5 If the download is a compressed file, it is opened in File Explorer.

6 Click or tap to close the File Explorer window after installing or extracting the download.

Continued

TIP

Downloads Not Listed Aren't Gone   Clearing the Downloads list with **Clear all** or removing an individual download from the list (step 3) does not remove the downloaded files from your device. If you want to remove a downloaded file, click the Open folder link to open the Downloads folder in File Explorer, and then delete it there. ■

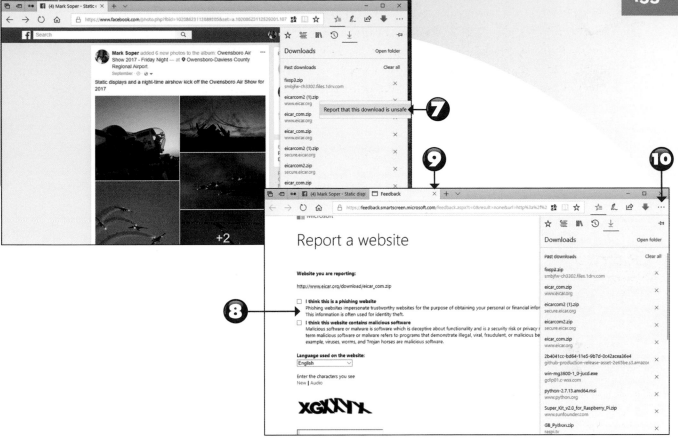

7 If the download is suspicious, right-click or press and hold it and click **Report that this download is unsafe**.

8 A new browser tab opens. Complete the form and submit it.

9 After the form is submitted, close the browser tab.

10 Click the **Settings and more** (three-dot) menu to close the Downloads menu.

End

TIP

Changing the Default Downloads Folder   To change the default downloads folder, open the **Settings and more** menu, click or tap **Settings**, click or tap **View advanced settings**, and click or tap the **Change** button in the Downloads section. ■

SETTING BROWSER PRIVACY, SERVICES, AND PLATFORM CONTROLS

The browser Settings, accessed from the bottom of the **Settings and More** (three-dot) menu, also enables you to configure privacy settings, protect your browser, and make it more efficient in page handling. Here are the options you can configure.

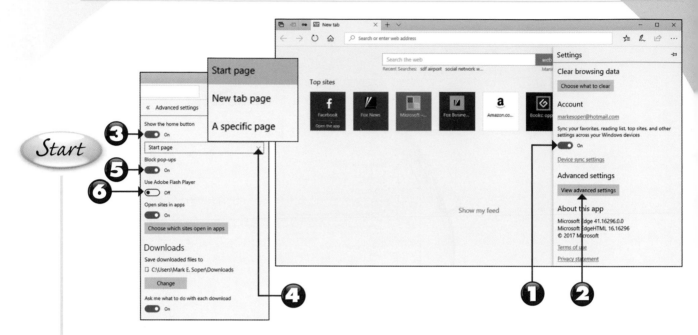

1 With browser Settings open, scroll down and turn on **Sync your favorites, reading list, top sites, and other settings across your Windows devices** to have the same information on all devices. This is handy if you use Windows 10 on more than one device.

2 Click or tap **View advanced settings**.

3 To display a Home button next to the Address box, click or press and drag to **On**.

4 Select what should be displayed when you click or tap the **Home** button.

5 Pop-ups are blocked by default; to permit them, click or press and drag to **Off**.

6 Leave the **Use Adobe Flash Player** setting turned off because it is a security risk. Enable it if a trustworthy site prompts you to use it.

Continued

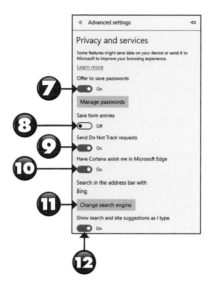

7 Scroll down to the Privacy and Services section. If you do not want Edge to save passwords you enter, click or press and drag the **Offer to Save Passwords** control to **Off**.

8 If you do not want Edge to save form entries, click or press and drag to **Off**.

9 To send Do Not Track requests to websites, click or press and drag to **On**.

10 To disable Cortana when using Edge, click or press and drag to **Off**.

11 Edge uses the Microsoft Bing search engine in the address bar. If you prefer a different search page that you have already used from within Edge, click or tap **Change search engine** and choose your favorite.

12 Leave this option enabled to make your searches easier.

Continued

TIP

Managing Passwords If you save your passwords with Edge, you can remove obsolete passwords by clicking or tapping **Manage passwords**. ■

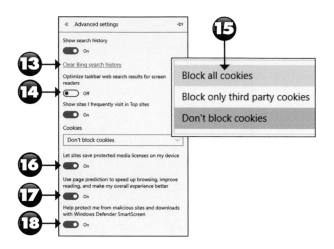

13 Click or tap to clear Bing search history.

14 Enable this if you use a screen reader.

15 Open the Cookies menu if you want to block third-party cookies or all cookies.

16 If you download protected media (TV, movies, music), leave this **On** so you can play it back on this computer.

17 Page prediction preloads pages to speed up browsing; leave this **On**.

18 SmartScreen Filter helps protect your browser from malicious sites; make sure this is turned **On** (may default to Off for some users).

End

NOTE

What the Privacy Settings Do If you block third-party cookies (step 15), you reduce the number of ads you see based on your recent search history. If you block all cookies (step 15), many e-commerce and e-banking websites won't work properly. If you turn on Do Not Track (step 9), you are requesting that websites and web apps do not track your activity. This setting also reduces the number of ads you see based on your recent search history. However, some websites disregard Do Not Track requests, so this setting is not a substitute for browser cookie management. ■

GROOVE MUSIC

Windows 10 FCU makes it easy to enjoy your audio collection with Groove Music, and you can now add Spotify. This chapter shows you how to play music with both apps.

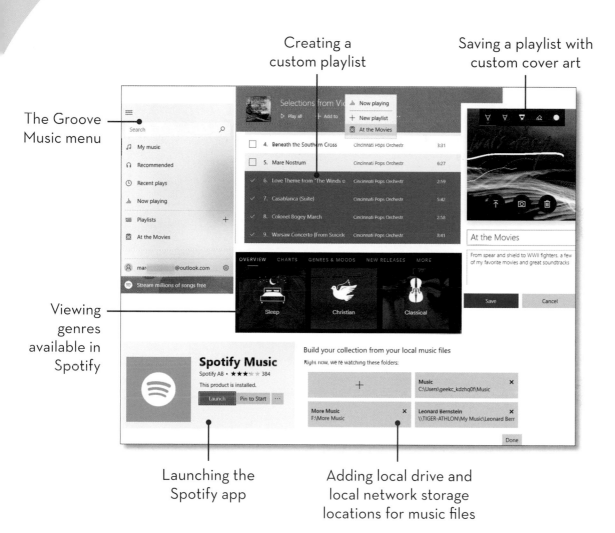

Creating a
custom playlist

Saving a playlist with
custom cover art

The Groove
Music menu

Viewing
genres
available in
Spotify

Launching the
Spotify app

Adding local drive and
local network storage
locations for music files

STARTING THE GROOVE MUSIC APP

The Groove Music app in Windows 10 FCU acts as a one-stop shop for your computer music needs. Whether you want to organize music files on your computer or tablet, listen to songs across devices, or access Spotify's enormous music catalog, the Groove Music app is the place to start. First, let's learn how to open the app and see its major features.

Desktop mode →

Start

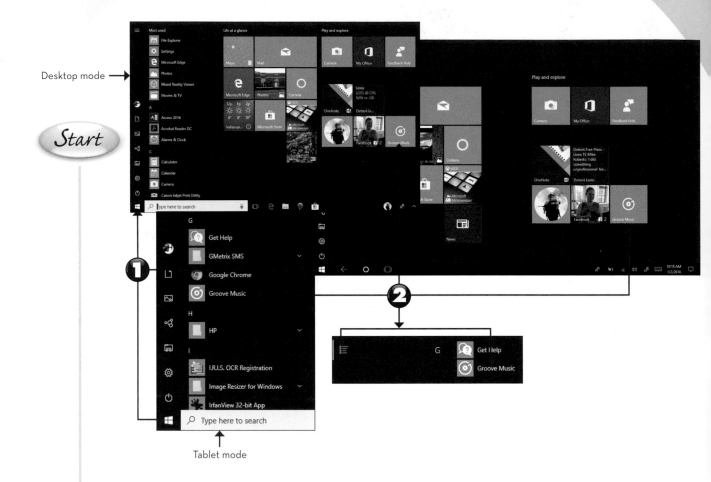

Tablet mode

1 Click or tap **Start** in Desktop mode or Tablet mode.

2 Desktop mode: If necessary, scroll down and click or tap **Groove Music**.
Tablet mode: If necessary, click or tap **All apps**, and then click or tap **Groove Music**.

Continued

NOTE

Playing Music from File Explorer   The first time you open a song in File Explorer, you might be prompted to choose a default app. Select Groove Music if you want to use it to play songs in File Explorer. ■

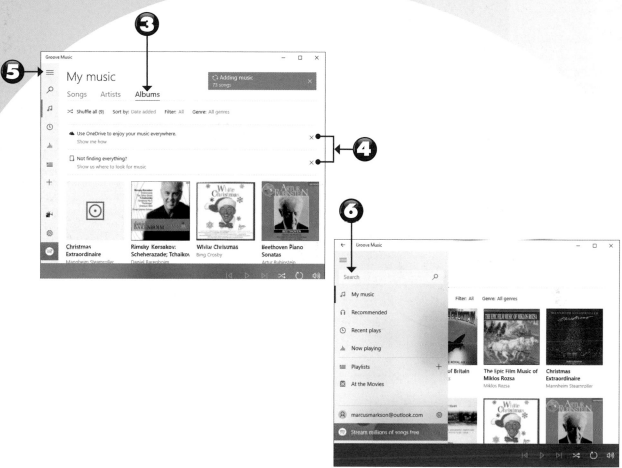

3 The Albums view is the default view.

4 Click or tap to close these notifications.

5 Click or tap to expand the menu.

6 In the expanded menu, note the Search box.

End

NOTE

Changing Settings To add locations to search for music, see "Selecting Music Folders," p. 149, this chapter. To learn how to sync files, including music, to OneDrive, see "Syncing Files with OneDrive," in Chapter 14, p. 296. ■

VIEWING AND PLAYBACK OPTIONS FOR YOUR MUSIC COLLECTION

The Groove Music app makes it easy to see the types of music in your collection and where it's located. Here's how to use these features.

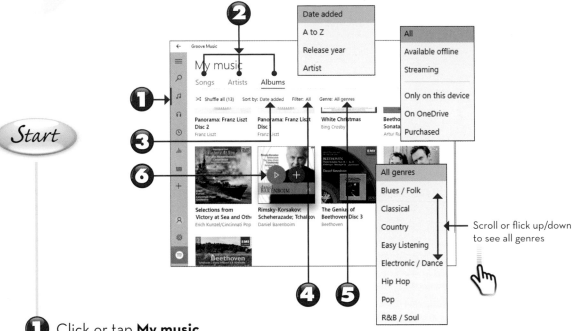

Scroll or flick up/down to see all genres

1 Click or tap **My music**.

2 Choose the view to use (Albums selected).

3 Click or tap to sort music.

4 Click or tap to filter music by location.

5 Click or tap to filter by genre.

6 To see the contents of an album, click or tap it.

Continued

NOTE

Music Locations In step 4, choose **Available offline** to see tracks that can be played back without an Internet connection. Choose **Streaming** to see tracks that require an Internet connection to play. Choose **Only on this device** to see tracks that are stored in the local Music folder. **On OneDrive** displays tracks that are stored in the OneDrive Music folder. **Purchased** displays tracks that were purchased from the Microsoft Store. ■

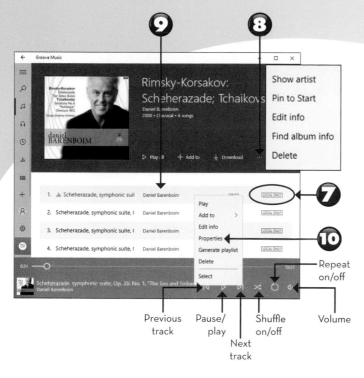

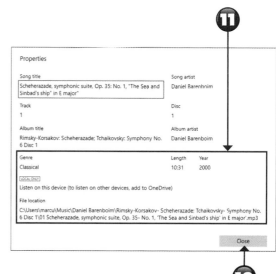

Repeat
on/off

Previous
track

Pause/
play

Next
track

Shuffle
on/off

Volume

7 Note that each track lists its location.

8 Click or tap for additional options.

9 Right-click a track for more options.

10 Click or tap **Properties** to learn more about the track.

11 Note the genre and location data.

12 Click or tap to close.

End

NOTE

Track Information   In step 7, tracks stored on OneDrive list ONEDRIVE
as the location. Tracks stored locally list LOCAL ONLY as the location. To
learn more about OneDrive, see Chapter 14. ■

CREATING A PLAYLIST

You can create a playlist (a collection of songs) from any selected tracks in your music collection. Here's how to make one, using a combination of selecting a single track from an album, an entire album, or selected tracks from an album.

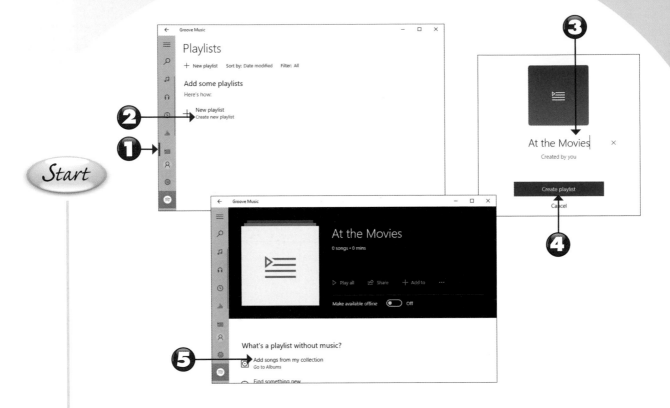

1 Click or tap **Playlists**.

2 Click or tap **Create new playlist**.

3 Enter a name for the new playlist.

4 Click or tap **Create playlist**.

5 Click or tap **Add songs from my collection**.

Continued

6 Click or tap **My music**.

7 Click or tap **Albums**.

8 Click or tap an album.

9 Click or tap a track.

10 Click or tap **Add to**.

11 Click or tap your playlist.

Continued

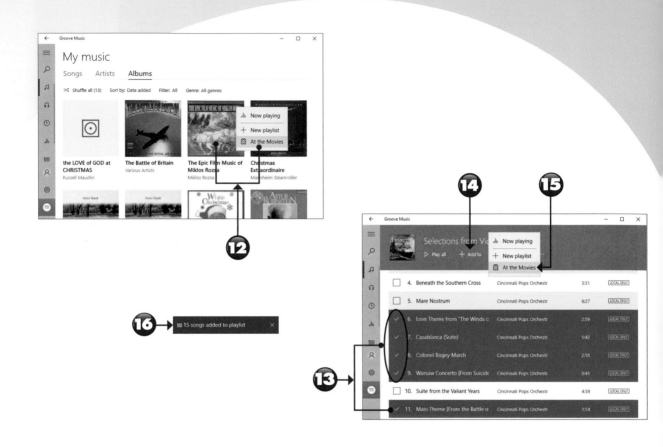

12 To add an album, right-click it and select your playlist.

13 To add multiple tracks from an album, open it and select the tracks.

14 Click or tap **Add to**.

15 Click or tap your playlist.

16 Click or tap to close the confirmation message.

Continued

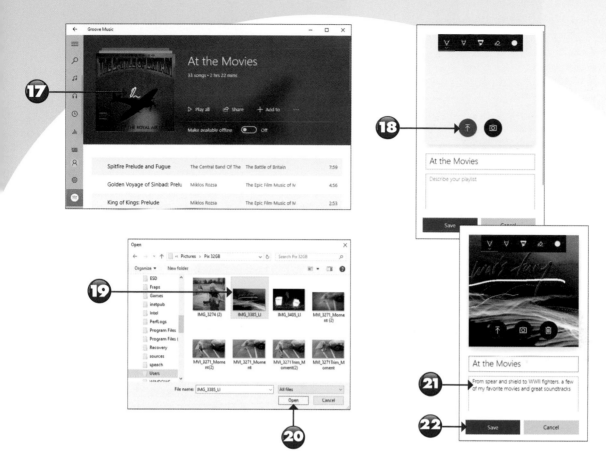

17 To change the playlist cover art, click the current playlist cover art.

18 Click or tap **Select an image.**

19 Navigate to a photo, and click or tap it.

20 Click or tap **Open.**

21 Add a description.

22 Click or tap **Save.**

End

PLAYING A PLAYLIST

Playing a playlist is as easy as playing an album or individual track.

Start

1 Click or tap **Playlists**.

2 Click or tap to select a playlist.

3 Click or tap to play the entire playlist.

4 Click or tap a track to play it.

End

SELECTING MUSIC FOLDERS

By default, Groove Music uses the current user's Music folder as the location for download-ing music and finding existing music tracks. However, Groove Music can also play music in other locations, including network folders. Here's how to configure this feature.

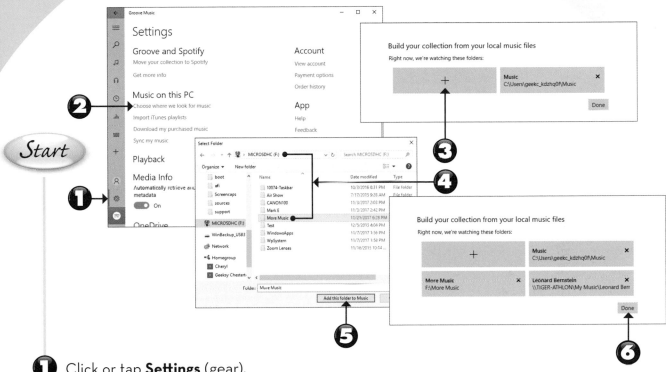

1. Click or tap **Settings** (gear).

2. Click or tap **Choose where we look for music**.

3. Click or tap the plus (+) sign.

4. Navigate to the folder you want to add and click or tap it.

5. Click or tap **Add this folder to Music**.

6. Repeat steps 3 through 5 for other folders if desired and then click or tap **Done**.

End

🔍 **TIP**

More Ways to More Music   Use the **Import iTunes playlists** option (steps 1 and 2) to access playlists you've already created. You can also add folders on your network (see step 6). ■

SEARCHING FOR MUSIC

The Groove Music search tool helps you find songs, artists, or albums in your collection. Here's how it works.

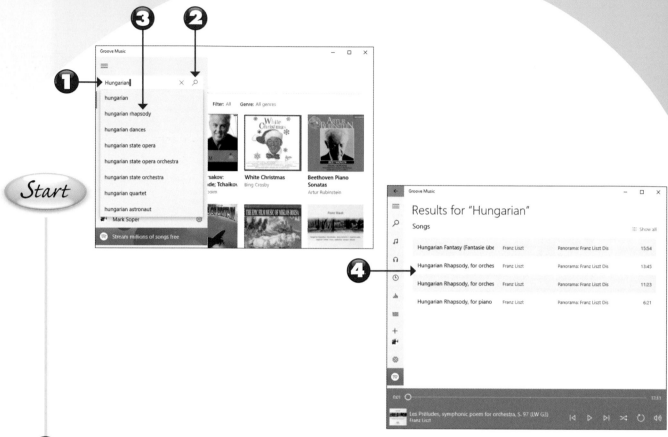

Start

1. Enter the music to search for (title, artist, or subject) into the Search box.

2. Tap the Search icon or press the **Enter** key on the keyboard.

3. Click or tap to select the artist, album, or song you want.

4. Note the matching songs.

Continued

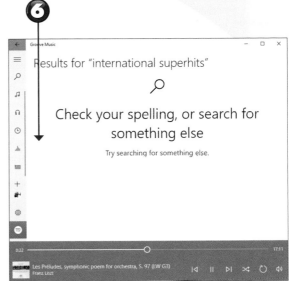

5 Repeat steps 1 through 3 to find more music.

6 The "Check your spelling" error message appears if there are no search matches in your music library.

End

SIGNING UP FOR SPOTIFY

At the end of 2017, Microsoft shut down its Groove Music service. As a replacement, it offers free access to the Spotify music streaming service. Here's how to add Spotify to your Windows 10 system by using the Spotify icon in Groove Music.

Start

1. Click or tap **Stream millions of songs free** (Spotify).

2. The Microsoft Store opens the Spotify Music page.

3. Click or tap **Get**.

4. Click or tap **Launch** to start Spotify.

Continued

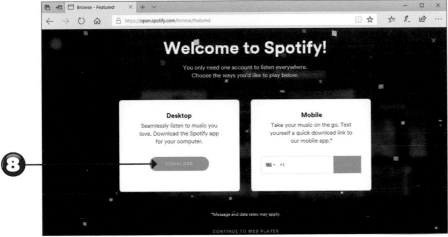

5 If you already have a Spotify account, log in.

6 Click or tap **Sign up** to create an account.

7 You can sign up for Spotify with either your Facebook account or your email address and a password you create.

8 From the **Welcome** dialog, click or tap **Download** to install the Spotify app.

Continued

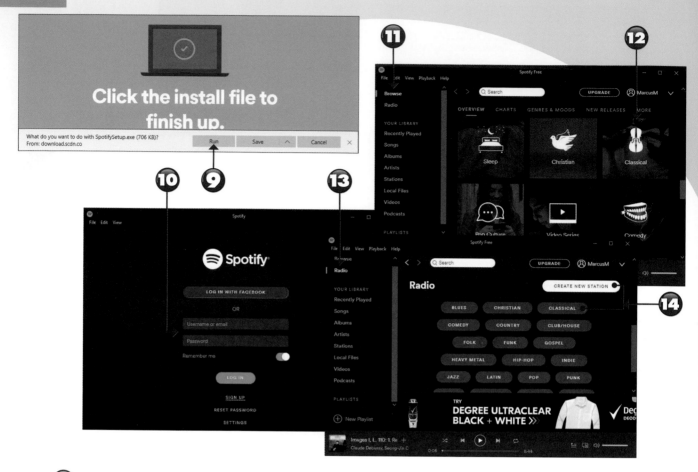

9 Click or tap **Run** to complete the installation.

10 Log in using the same method you chose in step 7.

11 Click or tap **Browse** to find music by genre.

12 Choose one or more genres.

13 Click or tap **Radio** to set up streaming music playback.

14 Click a genre, and then click **Create new station**.

End

TIP

Create More Focused Music Choices Use the search tool visible in steps 13 and 14 to search for specific composers or artists to stream or add to playlists. ■

Chapter 9

TAKING, EDITING, AND SHARING PHOTOS AND VIDEOS

Windows 10 FCU includes the Camera app so you can take digital photos and videos with your device's webcam, front-facing camera, or rear-facing camera. Once taken or recorded, you can view and edit them using the Photos app. In this chapter, you learn how to use the Camera and Photos apps. The instructions in this chapter are written for Tablet mode, but Camera and Photos work in either Desktop or Tablet modes.

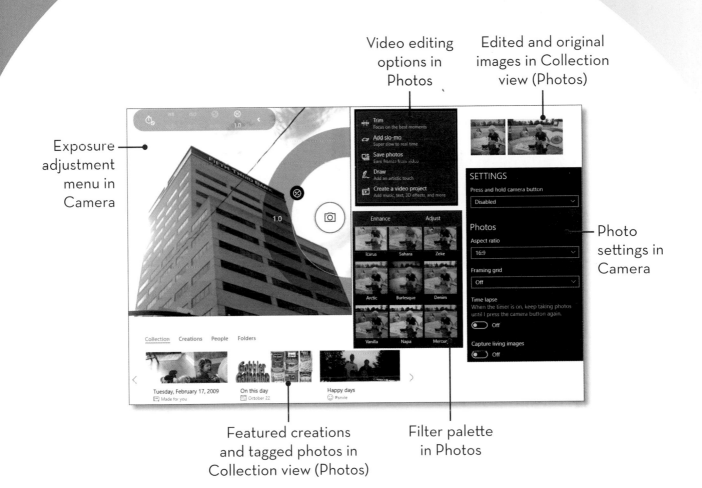

Video editing options in Photos

Edited and original images in Collection view (Photos)

Exposure adjustment menu in Camera

Photo settings in Camera

Featured creations and tagged photos in Collection view (Photos)

Filter palette in Photos

STARTING THE CAMERA APP

The Camera app is a default app that installs with Windows 10 FCU. Camera is usually available from the Start menu. If it is not located there, you can open it from All Apps. Both still photos and videos are stored in the Camera Roll folder inside the current user's Photos folder.

16×9 widescreen is the default setting for most front-facing cameras. Some tablets have main cameras with a 4×3 ratio.

Start

Some tablets offer a third mode for shooting panoramas.

① If the Start menu is not visible, tap or click **Start**.

② Tap or click **Camera**.

③ If the Camera app is not visible, you can tap or click **All apps** and scroll to the app.

④ Tap or click the **Change camera** icon to switch between front-facing camera and main camera.

⑤ Tap to take still photos.

⑥ Tap to switch to video mode.

End

NOTE

First-Time Only Setting The first time you start Camera on a new system, you are asked whether you want to allow the app to use location features. Camera remembers your choice and won't ask you again. You can change this setting through the Privacy settings available in the Windows Settings dialog box. (See Chapter 19 to learn more about viewing and changing settings.) ■

NOTE

The "Missing" Camera Switching Icon If your device doesn't have a main camera, the **Change camera** icon in step 4 isn't present. The front-facing camera is used mainly for shooting selfies (self-portraits). ■

SELECTING CAMERA SETTINGS

Some tablets have cameras that include advanced exposure and color settings. Some tablets offer more options in Camera mode than in Video mode. Here's how to open the advanced menu and use the options your tablet includes.

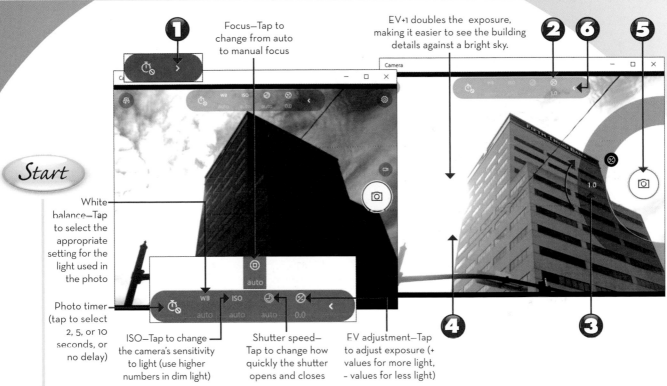

Focus—Tap to change from auto to manual focus

EV+1 doubles the exposure, making it easier to see the building details against a bright sky.

White balance—Tap to select the appropriate setting for the light used in the photo

Photo timer (tap to select 2, 5, or 10 seconds, or no delay)

ISO—Tap to change the camera's sensitivity to light (use higher numbers in dim light)

Shutter speed— Tap to change how quickly the shutter opens and closes

EV adjustment—Tap to adjust exposure (+ values for more light, - values for less light)

Start

① Tap the right arrow at the top center to see which adjustments are available.

② Tap an adjustment (EV in this example).

③ Drag the control wheel to the setting desired (+1 EV in this example).

④ The live preview changes to show the effect.

⑤ Tap to take the picture.

⑥ Tap to close the advanced menu and return to normal settings.

End

NOTE

Adjustments Vary by Camera Some built-in cameras don't have adjustments. If no right arrow is visible next to the **Photo timer** button, the camera doesn't have adjustable features. ■

NOTE

Learn More About Camera Controls To learn more about how white balance, ISO, shutter speed, and EV adjustments can improve your pictures with any type of device, see my book *The Shot Doctor: The Amateur's Guide to Taking Great Digital Photos*, Que Publishing, 2009. ■

USING VIDEO MODE

When you select Video mode in the Camera app, you can shoot MPEG4 video files with your device. Here's how to use this feature.

Start

1. Tap or click to switch to Video mode.

2. Tap or click to start recording.

3. Tap to change video camera settings.

4. Tap to change white balance settings.

5. Tap to change EV adjustment (exposure) settings.

6. Tap to close the adjustments menu.

Continued

7 Tap or click to pause recording at any time.

8 The elapsed recording time is shown here.

9 Tap or click to stop recording.

End

NOTE

Pinch to Zoom In either Camera or Video mode, you can use the touchscreen to zoom. Touch the screen with two fingers and move them apart to zoom in (larger image). To zoom back, move your fingers closer together. Note that this is a digital zoom (enlarges pixels), so image quality declines as you zoom in. ∎

CHANGING CAMERA APP SETTINGS

You can change the proportions (widescreen or standard), recording quality, and other settings with the Camera app's Settings menu. Here's how to discover what your device's camera can do. Note that details such as resolutions, recording rates, and other features shown here vary based on a particular device's camera features and which camera (main or front-facing) you have currently selected. In this example, we have the main camera selected.

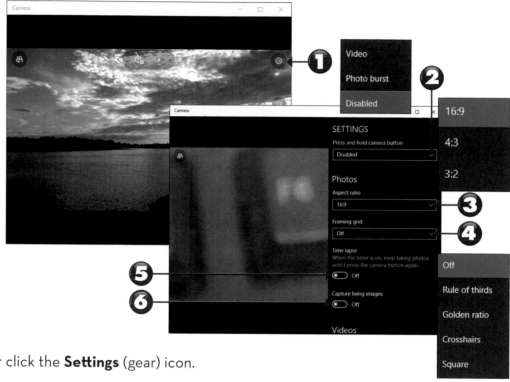

1 Tap or click the **Settings** (gear) icon.

2 Tap to open the **Press and hold camera button** menu to change the button's behavior.

3 Tap to open the **Aspect ratio** menu to select the proportions of your photos.

4 Tap to open the **Framing grid** menu to select a framing grid type.

5 Slide to **On** to enable time-lapse photography (also requires selecting a picture delay on the main Camera dialog).

6 Slide to **On** to capture a still image and video clip combination (Living image).

Continued

NOTE

Living Images When you view a living image, you see a brief video clip (up to 1 to 3 seconds long depending upon the device) followed by the still image. You can share either the video clip or the still image from within the Photos app. ∎

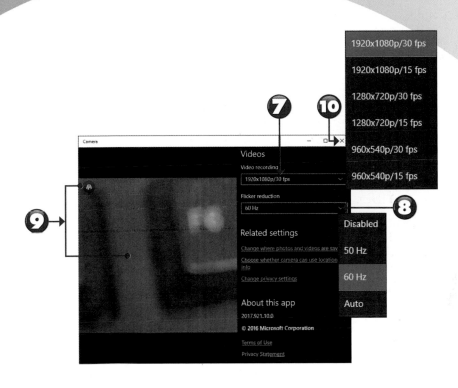

7 Tap or click to select the video size and frames per second (fps) shooting rate.

8 Tap or click to select a flicker reduction rate (if needed).

9 To change the settings for the other camera, tap the screen to close the Settings menu, tap the **Camera switch** icon to switch to the other camera, and then reopen the **Settings** menu.

10 To close the Camera app in Desktop mode (shown), click the X in the upper-right corner of the Camera window. To close the Camera app in Tablet mode, drag the top of the window down until the window disappears.

End

NOTE

Why Available Settings Vary   The settings shown in this exercise are based on the Microsoft Surface Pro 3 Windows tablet using its main (rear-facing) camera. Other tablets, laptops, and webcams might have different settings (for example, some offer digital video stabilization), and available resolution settings vary depending on the tablet model and whether you have selected the main or front-facing camera. ■

USING THE PHOTOS APP: COLLECTIONS

In Windows 10 FCU, the Photos app has been significantly upgraded to add more creative options for both photos and videos. Here's how to start it and put the default Collections view to work.

Click/tap to create a new video

A photo/video created on this date in a previous year

A photo album you created with Photos

Start

1 Click or tap **Start**.

2 Click or tap **Photos**.

3 The default **Collection** view now shows featured slideshows made for you by Photos, photos from this date, and other tagged or featured content.

Continued

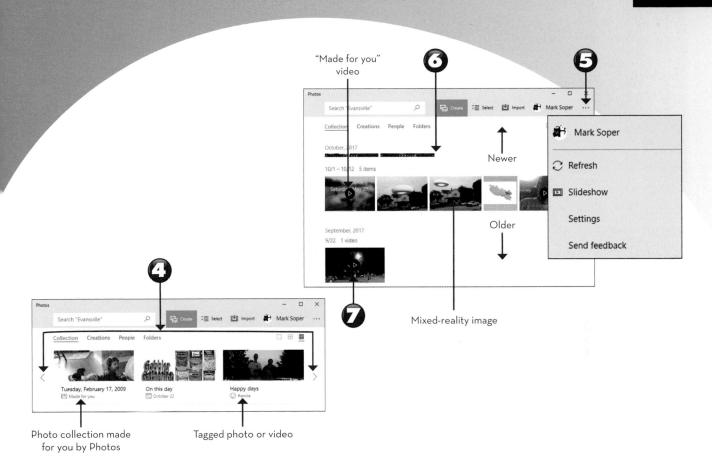

"Made for you" video

Newer

Older

Mixed-reality image

Photo collection made for you by Photos

Tagged photo or video

4 Scroll left or right for additional options.

5 Click or tap for options such as Refresh and Slideshow (current collection) and Settings.

6 Scroll down to see photos and videos from newest to oldest, sorted by month.

7 Click or tap to play a video or view a photo.

Continued

When you play a video, click or tap the bottom of the playback window to see playback and editing controls.

Tap or click to return to Collection.

Continued

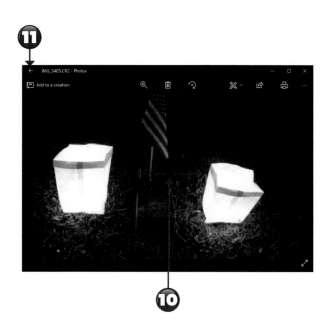

10 When you view a photo, move the mouse to the left or right edge and click or swipe left/right to view a different photo.

11 Click or tap the back arrow to return to Collection view.

End

NOTE

Editing Photos and Videos   To edit videos with Photos, see "Trimming Your Video," p. 176 and "Adding Slow-Motion Effects to Your Video," p. 178 (both in this chapter). To edit photos, see "Cropping Your Photo," p. 172, "Using the Enhance Menu," p. 173, and "Using the Adjust Menu and Saving Changes," p. 174 (all in this chapter). ▪

USING THE PHOTOS APP: CREATION AND VIDEO REMIX

The Creation view is a new feature in Photos that provides quick access to albums and slideshows you created or those created for you by Photos. Here's how to review those albums and use the new Video Remix feature to automatically create a video, complete with music and a title slide.

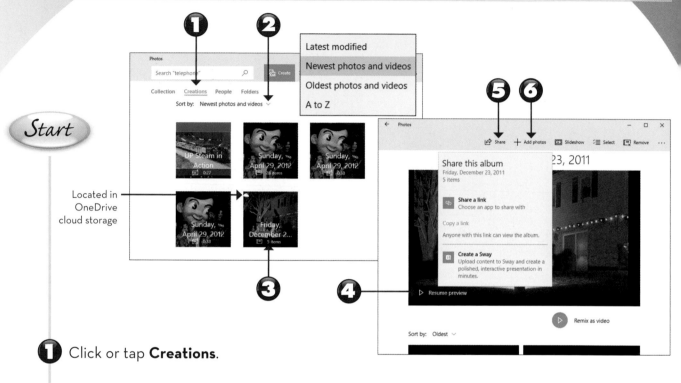

Start

Located in OneDrive cloud storage

1 Click or tap **Creations**.

2 Click or tap **Sort by** to change the sort order.

3 Click or tap an album.

4 The album opens. Tap the pause control to pause playback.

5 Click or tap **Share** to share the album.

6 Click or tap **Add photos** to add more pictures.

Continued

NOTE

Sharing an Album with Microsoft Sway   Microsoft Sway enables users to create interactive presentations that automatically adjust to different device screen sizes and orientations (vertical or horizontal). To learn more or to sign up for Sway (it's free!), go to https://sway.com. ∎

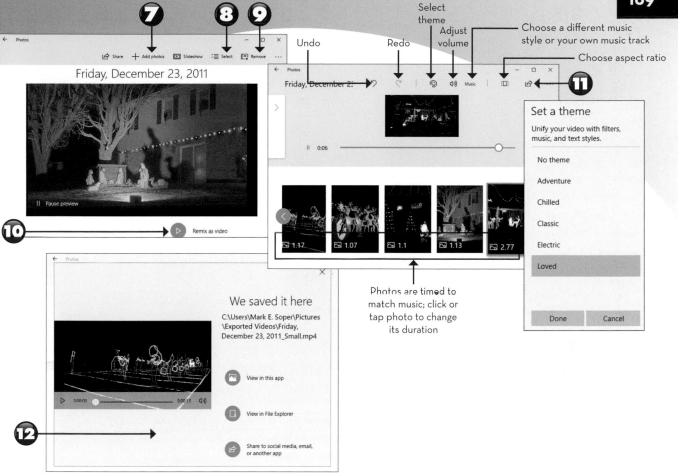

Select theme

Adjust volume

Choose a different music style or your own music track

Undo

Redo

Choose aspect ratio

Photos are timed to match music; click or tap photo to change its duration

7 Click or tap **Add photos** to add more photos to your album.

8 Click or tap **Select** to choose which photos to print, remove from the album, or share.

9 Click or tap **Remove** to remove this album (but not remove the pictures or videos in the album).

10 Click or tap **Remix as video** to convert the album into a video with music.

11 After editing, click or tap the **Share** icon to create a video file (small, medium, or large).

12 After the video is saved, choose how you want to play it back or share it.

End

USING THE PHOTOS APP: FOLDERS

The Folders menu is where you decide which folders contain your pictures. By default, your local Pictures folders and OneDrive are listed. Want to access other folders on your device or a network drive? Read on.

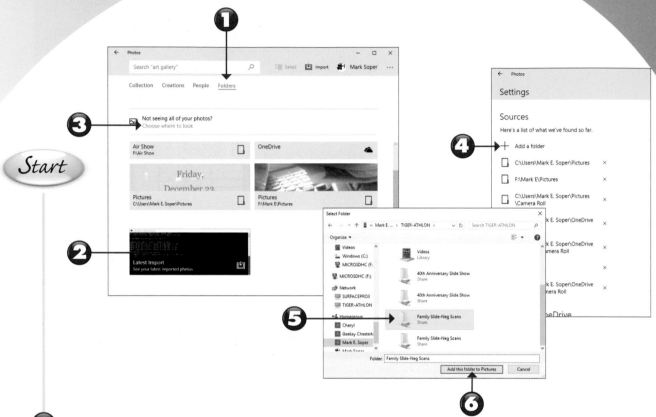

Start

1 Click or tap **Folders**.

2 Click or tap to see the latest content you imported from another drive or device.

3 Click or tap to add another location.

4 Click or tap **Add a folder**.

5 Navigate to the folder and click or tap it.

6 Click or tap **Add this folder to Pictures**.

End

SELECTING PHOTO OPTIONS

After you select a photo in the Photos app, you can print it, view camera information, rotate it, or use it in various places on your device. Here's an overview of these options.

Scroll down/flick up to see camera, folder path, and picture location.

1 Click or tap to discard the photo.

2 Click or tap to rotate the photo.

3 Click or tap **More**, **Slideshow** to view the photo as part of a slideshow.

4 Click or tap **Set as** to use the photo on the Lock screen, background, or Photos tile.

5 Click or tap **File info** to see exposure and camera information.

6 Click or tap to close File info.

Start

End

CROPPING YOUR PHOTO

Want to crop your photo so you can use it in a particular frame or for a special project? Here's how.

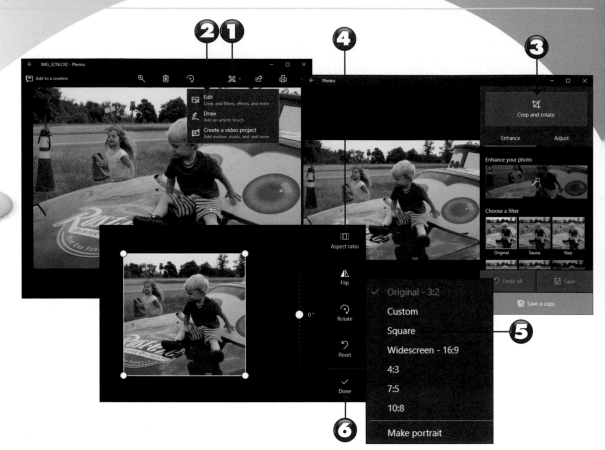

Start

End

1. With a photo selected, click or tap to open the **Get creative with this photo** menu.

2. Click or tap **Edit**.

3. Tap or click **Crop and rotate**.

4. Click or tap aspect ratio.

5. Choose the cropping desired.

6. Click **Done** to complete the crop.

USING THE ENHANCE MENU

Photos also includes sharpening tools and special effects filters in its Enhance menu. Here's how to use these features.

No filter
(original)

Start

1 Click or tap Enhance.

2 Click or tap **Enhance your photo**.

3 Drag the bar to the right to sharpen; drag to the left to blur.

4 To use a filter, scroll down or flick up to the **Choose a filter** palette.

5 Click or tap the desired filter. The preview window shows the changes you made.

End

USING THE ADJUST MENU AND SAVING CHANGES

Use the Adjust menu to change brightness, enhance or reduce color intensity, adjust clarity, add or change vignetting, and more. Here's how to use these features.

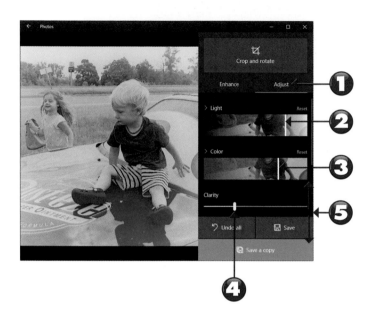

Start

1 Click or tap **Adjust**.

2 Drag the **Light** bar to the right to brighten, or to the left to darken.

3 Drag the **Color** bar to the right to intensify color, or to the left to reduce color.

4 Drag the **Clarity** control to the right to make the image clearer, or to the left to make the image softer.

5 Scroll down or flick up for more adjustments.

Continued

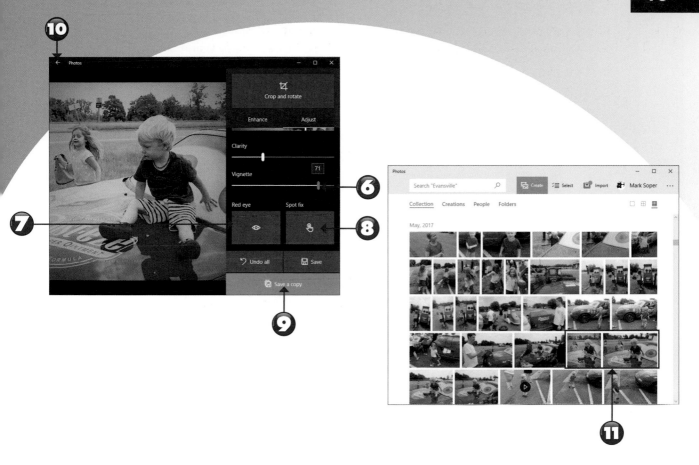

6 Drag the **Vignette** control to the right to darken image corners, or to the left to lighten image corners.

7 Click or tap to use the **Red eye** tool.

8 Click or tap to use the **Spot fix** tool.

9 Click or tap to save a copy of your photo with the edits you made.

10 Click or tap to return to the **Collection** view.

11 The edited version (left) compared to the original version (right).

End

TRIMMING YOUR VIDEO

Photos offers tools you can use to trim, add slow motion, adjust brightness, and add effects to your videos. In this example, we create a shortened video using Trim.

Start

① After opening the video, click or tap the playback window to display editing controls.

② Open the editing menu.

③ Click or tap **Trim**.

④ Drag this marker to the desired start of the trimmed video.

⑤ Drag the trim marker to the desired end of the trimmed video.

Continued

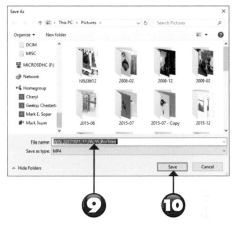

6 Drag this marker to the trim marker.

7 Click or tap **Play** to preview the trimmed video.

8 Click or tap **Save as** to save a copy of the video.

9 Photos adds "Trim" to the end of the original name.

10 Click or tap to save the trimmed video to the Pictures folder.

End

TIP

Saving a Video to a Different Folder To save your video to a different folder (such as your Videos folder), navigate to that folder before you click or tap the **Save** button (step 10). ■

ADDING SLOW-MOTION EFFECTS TO YOUR VIDEO

Slow-motion effects can make an ordinary video a lot more interesting to watch. Learn how to add your choice of slow-motion effects in this exercise.

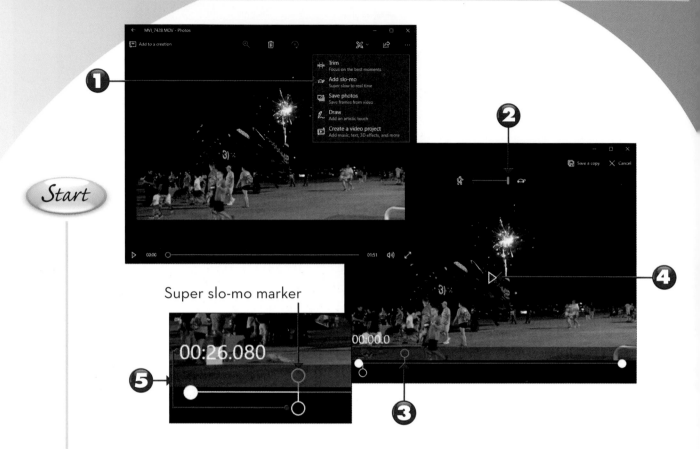

Super slo-mo marker

Start

① From the editing menu, click or tap **Add slo-mo**.

② Drag the slider to super-slow motion (toward the turtle icon).

③ Click or tap the timeline at the point where you want slow motion to take effect.

④ Click or tap **Play**.

⑤ When playback arrives at the blue marker, it becomes super slow for a few moments.

Continued

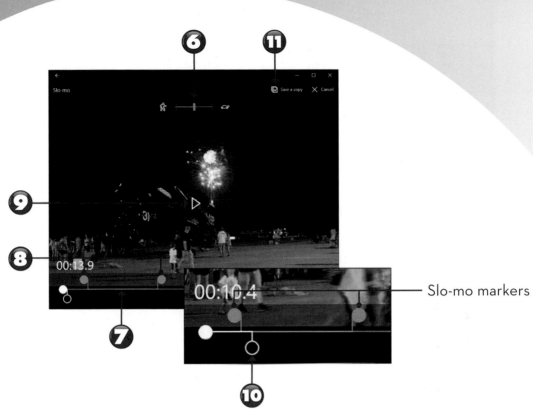

Slo-mo markers

6 Drag the slider to slow motion (between the icons).

7 Click or tap the timeline to place the slow-motion markers.

8 Drag them to indicate where to start and stop slow motion.

9 Click or tap **Play**.

10 When playback arrives at the first marker, it slows down until the second marker is passed.

11 Click or tap to save changes.

End

NOTE

Saving a Slo-Mo Video File   Photos uses the original name but appends an underscore (_) character: for example, the default name of the slow motion version of MVI-7428 is MVI-7428_. You can edit the name before you save it. See steps 9 and 10 of the exercise "Trimming Your Video," this chapter, p. 176, for an example of the video save dialog. ■

ENJOYING VIDEOS, TV, AND MOVIES

Windows 10 FCU includes the easy-to-use Movies & TV app, which helps you view both homemade and commercial video (TV, movie) content. It now supports 360-degree video and has a brand-new interface for easier operation. In this chapter, you learn how to use Movies & TV to find and play your own video content and visit the Microsoft Store for TV and movie content. Movies & TV normally runs full-screen, but the examples in this chapter show this app in a window to save space.

Mini playback
window

Download quality
○ HD
○ SD
◉ Ask every time

Download location
Modify your storage settings

Download devices
Show my download devices
Remove this device
Learn more

Your videos
Restore my available video purchases
Choose where we look for videos

Playback
Always start videos in full screen
◯ Off

Configuring
the Movies
& TV app

Playback
controls

0:07:32   0:03:57

Explore **Purchased** Personal

Refine: Most recent, All, All

Viewing
purchased
TV episodes

1 season   1 season   2 seasons   1 season

The Man From   The Weird Al Show   Downton Abbey   MacGyver
U.N.C.L.E. - The Compl

Build your collection from your local video files

Right now, we're watching these folders:

+

Videos   ✕
C:\Users\Mark E. Soper\Videos

Videos   ✕
F:\Mark E\Videos

360° videos: All
Rocket Launch 360: Delta IV NROL-45
Littlstar

Visit website

Adding folders to
watch for video files

Playing back a
360-degree video

FINDING YOUR VIDEOS

You can use the Movies & TV app to view video content you create with a camcorder, digital SLR, mirrorless camera, or smartphone. Here's how to get started.

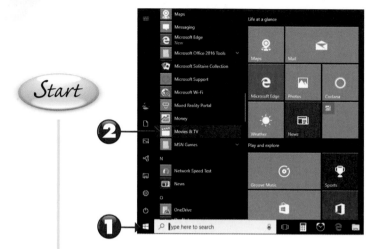

Start

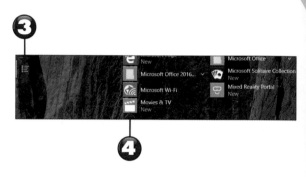

① Click or tap **Start** in Desktop mode.

② Click or tap **Movies & TV**.

③ Click or tap **All apps** in Tablet mode.

④ Click or tap **Movies & TV**.

Continued

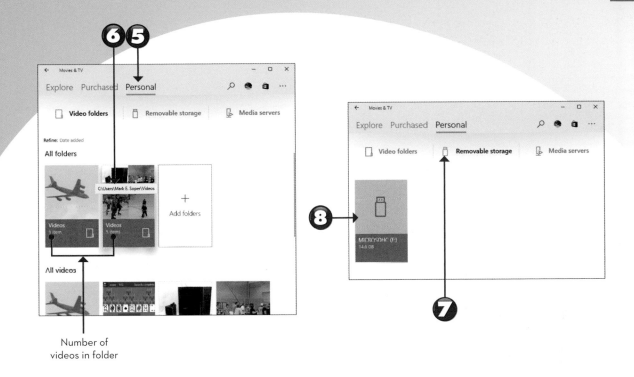

Number of
videos in folder

5 The **Personal** view displays the contents of your default video folders.

6 Hover the mouse over a folder to see its location.

7 Click or tap **Removable storage** to look for videos on memory cards or USB flash drives.

8 Click or tap a drive to see its video contents.

Continued

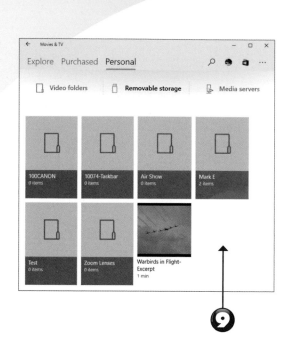

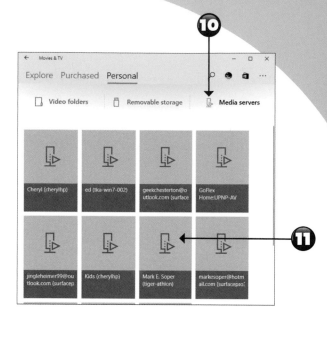

9 View the contents of the flash drive selected in step 6.

10 Click or tap **Media servers** (devices that provide streaming media on your network).

11 Click or tap a media server.

Continued

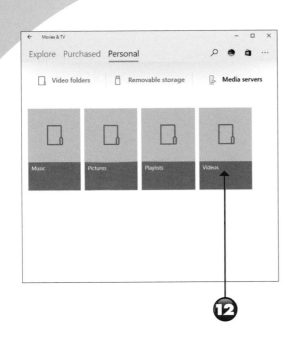

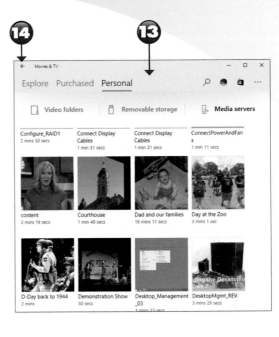

12 Click or tap **Videos**.

13 Click or tap through additional folders as needed to see the videos stored on the media server.

14 Click or tap to return to the previous level.

End

NOTE

More About Media Servers Depending upon the speed of your network and the number of videos stored on a media server, it might take several minutes before the contents of a media server's video folder (step 11) are visible. If Media Servers are not available, make sure Network Discovery is enabled (see Chapter 20 for details). ■

ADDING A LOCATION TO LOOK FOR VIDEOS

The Movies & TV app looks in the current user's Videos folder for videos. However, you can also check other folders, such as external drives, network locations, and Camera Roll (the folder used for storing photos and videos shot with your device's onboard camera). Here's how to configure Movies & TV to find videos in other folders, using Camera Roll in this example.

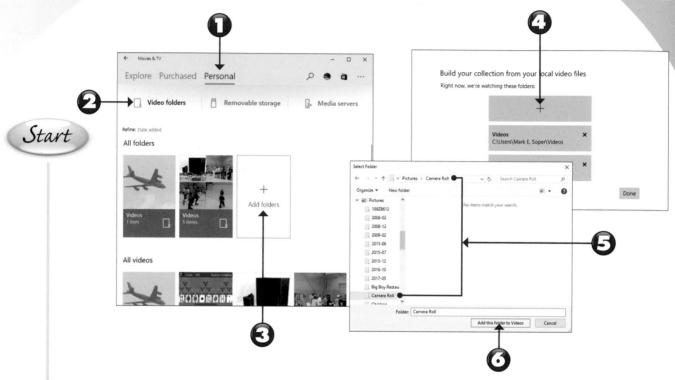

1 Click or tap **Personal**.

2 Click or tap **Video folders** (if it not already displayed).

3 Click or tap **Add folders**.

4 Click the plus (+) sign to add another folder.

5 Navigate to the folder location and click or tap the folder.

6 Click or tap **Add this folder to Videos**.

Continued

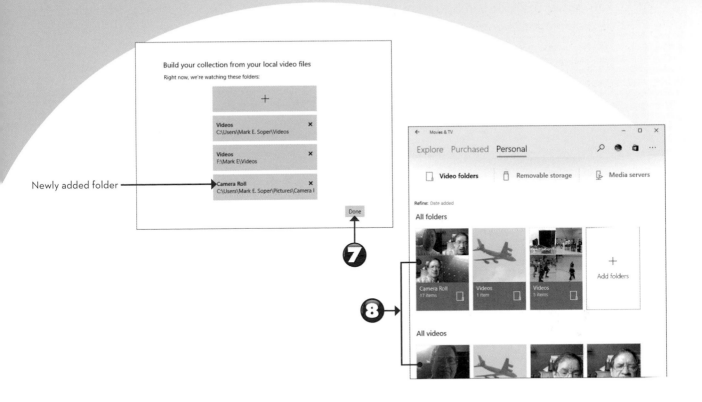

Newly added folder

7 Repeat steps 4 through 6 as needed and then click **Done**.

8 Results from the new folder appear in the **All folders** and **All videos** views.

End

TIP

Removing a Folder To prevent Movies & TV from displaying the contents of a folder, click the X on the right side of the folder listing in the **Build your collection** dialog (steps 4 or 7). ▪

PLAYING A VIDEO

You can play a video in a window or full screen using the Movies & TV app. You can quickly display playback controls to help you adjust volume, change the aspect ratio, or pause the video.

Start

1. Open the **Personal** category.

2. Click or tap the video location.

3. Click or tap a video to play.

4. The video file begins to play.

5. Move the mouse or touch the bottom of the playback window to display playback controls.

6. Click or tap to show full-screen.

Continued

7 Click or tap here to pause/continue playback.

8 You can click or press and drag to go to a particular moment in the video.

9 To adjust volume, click or tap here and drag the volume slider.

10 Click or tap to go back 10 seconds or go forward 30 seconds.

11 Click or tap to return to windowed playback.

End

PLAYING A VIDEO IN MINI VIEW

In addition to windowed and full-screen playback, you can play back your videos in a small window (mini view). Here's how.

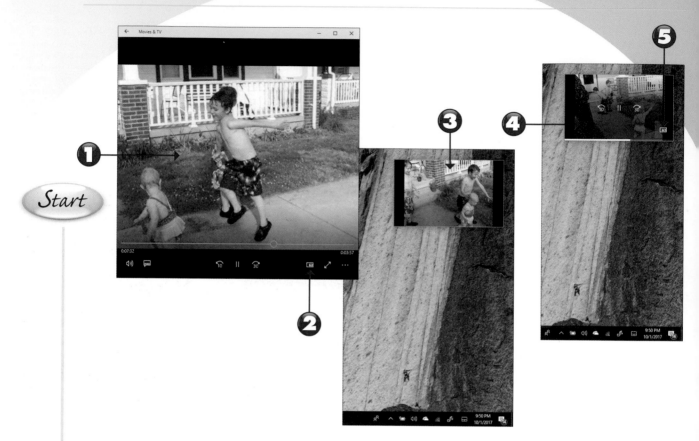

1. Start your video playback in normal window or full-screen modes.

2. Click or tap the **mini view** button.

3. The video continues to play in mini view.

4. Hover the mouse or tap the playback window to display the menu.

5. Click or tap the **Leave mini view** button to return to the previous playback mode.

CASTING VIDEO TO A DEVICE

If your computer screen isn't big enough for you to enjoy your video, use the screen casting feature built into Movies & TV to send a video to a smart TV or set-top box. Here's how.

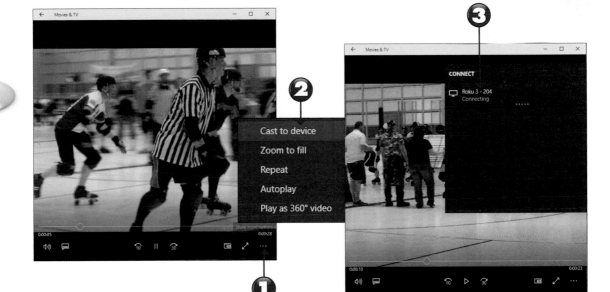

From windowed or full-screen playback modes, click or tap the **More** (three-dot) icon.

Click or tap **Cast to device**.

Click or tap the device you want to use.

NOTE

Casting and Media Server Content If you want to cast a file stored on a media server, connect to the folder using the Add a location feature covered earlier in this chapter, or copy the file from the server to a local drive using File Explorer. ■

BUYING OR RENTING A MOVIE OR TV SHOW

You can shop for TV shows and movies from the Microsoft Store or from within the Movies & TV app. Using your Microsoft account, you can purchase items for downloading or streaming. This example demonstrates buying an episode of a TV series.

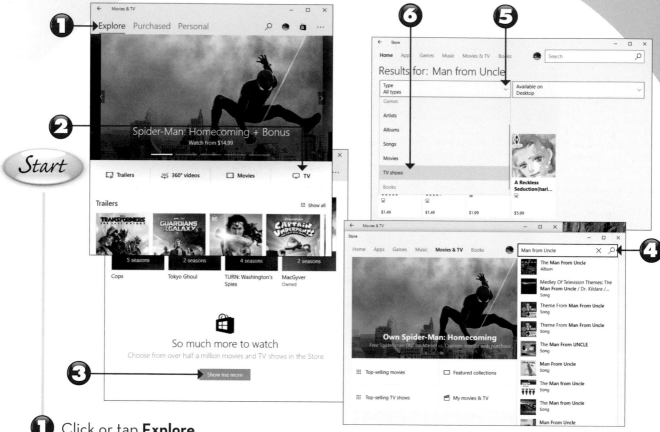

1 Click or tap **Explore**.

2 Click or tap **TV**.

3 Scroll through the featured shows. If you find a show you like, click or tap it. Otherwise, click or tap **Show me more**.

4 Type the name of the TV show you are looking for and press the **Enter** key on the keyboard or click/tap the Search icon.

5 Open the **Type** menu.

6 Select **TV shows** from the drop-down menu.

Continued

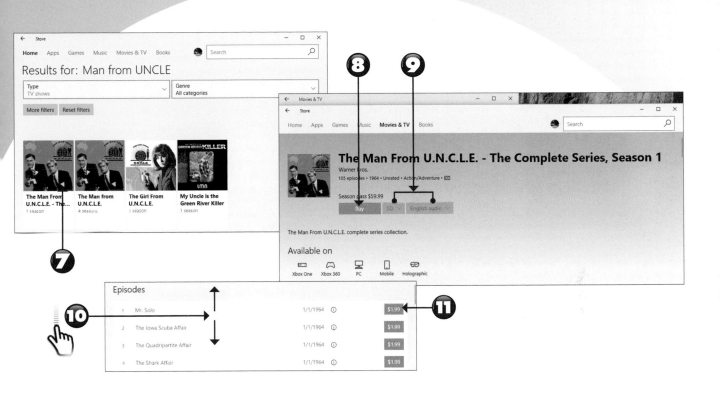

7 Click or tap the matching series.

8 Click or tap **Buy** to buy a season pass.

9 If different formats or languages are available, open the menus to select.

10 To view individual episodes to purchase, scroll down or flick up.

11 Click or tap an episode to buy.

Continued

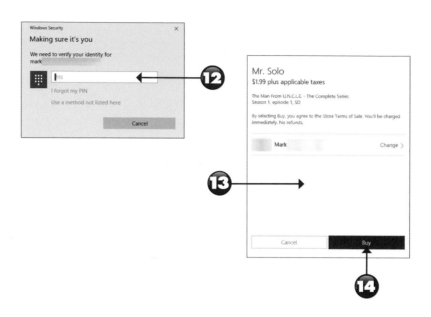

12 Sign in to your Microsoft account as prompted.

13 Review purchase details.

14 Click or tap **Buy**.

Continued

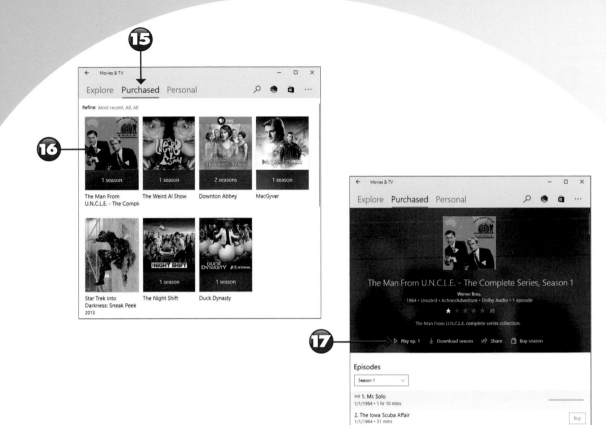

15 Click or tap **Purchased** in the Movies & TV app.

16 Click or tap your new series.

17 Click or tap the **Play ep.** button.

End

NOTE

Playback Controls The same playback controls available for your own videos are also used for watching TV shows and movies. ■

PLAYING 3D VIDEOS

Movies & TV can now play 360-degree videos. Here's how to try this great new feature.

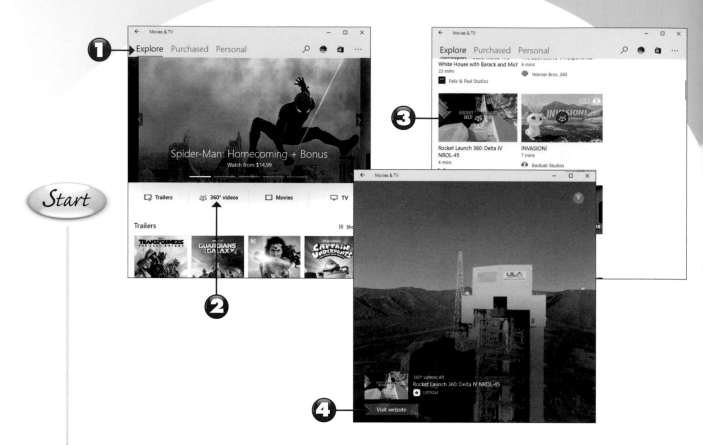

Start

1 Click or tap **Explore**.

2 Click or tap **360° videos**.

3 Click or tap a video.

4 The video begins to play. Click or tap the **View website** button to learn more about the video.

Continued

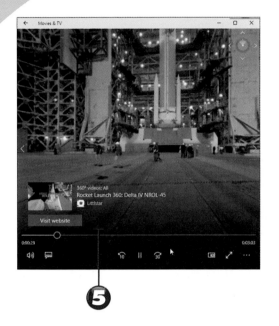

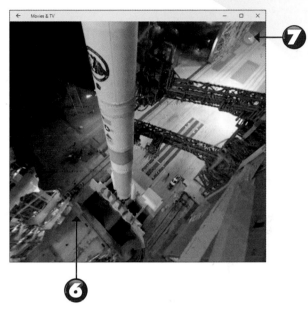

5 Click or tap the playback window to display standard playback controls.

6 Click and drag or press and drag the playback window to change the playback angle.

7 The indicator shows the direction and rotation angle.

End

USING SEARCH TO FIND LOCAL AND MICROSOFT STORE MEDIA

The Movies & TV app's powerful search feature can look for matches within your existing collection of videos, movies, or TV shows as well as matches in the Microsoft Store. In this example, you learn how this feature makes finding your favorite content easier.

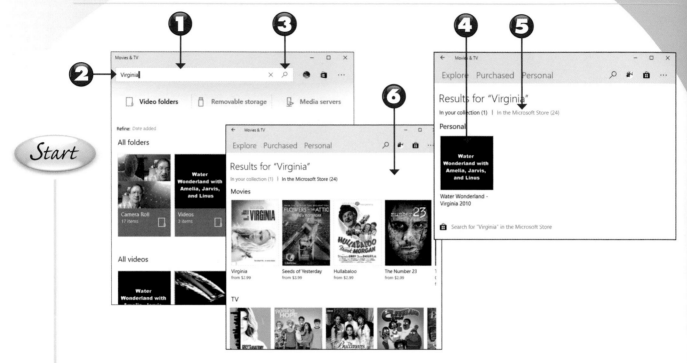

Start

1. Click or tap the **Search** window.

2. Enter a search term or phrase.

3. Press the **Enter** key on the keyboard or click or tap the **Search** icon.

4. The app lists matches from your own content; you can click or tap to choose a video to play.

5. Click or tap **In the Microsoft Store** to see movie & TV results from the Microsoft Store.

6. The results from the store are displayed.

End

TIP

Finding More Results To find games, apps, or other types of results, scroll down to the bottom of the results window shown in step 6 and click or tap **Search for "search term" in the Microsoft Store**. ■

Use the Settings menu to view and change the settings used for the Movies & TV app. Here's what to expect.

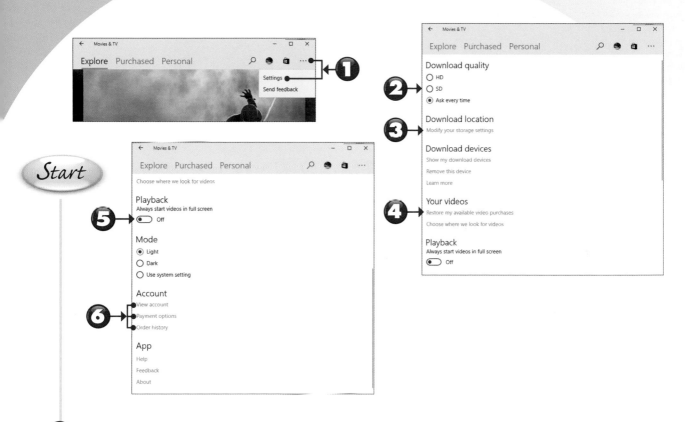

1 Click or tap the **More options** (three-dot) icon, and then click/tap **Settings**.

2 Change download quality settings if you prefer HD or SD as the default.

3 Click or tap this link to change the default download folder for movies and TV.

4 If your video purchases are not showing up on this computer, click or tap **Restore my available video purchases**.

5 To play back videos in full-screen by default, set to **On**.

6 Click or tap these links to view account, payment, or order history information.

End

Chapter 11

CONNECTING WITH FRIENDS

Windows 10 FCU offers a variety of ways you can connect with people, ranging from email to social media to face-to-face connections over your computer. In this chapter, you learn how to use several key communications apps and features of Windows.

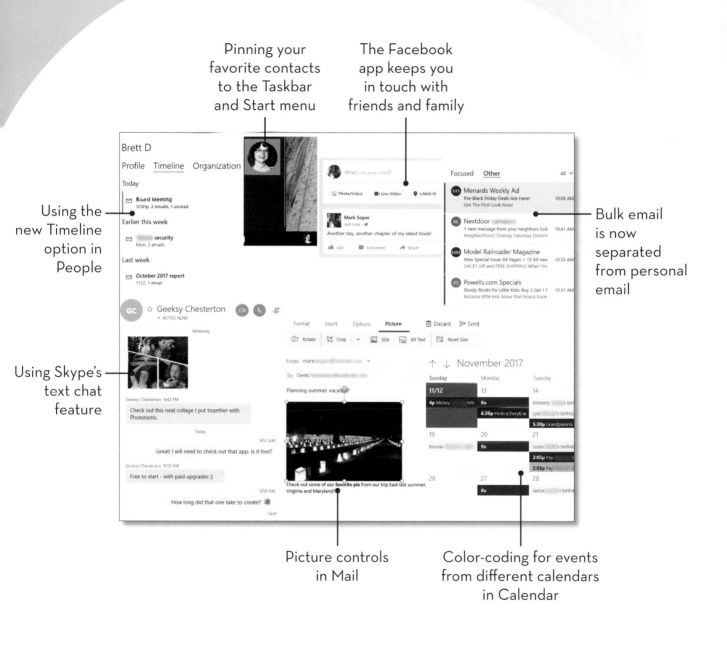

Pinning your favorite contacts to the Taskbar and Start menu

The Facebook app keeps you in touch with friends and family

Using the new Timeline option in People

Bulk email is now separated from personal email

Using Skype's text chat feature

Picture controls in Mail

Color-coding for events from different calendars in Calendar

USING THE PEOPLE APP

The People app enables you to compile and maintain a list of contacts. You can import existing contacts from your email clients and add photos, addresses, and much more information.

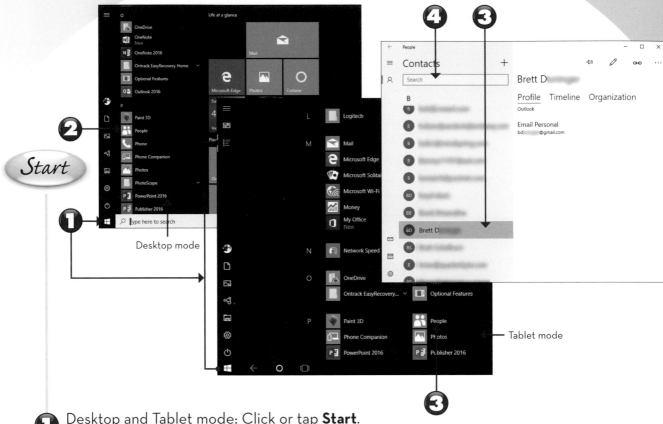

Desktop mode

Tablet mode

Start

1 Desktop and Tablet mode: Click or tap **Start**. In Tablet mode, then click or tap **All Apps**.

2 Click or tap **People** (Desktop and Tablet mode).

3 The People app opens with your contacts displayed in the left column. Click or tap a contact name to view that contact's information.

4 Use the **Search** box to search for a specific contact.

Continued

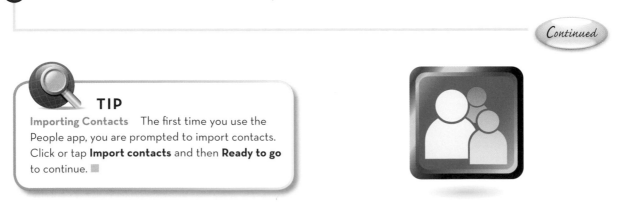

TIP

Importing Contacts The first time you use the People app, you are prompted to import contacts. Click or tap **Import contacts** and then **Ready to go** to continue. ■

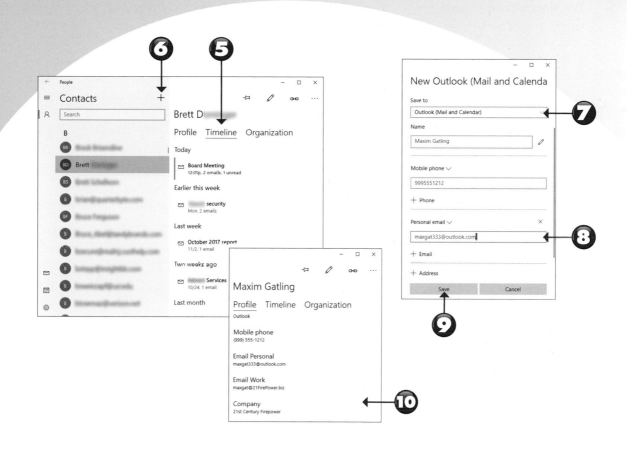

5 Click or tap **Timeline** to see previous communications with the contact.

6 Click or tap the **+** to start a new contact.

7 Select where to save the contact if you have more than one account.

8 Fill out the contact form; click or tap a text box or field and enter the contact information.

9 Click or tap **Save** when you finish entering contact information.

10 The new contact is added to your list.

End

ADDING PEOPLE TO YOUR TASKBAR

Windows 10 FCU enables you to add up to three of your favorite people to the Taskbar so they're only a click or a tap away. Here's how.

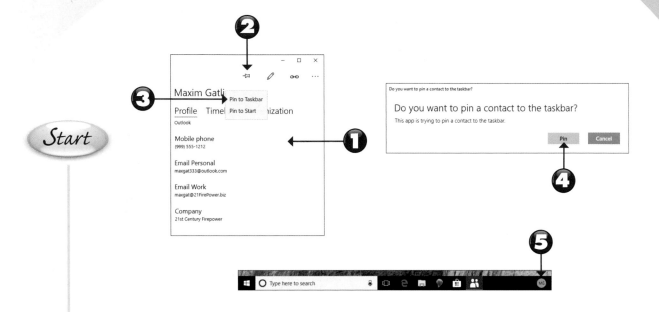

Start

1 Open the contact you want to add to the Taskbar.

2 Click or tap the pushpin icon.

3 Click or tap **Pin to Taskbar**.

4 Click or tap **Pin**.

5 The contact is pinned to your Taskbar.

End

TIP

Pinning a Contact to the Start Menu If you prefer to have your favorite contacts on the Start menu, choose **Pin to Start** in step 3. ■

ADDING A PICTURE TO YOUR CONTACT

Want to have a picture for a Start menu or Taskbar contact? When you add a picture to your contact, it appears whenever you pin the contact. Here's the process.

1. Open the contact and click or tap **Edit** (pencil icon).

2. Click or tap **Add photo**.

3. Choose a photo.

4. Adjust cropping and click or tap **Done**.

5. Click or tap **Save**.

6. Contacts pinned to the Start menu and Taskbar.

NOTE

Using Photos To locate the photo you want to use, Contacts opens the Photos app. To learn more about Photos, see Chapter 9, "Taking, Editing, and Sharing Photos and Videos." ■

CONNECTING TO FACEBOOK WITH THE FACEBOOK APP

You can use the free Facebook app in the Microsoft Store to keep up with the latest Facebook postings, add status updates, and upload photos to your profile page. If you don't already have the Facebook app, you must install it from the Microsoft Store first.

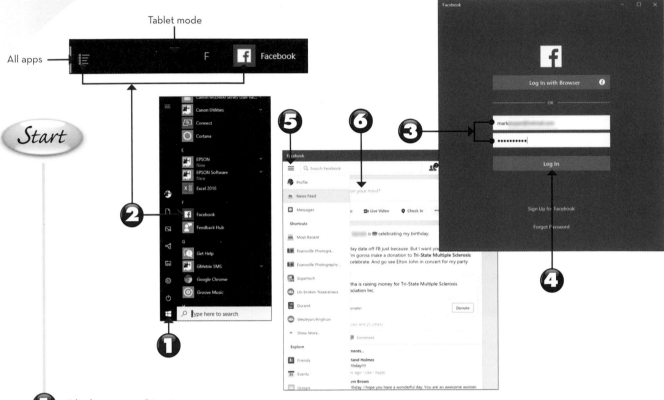

1 Click or tap **Start**.

2 Click or tap **(All apps**, Tablet mode), **Facebook**.

3 Click or tap the Email box and enter your email login, and then enter your password in the Password box.

4 Click or tap **Log In**. You might be prompted to connect with nearby places, friends, and more; access your current location; or sync your profile picture and cover photo to your Windows account and Lock screen. Click or tap **Yes** or **OK** to do any of these.

5 By default, the app shows your News Feed. Click or tap the Menu icon to expand the menu.

6 To update, click or tap in the Publisher box ("What's on your mind?").

Continued

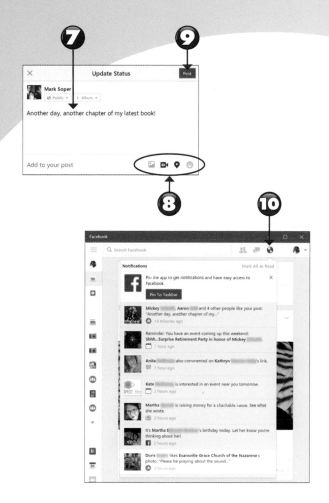

7 Type your status update.

8 Add other content (photos, videos, and more) if desired.

9 Click or tap **Post**.

10 To view notifications from Facebook and other users, click or tap the **Notifications** icon.

11 Click or tap the down-arrow next to your profile picture to view the activity log, Facebook settings, and other account management options.

End

TIP

App Screen Size Depending on how your app screen is sized, you might be able to view all the Facebook features without having to open hidden items. You can click and drag a border or press and hold a border to resize a window. ■

STARTING MAIL

Windows Mail works with Microsoft's web-based Outlook.com email service and many other email services, including Gmail, Yahoo! Mail, and Exchange. Mail automatically detects the email you used to create your Microsoft account and adds it as your first account. In this task, you learn how to navigate the Mail app.

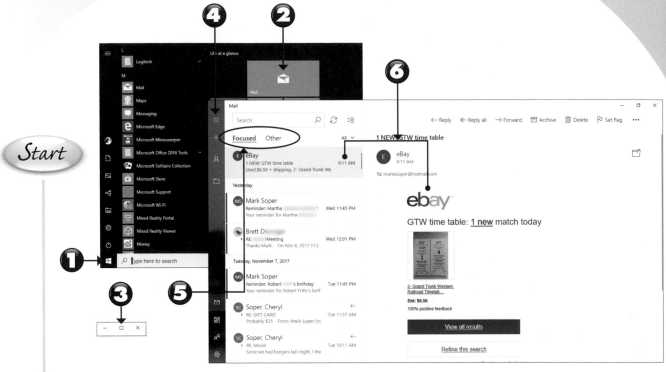

1 Click or tap **Start** to open the Start menu.

2 Click or tap **Mail**.

3 Click or tap the **Maximize** button to view the Mail app full screen. (This enables you to view the content of messages in a separate pane from the list of messages in your inbox.)

4 Mail opens with the default account's Inbox selected. If you have additional accounts added, click or tap to select any account.

5 **Focused** messages are addressed specifically to you. To see ads and other messages sent to groups, click or tap **Other**.

6 To view any message in the Inbox, click or tap the message.

Continued

NOTE

First-Time Use When you first start Mail, a Welcome window might appear; click or tap **Get Started**. You'll then see another first-time use window that lists your default account (or accounts), along with an option to add more accounts; click or tap **Ready to go** to begin. ■

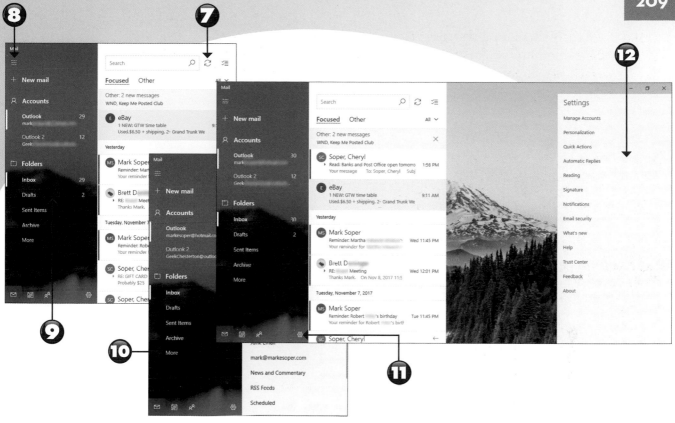

7 Click or tap **Sync this view** to download new messages.

8 Click or tap **Menu** to hide or display the left pane listing the main Mail components.

9 Click or tap a folder name to view the folder's contents.

10 Click or tap **More** to view additional Mail folders.

11 Click or tap **Settings**.

12 The Settings panel opens; use this panel to find settings for controlling accounts, adding a signature, specifying how email is marked, and more.

End

TIP

Using Another Email Client? If you're using a web-based email service, such as Yahoo! or Google, you can use your web browser to access messages rather than using the Mail app. ■

NOTE

Setup Help If you're using an Outlook email account, one of the easiest ways to start setting up your email is to utilize the links found in the Outlook.com team's introductory email. Just click or tap the message to open it, and then follow the instructions and links provided. ■

ADDING AN EMAIL ACCOUNT

You can add accounts from other email providers to the Windows 10 FCU Mail app and check your messages in one convenient spot. You might have a work email and a home email account, for example, or a Google and a Yahoo! Mail account. You can add them to Mail. Here's how.

Start

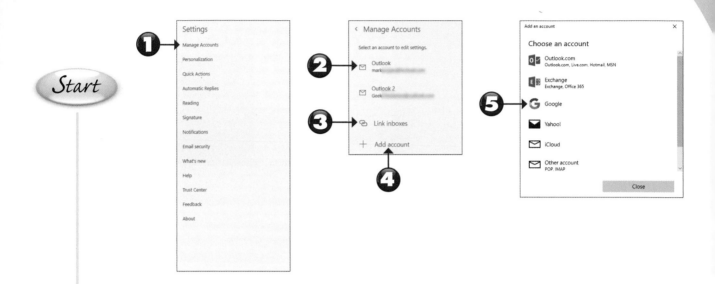

1 From the Settings menu, click or tap **Manage Accounts**.

2 Click or tap an account to make changes to its settings.

3 To combine inboxes from multiple accounts, click or tap **Link inboxes**.

4 To add an email account, click or tap **Add account**.

5 Click or tap an account type.

Continued

NOTE

Updating Account Settings   During the Add account process, you might be prompted to **Get the most out of your (email) account**. By clicking or tapping **Next**, your third-party account will get features comparable to Outlook.com accounts (focused inbox and others). To skip, click or tap **Add account without new features**. ■

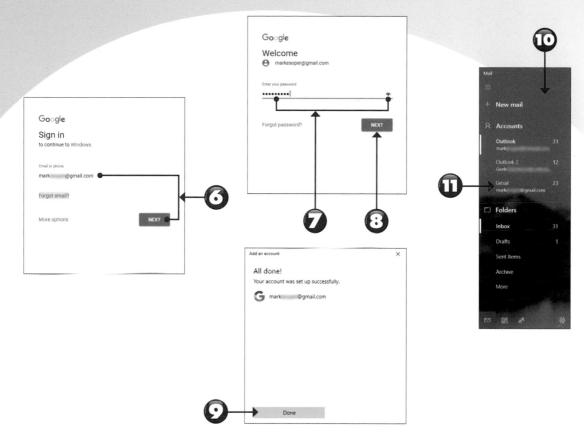

6 Enter the username for the email account and click or tap **Next**.

7 Enter the password. If you want to see what you've typed, click or tap the eye icon.

8 Click or tap **Next**.

9 Depending on your email provider, you might encounter additional windows to finish the process; click or tap to fill in the appropriate information as prompted. Click or tap **Done** when the account is successfully added.

10 Note that all the email accounts you've added appear in the Accounts section of the left pane.

11 Click or tap an account to use it.

End

NOTE

Edit an Account If you need to make changes to an account's settings or delete the account entirely, click or tap the account. This opens a window with the account's name, settings, and an option for removing the account from your Mail app. Simply make your changes and click or tap **Save** when finished. ■

COMPOSING AND SENDING AN EMAIL MESSAGE

You can easily compose a new email message and send it on its way. The Mail app lets you add simple formatting, insert pictures or links, attach files, and even check your spelling before you hit the Send button. In this task, you learn to quickly create a message and add a file attachment.

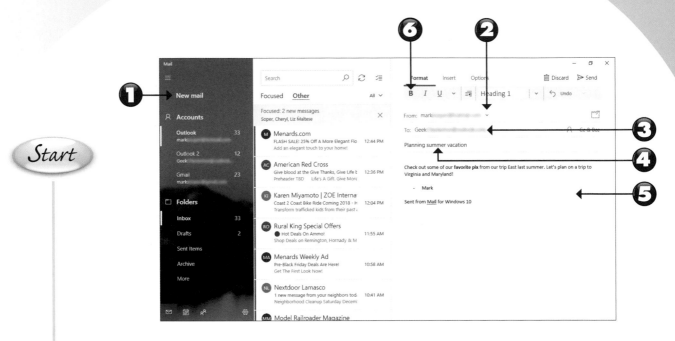

Start

1 With the Mail app open, click or tap **New mail**.

2 If you use more than one account, click or tap the **From** field and choose the account.

3 Click or tap the **To** field and enter the email address for the person to whom you want to send a message. If you're sending the email to multiple people, include a semicolon between addresses.

4 Click or tap the **Subject** field and give your message a heading or title.

5 Click or tap the blank area below the Subject field and enter your message text.

6 Add bold or other enhancements as desired.

Continued

TIP

Use a Contact As you're typing an email address in the **To** field, a list of possible matches might appear courtesy of the People app (your digital address book of contacts). If the name matches a contact, you can click or tap it to finish the entry.

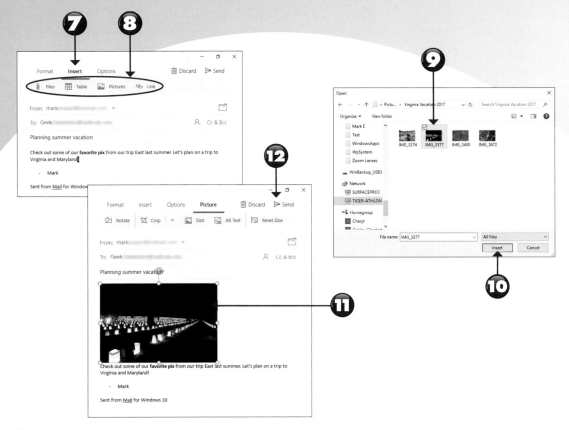

7 To add a file attachment, click or tap the **Insert** tab.

8 Click or tap **Files** to attach a file or **Pictures** to attach a picture. You can also insert a table or a link to a web page.

9 Navigate to the file you want to attach; click or tap the filename.

10 Click or tap **Insert**.

11 Mail adds the file attachment or photo.

12 Click **Send** when you're ready to send the file.

End

NOTE

Check Your Folders To see a list of sent emails for an account, click or tap the **Sent Items** folder in the Folder pane. Mail pins the Sent Items and Drafts folders to the Folders pane by default. To pin other folders, first click or tap the **More** button at the bottom of the account listed in the Folder pane. (You might need to scroll to view the option.) Next, right-click or press and hold a folder name and click or tap **Favorites**. You can also use the same technique to unpin folders from the pane, but you should choose **Remove from Favorites**. ■

READING AND REPLYING TO MESSAGES

Mail lists the email messages for each account in the main window, along with a brief peek at the content of each. You can read individual messages in their entirety in a separate window. You can also reply to a message from within the message window.

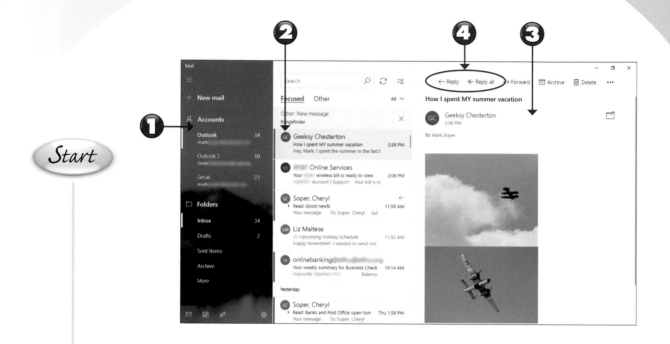

Start

1 From Mail's navigation pane, click or tap the email account or Inbox you want to view.

2 Click or tap the message you want to read.

3 The message opens on the right side of the app window, along with a toolbar of commands.

4 To reply to a message, click or tap **Reply**. If the message went to multiple people, you can reply to all of them using **Reply All**.

Continued

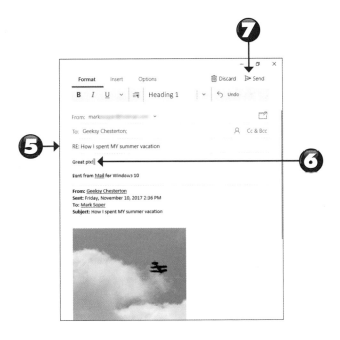

5 Mail automatically fills in the sender's email address and adds RE: to the subject line to indicate the message is a reply. Mail also includes the original message text.

6 Type your message reply here.

7 Click or tap **Send**.

End

NOTE

Reading Conversations If you're corresponding with the same person (or persons) with replies back and forth, you can click or tap the message in the main Mail window to view each reply as a submessage to the original message. This lets you see the conversation's progress as each person responds. ■

FORWARDING MESSAGES

It's easy to forward a message to another person. Mail automatically inserts FW: in the subject title to indicate a forwarded message, but you can delete the FW: if you want to.

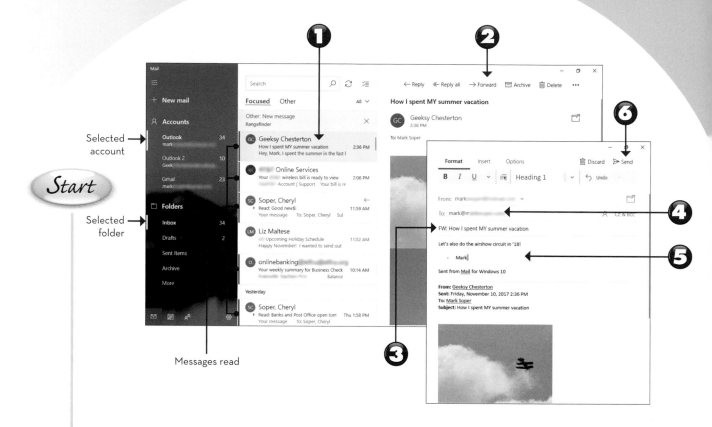

1 From your account's Inbox in Mail, click or tap the message you want to forward.

2 Click or tap **Forward**.

3 Note that Mail automatically adds FW: to the subject line to indicate the email is a forwarded message.

4 Click or tap the **To** box and type in the email address you want to send to.

5 You can add any additional message text here.

6 Click or tap **Send**.

End

DELETING MESSAGES

To help keep your Inbox lean and clean, it's a good practice to delete messages you no longer want to keep. You can use the Select feature to choose multiple messages for deletion.

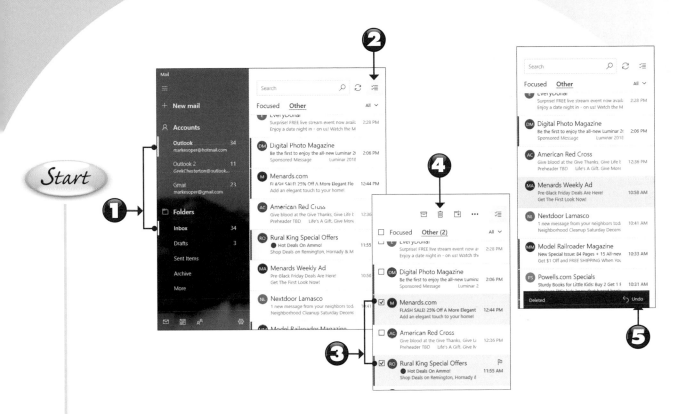

1. From your Mail account's Folders pane, click or tap the Inbox or folder you want to view.

2. Click or tap **Enter selection mode**.

3. Click or tap the check box for the message or messages you want to delete.

4. Click or tap **Delete**.

5. To undo the deletion, click or tap **Undo**.

TIP

Quick Delete You can move the mouse pointer or your finger over an email message to reveal a Delete (trash can) icon at the right side of the highlighted message. Click or tap the **Delete** icon to delete the message. ■

FLAGGING MESSAGES

You can use Mail's flagging tool to flag a message. When you add a flag, it's easier to spot the message in the list later, such as flagging an important message you want to reread or respond to at a later time. Start by opening the email account you want to use.

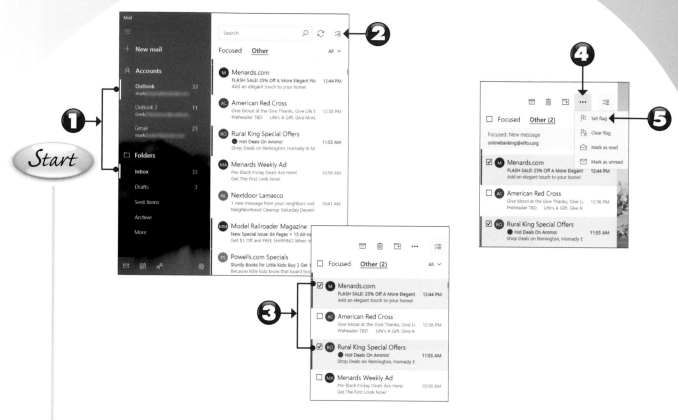

Start

① From your Mail account's Folders pane, click or tap the Inbox or folder you want to view.

② Click or tap **Enter selection mode**.

③ Click or tap the check box for the messages you want to mark.

④ Click or tap **Actions**.

⑤ Click or tap **Set flag**.

Continued

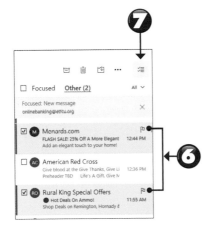

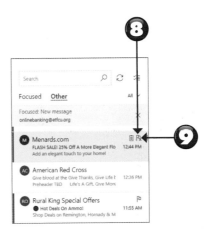

6 Mail adds a flag icon to the messages.

7 Click or tap the **Exit selection mode** icon.

8 To clear a single flag, float the mouse over the flag until the **Clear flag on item** symbol appears.

9 Click or tap the symbol to remove the flag.

End

TIP

More Options Right-click a message to see additional options (Archive, Move, Move to Junk, Move to Other, Always Move to Other). ▪

TIP

Quick Flagging and Group Unflagging You can also hover the mouse pointer over or tap and hold an email message and select **Delete** or **Set flag** to delete or flag the selected message. To unflag several messages, select them, and then click the flag on any selected message. ▪

CREATING AN EMAIL SIGNATURE

A signature is information, typically text, that appears appended to every email message you send, rather like a sign-off to your message. A signature can be as simple as your name and contact information, a website URL, your favorite quote, or your company name and number.

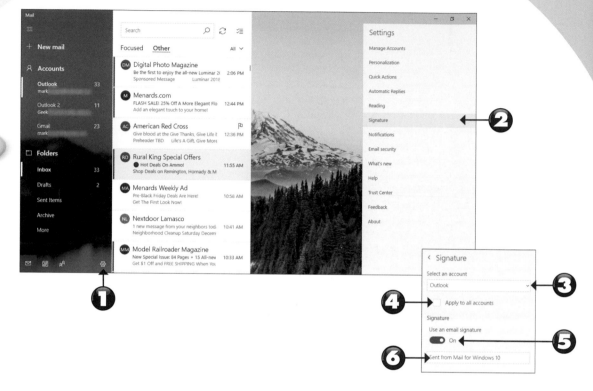

Start

1. Click or tap **Settings**.

2. Click or tap **Signature**.

3. If you have more than one account, select the account to use.

4. To use the same signature for all accounts, click or tap the empty **Apply to all accounts** check box.

5. If it is not currently selected, toggle the **Use an email signature** control to **On**.

6. Note Mail's default signature.

Continued

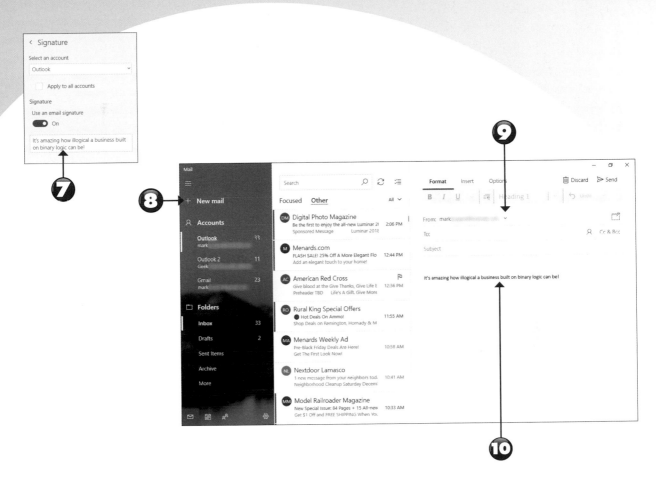

7 Click or tap the signature box, and type your own signature text.

8 To view your new signature, click or tap **New mail**.

9 Select the account that uses the signature you created.

10 The signature automatically appears at the bottom of the new message.

End

NOTE

Turn Off Signatures If you don't want to include a signature with your emails, you can turn off the feature. Click or tap **Settings**, **Signature**. Drag the **On/Off** button to the **Off** position.

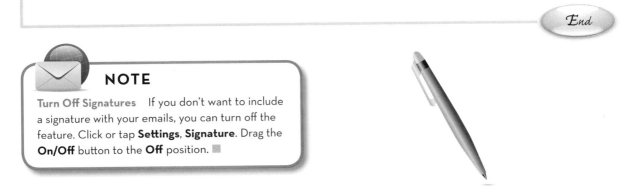

USING THE CALENDAR APP

You can use the Calendar app to keep track of appointments you make with friends, colleagues, and others. Calendar helps you remember important birthdays and special occasions, events, and other daily, weekly, or monthly activities you pursue. You can flip back and forth between daily, weekly, or monthly view and check out your work-week schedule, too.

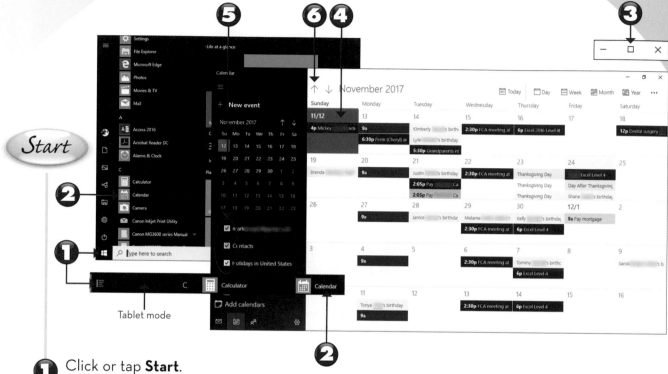

Tablet mode

1 Click or tap **Start**.
Click or tap **All apps**.

2 Click or tap **Calendar**.

3 Click or tap the **Maximize** button to display the Calendar app full screen.

4 Calendar opens in Month view.

5 If you're using several email and social media accounts, Calendar already inserts items such as birthdays and anniversaries for you. See the color-coding in the left pane to determine the source for each calendar event.

6 Use up/down or left-right arrows to move between months.

Continued

NOTE

First-Time Use   When you see the Welcome screen in Calendar, click or tap **Get started** and then follow the onscreen instructions to proceed. ■

NOTE

Associate Your Accounts   When you set up a third-party email account such as Yahoo! or Gmail and agree to **Get the most out of your account**, its email, calendar, and contacts are synced and available to Calendar. ■

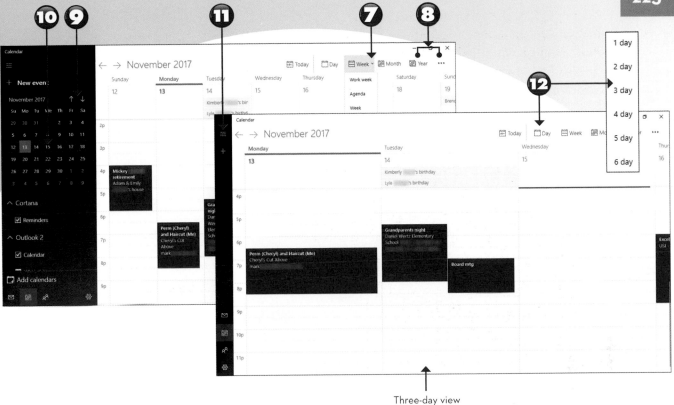

Three-day view

7 To select the week view desired, open the Week menu and select **Work week, Agenda**, or **Week**.

8 To select another view (**Month, Year**), click or tap it.

9 Use the navigation calendar to view a particular date; click the arrows above the navigation calendar to move to the previous (up-arrow) or next (down-arrow) month.

10 Click or tap the date you want to view.

11 To toggle details on the navigation bar on/off, click or tap the **Menu** button.

12 To display a range of dates, click or tap **Day** and choose the number of days to display.

End

NOTE

Turn Off Calendars Account calendars are listed below the navigation calendar, including the Birthday calendar with Facebook birthdays. You can uncheck a calendar to turn off its display as part of your main calendar. For example, if you uncheck the Birthday calendar, you no longer see your friends' birthdays listed in the calendar display.

SCHEDULING AN APPOINTMENT WITH CALENDAR

It's easy to set up an appointment using Calendar. Appointments are called *events* in Calendar's lingo. You can set up a quick event using the pop-up box, or you can fill out more details for an event using a form. In this task, you learn how to schedule a basic or detailed appointment.

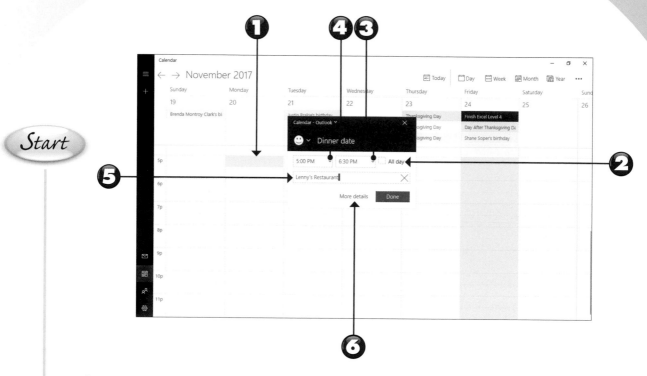

1 With Calendar open, navigate to the date to which you want to add an appointment, and click or tap the date. If you're in Day, Work week, or Week view, you can click or tap a specific time.

2 To set a specific time, clear the **All day** check box.

3 Enter the start and ending times.

4 Enter a title for the event.

5 Enter a location for the event.

6 To add additional information, click or tap **More details**.

Continued

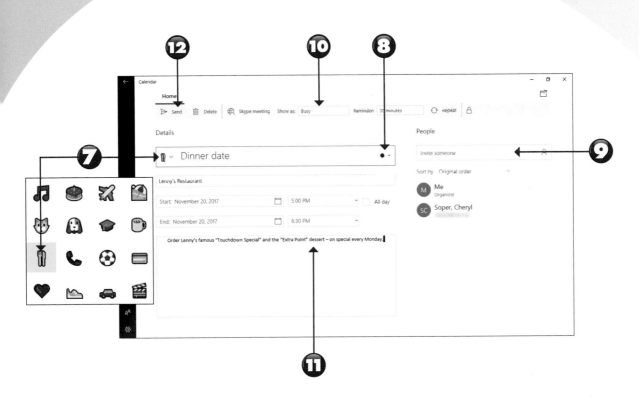

7 To change the icon for the event, click or tap and select an icon.

8 Optionally, to choose a different calendar to post the event to, click or tap here and choose another calendar.

9 Click or tap to invite someone to the event.

10 To change how the event appears on shared calendars, click or tap the **Show as** menu and select **Free**, **Tentative**, **Busy**, or **Out of office**.

11 Click or tap to add additional information about the appointment.

12 Click or tap **Send** to save the event and invite any selected attendees. (If no one else is invited, click **Save and Close**.)

End

SCHEDULING AN ALL-DAY EVENT

An all-day event is anything that lasts for the entire day, such as a birthday or a conference you're attending. All-day events appear listed at the top of a date in Day, Week, or Work week view.

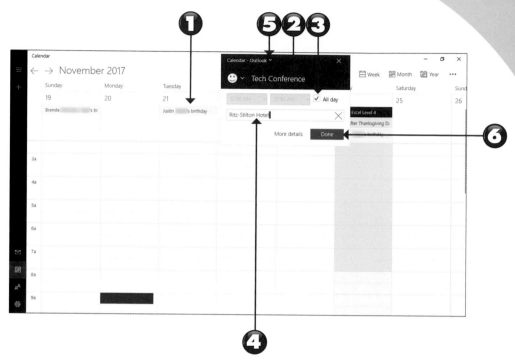

Start

1 From Calendar, click or tap the date to which you want to add an appointment.

2 Click or tap the **Event name** box and enter a name for the all-day event, such as Tech Conference.

3 If it is not already checked, click or tap the **All day** check box. The box must be checked to record the event as an all-day item.

4 Enter a location (optional).

5 If you need to add the event to a different calendar, select the calendar.

6 Click **Done** when finished.

End

TIP

Easy Edits   You can always make changes to items on your schedule. Just click or tap the event on the calendar to open the form window and make your changes. ■

SCHEDULING A RECURRING APPOINTMENT

If your schedule involves regular appointments, such as a weekly staff meeting, you can set a recurring event. Using the Repeat feature, you can specify how often the event occurs and when it stops recurring.

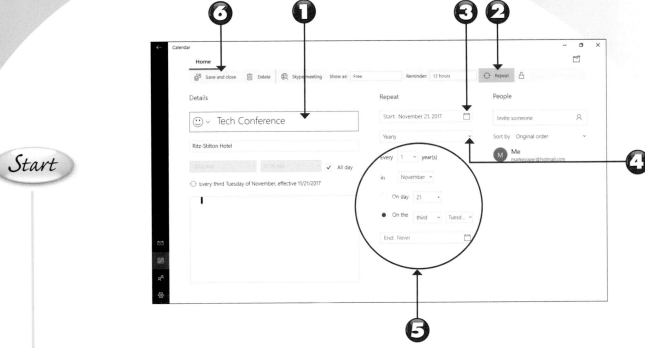

1 Open the Event form and fill out the appropriate appointment details.

2 Click or tap **Repeat**.

3 Click or tap **Start** to choose a date from a pop-up calendar when the recurring event begins.

4 Click or tap the **Occurrence** arrow and choose how often the event repeats: Daily, Weekly, Monthly, or Yearly.

5 Set the end date and other relevant details for the recurring event. (These details differ by type of occurrence; an event recurring weekly has different details than one recurring monthly.)

6 Click or tap **Save and close**. (If you invited anyone, click **Send**.)

End

NOTE

Editing Recurrences   You can make changes to a repeating appointment by clicking or tapping the event on the calendar. This opens the form where you can click or tap **Edit series** to change how often the appointment repeats. To remove the appointment entirely, click or tap **Delete**.

SETTING AN APPOINTMENT REMINDER

Calendar has a handy feature for helping you remember upcoming events on your calendar. The Reminder feature lets you set an alarm that notifies you with a prompt box when the appointment draws near. The default is 15 minutes prior.

Start

1 Open the event's form.

2 Click or tap the **Reminder** drop-down arrow.

3 Click or tap a reminder time.

4 Click or tap **Save and close**.

5 When the specified reminder time arrives, a notification reminder box pops up onscreen; click or tap **Snooze** to ignore it for a few minutes, or click or tap **Dismiss** to close the reminder.

End

TIP

Removing a Reminder To remove a reminder, reopen the form, click or tap **Reminder**, and choose **None** from the drop-down menu. ■

HIDING AND DISPLAYING CALENDAR'S FOLDERS PANE

The left side of the Calendar app lists your folders, a navigation calendar, and icons for accessing Mail, Settings, and more. You can hide the pane to free up more viewing space for the calendar display.

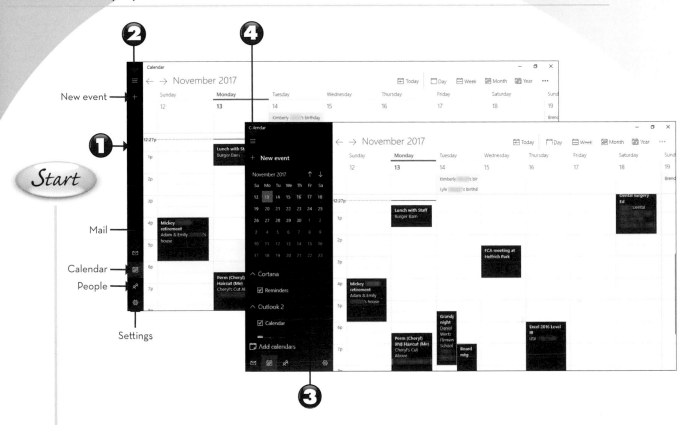

New event

Start

Mail

Calendar

People

Settings

1 When the Calendar app's left pane menu is hidden, you can still access most icons.

2 Click or tap to display the pane.

3 When the pane is open, you can also add or hide calendars.

4 Click or tap to hide the pane again.

End

TIP

Switching You can switch between the Calendar, Mail, and People apps. Click or tap the **Mail** icon to view mail; click or tap the **People** icon to view contacts; click or tap the **Calendar** icon to view your schedule. ■

STARTING SKYPE

You can use the Skype app, included free with Windows 10 FCU, to make face-to-face video calls over the Internet. You can also use Skype to send and receive text messages and voice calls around the world. Because Skype clients are available for Android, iOS, MacOS, Linux, Kindle Fire HD, and Xbox One, you can use Skype for all of your voice, video, and text chat needs. Here's how to get started with Skype in Windows 10 FCU.

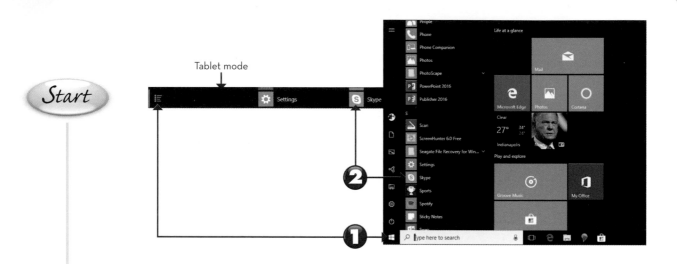

Tablet mode

Start

1 Click or tap **Start**.
Click or tap **All apps**.

2 Click or tap **Skype**.

Continued

NOTE

Requirements You need a webcam and a microphone (which are built in to most laptop PCs) to use Skype. Your Microsoft account is also your Skype account. However, if you use a local account, you must create a separate Skype account. The first time you use Skype, you are prompted to allow access to your contacts, camera, and microphone. ■

Continued

3 Review the new features; then click or tap **Close**.

4 Skype opens with the Recent Conversations panel displayed.

5 Click to reopen a recent conversation.

6 To change your online status, click or tap your name or picture at the top of the navigation pane.

TIP

Testing, Testing   To quickly test your device's sound, click or tap **Echo/Sound Test Service** located in the **Contacts** category. Click or tap the **Call** button and follow the instructions to conduct a sound test. ▇

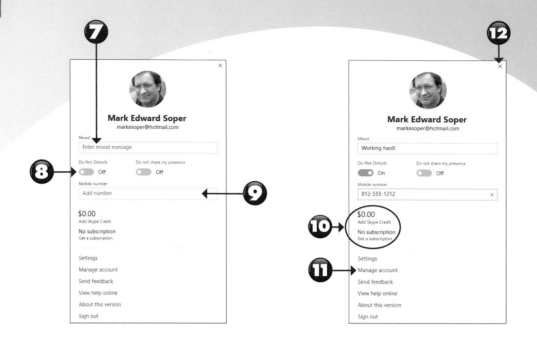

7 Click or tap the Mood box and enter text that describes your mood.

8 Set your status to **Do Not Disturb** or **Do not share my presence** by dragging the appropriate slider to **Off**.

9 Add your mobile number if you want to use your mobile number to receive Skype calls.

10 If you want to call phone numbers with Skype, click or tap one of these to add credit or buy a subscription.

11 Click or tap to manage your Skype account online.

12 Click or tap to close this dialog and return to Skype's recent conversations.

End

NOTE

Configure Settings To find settings for Skype, click or tap the **Settings** link in the user pane. The Settings page includes settings for audio, video, microphone, notifications, and more. ■

ADDING CONTACTS WITH SKYPE

You can add contacts to Skype for people you communicate with the most. You add a contact when you send your first message to a given person, and that person accepts your message.

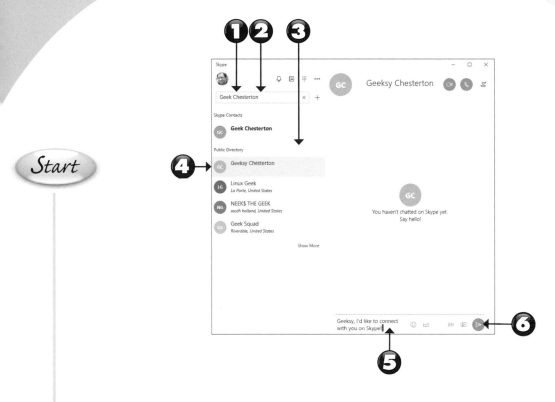

1. From either Skype's Recent conversations or Contacts tab, click or tap in the **Search Skype** box.

2. Type the name of the person you want to find and press the Enter key.

3. Any Skype contacts matching the name are listed first, followed by possible matches from the public directory of Microsoft accounts and Skype users.

4. Click or tap a match to set up as a contact.

5. Type a message to this person in the **Type a message** field.

6. Click or tap **Send**.

ACCEPTING A SKYPE CONTACT

When a Skype user sends you a message, you have the option to accept it (making yourself one of the sender's contacts, and setting the sender as one of your contacts) or blocking it. Here's what that process looks like.

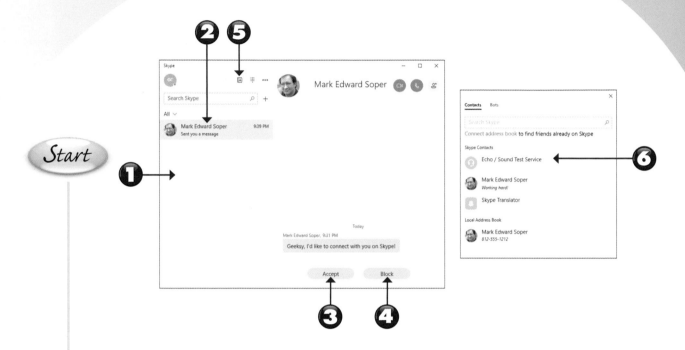

1 The Skype user's message shows up in your Recent conversations pane.

2 Click or tap the message.

3 Click or tap **Accept** to become a contact.

4 Click or tap **Block** to avoid becoming a contact.

5 Click or tap the **Contacts** (address book) icon to see your contacts.

6 View your contacts.

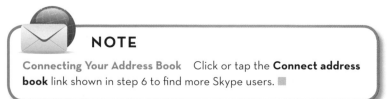

NOTE

Connecting Your Address Book   Click or tap the **Connect address book** link shown in step 6 to find more Skype users. ■

TEXT MESSAGING WITH SKYPE

Skype supports instant messaging to your friends, family, and co-workers. Text messages appear as a conversation in the contact window.

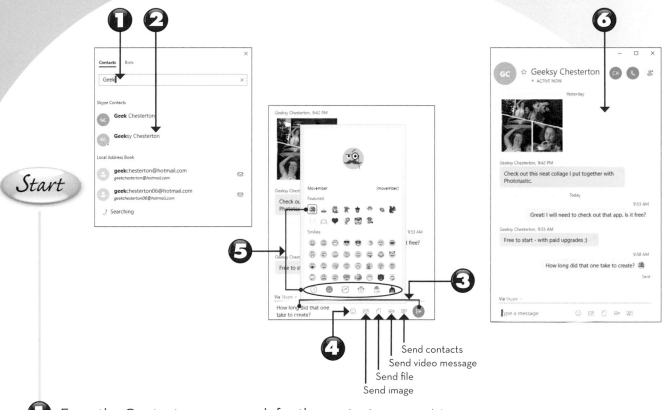

Send contacts
Send video message
Send file
Send image

1 From the Contacts pane, search for the contact you want to message.

2 Click or tap the contact.

3 Click or tap the **Type a message** box, type your message text, and add any additional content. Click or tap **Send** when finished.

4 To add an emoticon or Moji (animated emoticon), click the **Insert emoticon or Moji** icon.

5 Choose a category and click or tap the one you want.

6 Note that messages scroll up, with the most recent message on the bottom.

End

NOTE

Starting a Messaging Session from Recent Conversations If your contact is listed in Recent conversations, you can click or tap the listing to start messaging. ■

PLACING A VIDEO CALL WITH SKYPE

With your webcam, you can place a face-to-face video call. When making a video call, Skype displays a few tools you can use, and it keeps track of the call duration.

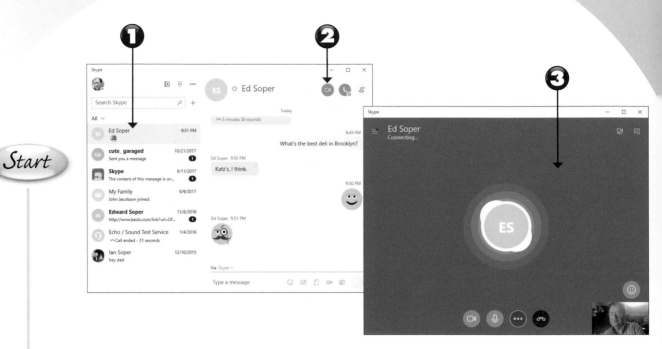

 Start

1 Click or tap the contact you want to call from Recent conversations (shown) or from Contacts.

2 Click or tap the **Video Call** icon.

3 Skype begins calling the other person for you.

Continued

NOTE

Voice Calls A voice call works the same way as a video call in Skype. Click or tap the **Voice Call** icon instead of the **Video Call** icon to place your call. When you're connected, only the microphone works; the video feed is turned off. ■

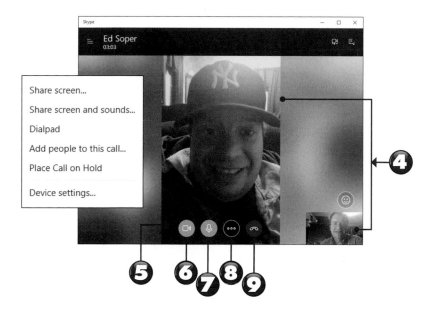

4 When the person accepts your call, the screen shows the view from that device's camera, with the view from your device's camera in the lower-right corner.

5 Mouse over or tap the screen to display Skype's call controls.

6 Click or tap the camera icon to turn off your video feed; the other user will see your profile picture instead.

7 Click or tap the microphone icon to mute the sound from your microphone.

8 Click or tap the menu (three-dot) button to display additional options.

9 Click or tap the hangup icon to end the call.

End

RECEIVING A CALL WITH SKYPE

When you receive a Skype call, a notification box pops up and you can choose to accept or decline the call. You can choose between taking a video call or a voice call.

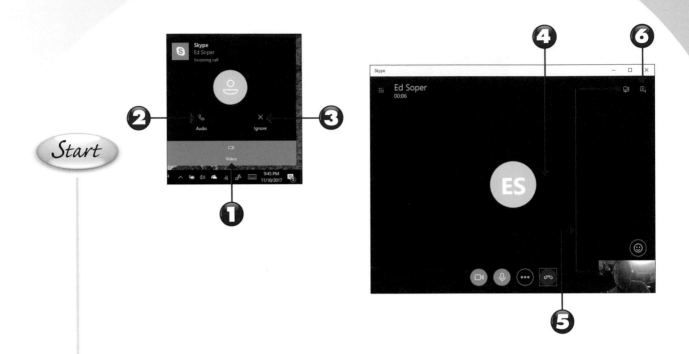

1 When an incoming Skype call arrives, a notification appears. Click or tap **Video** to accept a video call.

2 Click or tap **Audio** to accept the call as audio only.

3 Click or tap **Ignore** to ignore the call.

4 Skype opens and starts the call.

5 If you have the wrong camera selected, click or tap the **Switch camera** icon to use the other camera.

6 To use text chat during a call you started or received, click the text chat button.

Continued

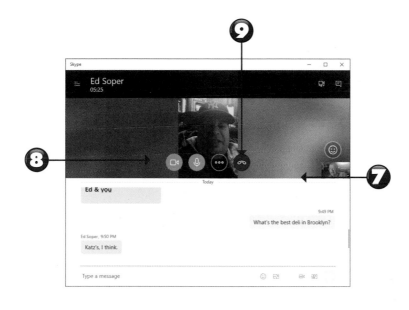

7 The screen splits and your call continues while the lower part of the screen can be used for chatting.

8 To see the call controls, mouse over or touch the call window.

9 To end the call, click or tap the hangup icon.

End

Chapter 12

NEWS, WEATHER, SPORTS, MAPS, AND MONEY

You can use Windows 10 FCU to keep abreast of the latest news and information the Internet has to offer. This chapter shows you how to use apps included with Windows 10 FCU to access headlines, maps, weather, sports, and financial news.

Using the Measure distance inking option in Maps

Viewing a radar map in Weather

The main menu in News

Selecting a team in Sports

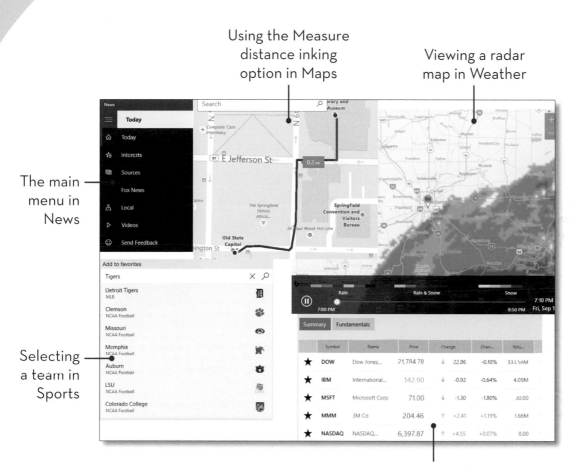

Viewing stocks and stock indices in Money

STARTING THE NEWS APP

Here's how to start up the Windows 10 FCU News (also known as MSN News) app. If you used News previously, some of these steps will not apply to you.

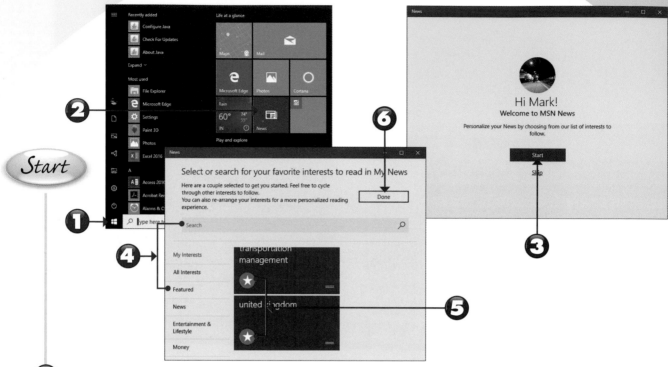

1 Click or tap **Start**.

2 Click or tap **News**.

3 Click or tap **Start** to personalize your news.

4 Click or tap a category or search for an interest.

5 Click or tap each interest you want to follow. Green stars indicate the ones you have selected.

6 When you are finished, click or tap **Done** to open the News app.

End

NOTE

Finding News, Weather, Map, Money, and Sports If these apps are not on the right pane of the Start menu on your device, scroll down or open All Apps to find them. For this chapter, we added them to the Start menu. See Chapter 4 to learn more about customizing the Start menu. They can also be installed from the Microsoft Store if they aren't installed on your system. ■

USING THE NEWS APP

The News app taps into the powerful Bing search engine to bring you the latest news and headlines from around the world or in your own locale.

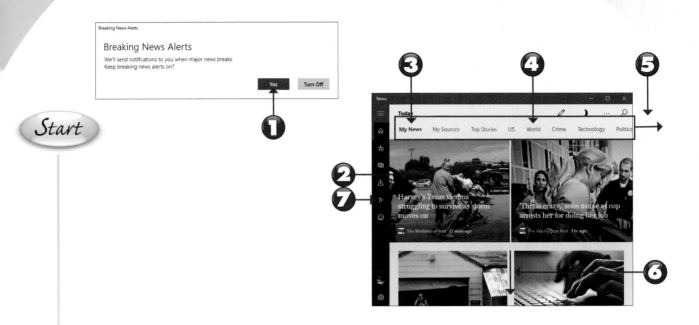

Start

1. Click **Yes** to receive breaking news alerts.

2. Click or tap a story to read more about it.

3. Click or tap **My News** to see stories matching the interests you set up.

4. Click or tap a category to view more news.

5. Scroll right to view more topic categories.

6. Scroll down to view more news in the current category.

7. Click to view news videos.

End

CUSTOMIZING NEWS

You can look up your favorite news sources and add them to the News app's Interests list. News stories from your favorite sites appear listed among the default content on the Home page. You can toggle the default topics on or off to control which news topics appear listed across the screen.

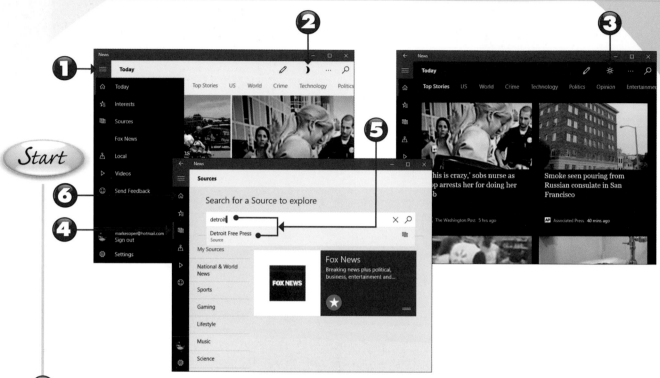

Start

1. Click or tap to expand the menu.

2. Click or tap to change to the dark theme.

3. Click or tap to change back to the default light theme.

4. Click or tap to add a new source.

5. Search for the source and click a match.

6. Click or tap anytime you want to return to the home screen.

Continued

TIP

Removing Interests or Sources To remove an interest or source, go to the appropriate menu and click or tap the green star. ■

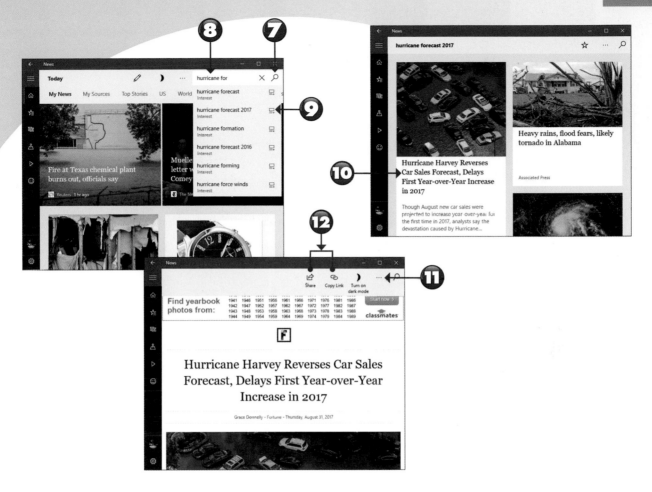

7 Click or tap **Search**.

8 Enter a search term or phrase.

9 Click a search result to see matching stories.

10 Click or tap a story to read it.

11 Click or tap to expand the top menu.

12 Use **Share** or **Copy Link** options to send stories to others.

End

STARTING THE WEATHER APP

You can use the Weather app (also known as MSN Weather in the Store) to check your local weather report, view forecasts, and track the weather in your favorite locations. If you have used the Weather app before, some of these steps might not apply to you.

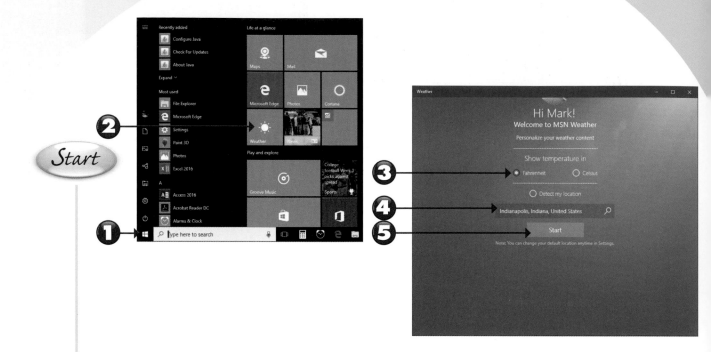

1 Click or tap **Start**.

2 Click or tap **Weather**.

3 Click or tap the temperature scale to use.

4 Enter your location (city, state, ZIP, or postal code). If more than one location matches, choose the right one from the list of matches.

5 Click or tap **Start**.

Continued

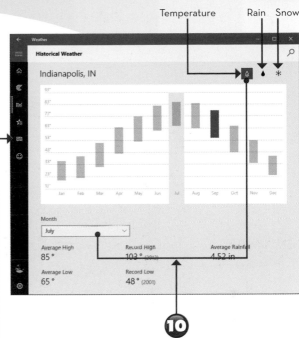

Temperature   Rain Snow

6 Note the current conditions and forecast.

7 Click or tap to see the radar.

8 Use the zoom controls to adjust the radar view.

9 Click or tap to see historical weather.

10 Select the month and data type (temperature, rain, snow).

11 Click or tap for weather news.

End

TIP

Weather on Your Start Menu To display weather for your home location on the Start menu, right-click or press and hold the Weather tile. Click or tap the three-dot button (touchscreen only); then click/tap **More**, **Turn live tile on**.

ADDING LOCATIONS TO WEATHER

Whether you're checking the weather before you travel or keeping an eye on the sky where friends or relatives live, Weather makes it easy to add more locations. Here's how.

Start

1. To check weather for a specific location, tap the **Home** button.

2. Click or tap in the **City or ZIP Code** box and type the location.

3. Click or tap the location from the list, or click or tap the **Search** icon to conduct a search.

4. Note that the Weather app window displays the current information and forecast for the designated place.

5. Click or tap the star to add this location to your favorites.

6. Click or tap **Close**.

Continued

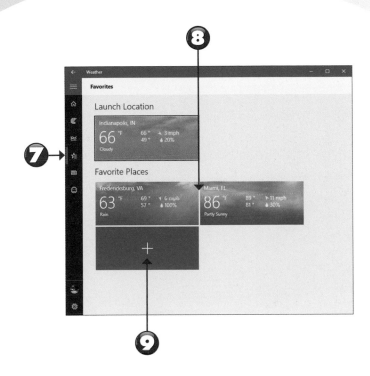

7 Click or tap **Favorites**.

8 Click or tap a location to see more weather details.

9 Click or tap to add another location.

End

TIP

Removing a Location from Weather Favorites   To remove a location, right-click or press and hold it, and then click or tap **Remove from Favorites**. ■

STARTING MAPS

The Maps app works with Microsoft's Bing website to help you find locations down the street or around the world. You can find directions, look up an address, or view your current location using this app. In this task, you learn how to start the improved Maps app for the first time.

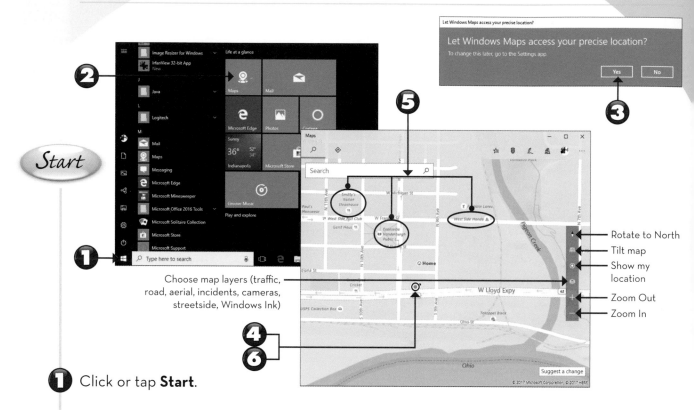

Choose map layers (traffic, road, aerial, incidents, cameras, streetside, Windows Ink)

Rotate to North

Tilt map

Show my location

Zoom Out

Zoom In

1 Click or tap **Start**.

2 Click or tap **Maps**.

3 The first time you run Maps, a prompt box appears asking whether Maps can use your precise location and location history; click or tap **Yes** (used in these lessons) or **No** to continue.

4 If you answered Yes in step 3, your location is marked on the map. If you are at home, it is marked Home.

5 Note that some businesses are listed on the map.

6 To display more information about what's nearby, click your location.

Continued

TIP

Easier Access in Tablet Mode In Tablet mode, if Maps is not pinned to the Start menu, tap **All apps** to view it. You can pin the Maps app (or other apps) to the Start menu so it's easy to access. Click or tap the **Start** menu, click or tap **All Apps**, right-click the **Maps** app name, and choose **Pin to Start**. ■

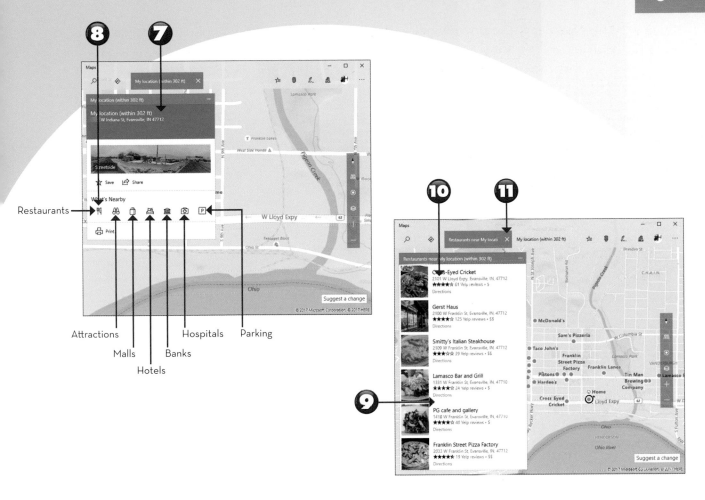

Restaurants

Attractions   Hospitals   Parking

Malls   Banks

Hotels

7 Note your location (accurate to within the distance listed).

8 Click or tap a business type to see what's nearby.

9 Maps displays a list of the nearest locations and shows them in addition to mapping additional locations.

10 Click or tap to get directions.

11 Click or tap to close the listing.

End

TIP

Moving and Zooming the Map   Use the scroll wheel on your mouse to zoom in and zoom out. Click and drag the map with your mouse to display a particular area.

GETTING DIRECTIONS

The Maps app also provides directions to your destination by car, transit (train/bus), or walking. Here's how.

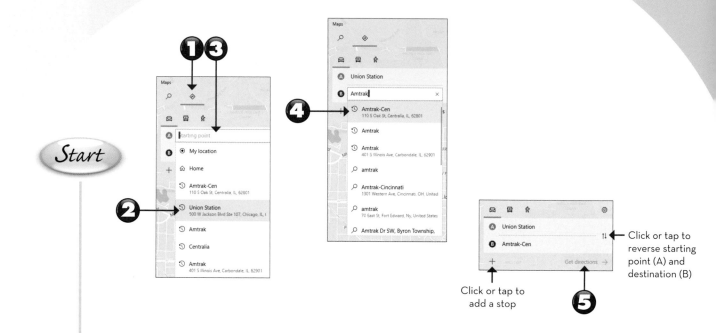

Click or tap to reverse starting point (A) and destination (B)

Click or tap to add a stop

Start

1 Click or tap **Directions**.

2 If the starting location (A) is listed in your search history, click or tap it.

3 If the starting location is not listed, search for it.

4 Search for or click/tap the destination (B).

5 Click or tap **Get directions**.

Continued

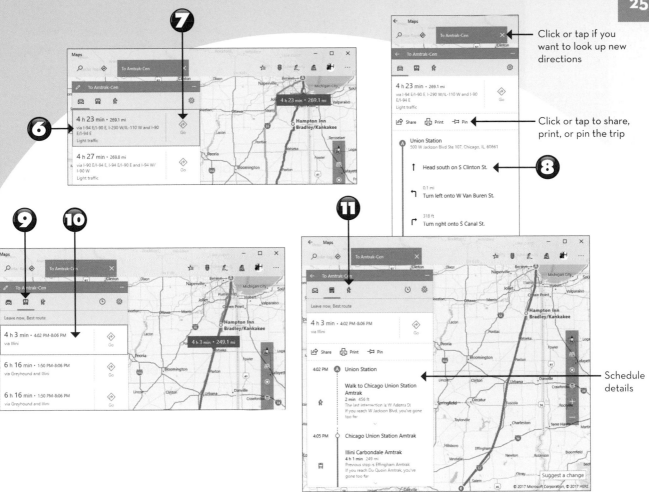

Click or tap if you want to look up new directions

Click or tap to share, print, or pin the trip

Schedule details

6 Each route lists estimated time, current traffic, mileage, and major highways.

7 The fastest route by car is listed first. Tap or click **Go** to start, or click the description for details.

8 Details of the trip shown in step 7 are listed here.

9 For transit directions, click the bus icon.

10 Transit directions (when available) list bus and/or train schedules and total time. Tap your preferred schedule for details.

11 For walking directions, click the walker icon. Depending upon the start and destination points, walking directions might not be available.

End

USING INK WITH MAPS

Maps has built-in support for Windows Ink, and now you can use it to measure distance as well as to point out details along the way. This example uses Windows Ink to help plan a walking tour of Springfield, Illinois.

1 Search for the location and select the best match.

2 Click or tap **Attractions**.

3 Click to close the window.

4 Click or tap **Ink**.

5 Click or tap **Measure distance**.

6 Select the ink color and marker tip size.

Continued

NOTE

Learning More About Windows Ink To discover more features of Windows Ink, see Chapter 13, "Using Windows Ink." ■

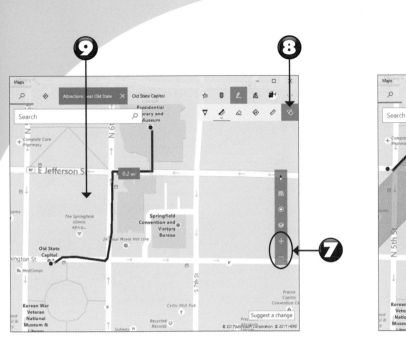

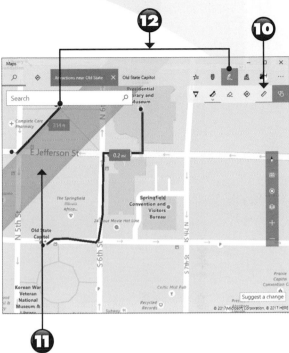

7 Adjust the zoom level so you can see the origin and destination.

8 If it is not highlighted, click or tap **Touch writing**.

9 Click or tap to start drawing on the map. As each travel segment is drawn, the distance is measured and displayed.

10 Click or tap the ruler to use it. Click to close it when you are done.

11 Drag the ruler into place. To rotate it with your mouse, hover over it and use the scroll wheel.

12 Click **Measure distance** and draw along the edge of the ruler for straight-line distance.

End

TIP

More Maps Features Click the Menu (three-dot) icon in the upper-right corner of the Maps app to share a map (email, URL, Cortana, Facebook, and so on), to print it, or to access settings for Maps. ■

USING THE MONEY APP

Whether you're browsing financial news or focusing on a single company, the Money app (also known as MSN Money) is ready to help. Here's how to get started. If you have already used Money in an older version of Windows, some of these steps may not apply to you. If it's not installed on your system already, you can get it from the Microsoft Store.

1 Click or tap **Start**.

2 Click or tap **Money**.

3 Click or tap **Start** to choose stocks and indices to follow.

4 Use Search to quickly locate your favorites.

5 Click or tap the stocks and indices you want to follow.

6 Click or tap **Done** to continue.

Continued

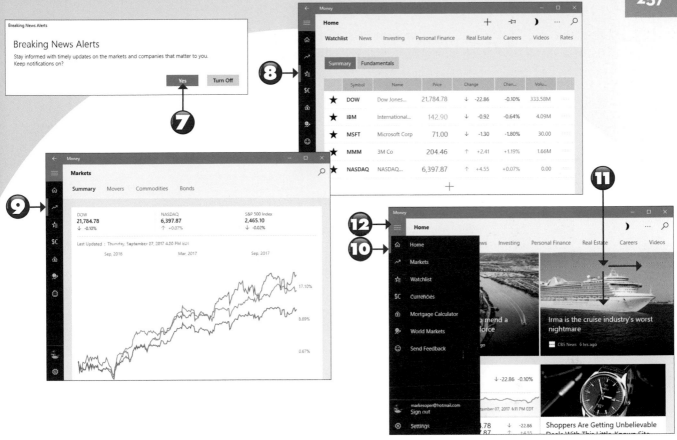

7 Click or tap **Yes** to get breaking news alerts on the stocks and markets you monitor.

8 Click or tap **Watchlist** for a summary of your stocks or indices.

9 Click or tap **Markets** to see a summary of the major stock indices.

10 Click or tap **Home** to display current stock information and news stories.

11 Scroll or flick down for more stories and to the right for more categories.

12 Click or tap to expand the menu.

End

TIP

Using Cortana If you've activated Cortana (the Windows 10 FCU digital assistant), you can view news by clicking or tapping the **Ask me anything** box next to the Start menu. Cortana lists the day's top headlines, displays any stocks you're watching, and shows your local weather report, all in a scrollable pop-up menu. ■

USING THE SPORTS APP

You can use the Sports app (also known as MSN Sports) to view the latest news and scores from athletic events around the world, including video clips and slideshows of the latest events. Let's get started!

1 Click or tap **Start**.

2 Click or tap **Sports**.

3 Click or tap a sport topic to view news, or scroll down the window to view other sports news stories.

4 To add your favorite teams to the front page, click or tap **Add Favorites**.

5 Type in all or part of the team name.

6 Click or tap your team.

Continued

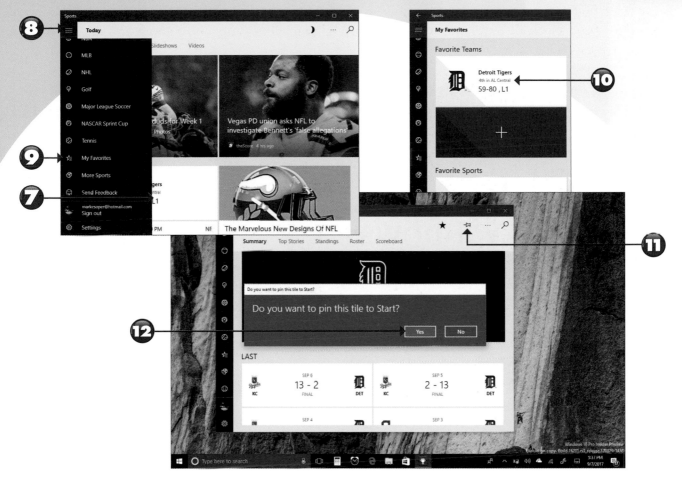

7 Your team(s) are listed on the Home page.

8 Click or tap to expand the menu.

9 Click or tap **My Favorites** to see more about your teams.

10 Click or tap your team to check scores, roster, and more.

11 To pin a team to the Start menu, click or tap the pushpin.

12 Click **Yes**.

End

Chapter 13

USING WINDOWS INK

The improved Windows Ink Workspace combines old and new pen-enabled apps to make your pen, touchscreen, or touchpad more powerful and easier to use for creating notes, reminders, and simple drawings. As you learn in this chapter, Windows Ink Workspace can also work with Cortana, Mail, Photos, and other apps.

Creating a Cortana reminder with Sticky Notes

Annotating a web page in Microsoft Edge with Windows Ink

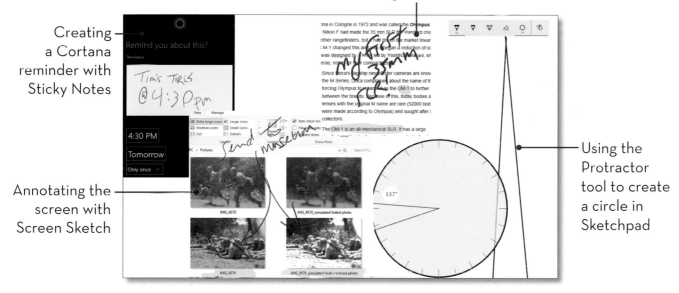

Annotating the screen with Screen Sketch

Using the Protractor tool to create a circle in Sketchpad

OPENING THE WINDOWS INK WORKSPACE

You launch the Windows Ink Workspace from the taskbar. Here's how to get started with it.

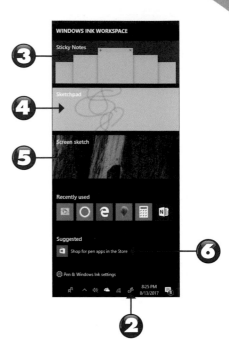

Start

1. If the Windows Ink Workspace icon is not visible, right-click the taskbar and click or tap **Show Windows Ink Workspace button**.

2. Click or tap the **Windows Ink Workspace** icon in the taskbar.

3. To create a sticky note, click or tap **Sticky Notes**.

4. To create a sketch you can save as an image file, click or tap **Sketchpad**.

5. To sketch over the current screen and save the result as an image file, click or tap **Screen sketch**.

6. To get more pen apps, scroll down and click or tap **Shop for pen apps in the Store**.

End

NOTE

Pen, Tablet, Touchpad, or Mouse   Windows Ink Workspace works with any of these input devices. ■

CREATING A STICKY NOTE

Windows lets you place sticky notes anywhere on your desktop, gives you a choice of colors, and lets you resize them as needed. You can create sticky notes in either Desktop or Tablet mode, but you can see them only in Desktop mode.

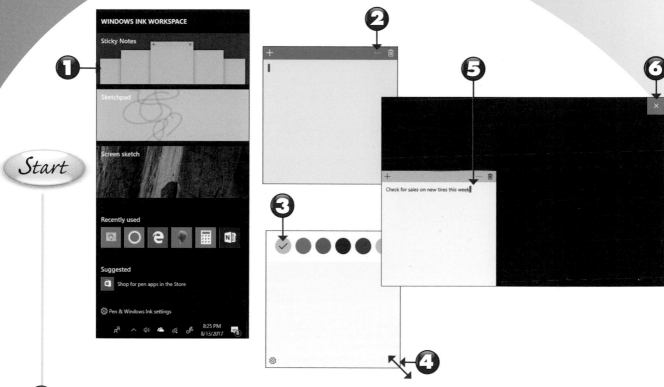

Start

1 From the Windows Ink Workspace, click or tap **Sticky notes**.

2 To change the note color, click or tap the three-dot menu button.

3 Click or tap your preferred note color.

4 To resize the note, hover over a corner or side. When the cursor changes to a double-headed arrow, click or press and drag an edge or corner, and then release.

5 Type or handwrite the note text.

6 Click or tap the **X** to return to the Windows desktop.

End

TIP

Drag It Anywhere To place the sticky note where you want it, click or press and hold the top border of the note touchpad, and then drag it into position. Release the mouse or touchpad button or move the pen or finger away from the screen to drop it. ■

CREATING A REMINDER USING STICKY NOTES

You can create a sticky note that Cortana can use to create a reminder. Here's how:

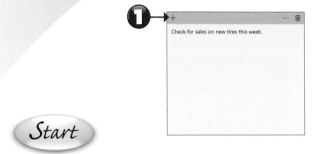

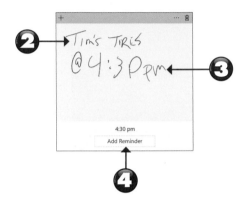

1 If you already have a note on the desktop, click the plus (+) sign to create a new note. Otherwise, open the Windows Ink Workspace and click/tap Sticky Notes.

2 Handwrite or type a note that includes a date or time.

3 The date or time portion of the note turns red. Click or tap the red text.

4 Click or tap **Add Reminder**. Click or log in if prompted.

Continued

NOTE

Enable Insights When you start Sticky Notes for the first time, you are prompted to enable Cortana's insights feature. This lets Cortana help you with reminders. ■

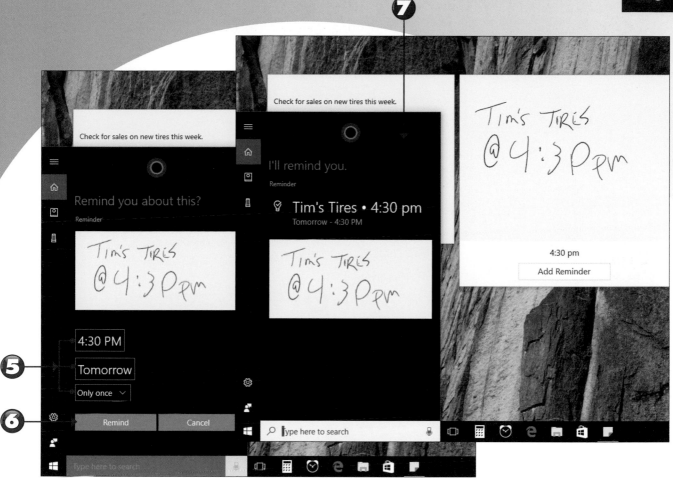

5 After Cortana finishes recognizing text, make any edits needed.

6 Click or tap **Remind**.

7 Look for the confirmation message from Cortana.

End

CAUTION

Troubleshooting Reminders with Sticky Notes If Sticky Notes does not recognize dates or times (step 2), make sure you have signed in to Cortana, are not using a local account (Cortana cannot provide reminders for local accounts), and have enabled Cortana insights in Sticky Notes. (See "Configuring Sticky Notes," later in this chapter, to learn how.) ■

DELETING A STICKY NOTE

You can delete a sticky note you no longer need. Here's how.

Start

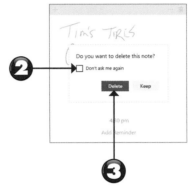

1 Click or tap the note's trashcan icon.

2 If you don't want to confirm deletions in the future, click or tap the **Don't ask me again** check box.

3 Click or tap **Delete** to remove the sticky note from your screen.

End

TIP

Goodbye Sticky Note, Cortana's Got Your Back   After you create a Cortana reminder with a sticky note, you can delete the sticky note. The reminder stays in Cortana. To learn more about Cortana, see Chapter 5, "Using Cortana Search." ■

CONFIGURING STICKY NOTES

In addition to changing the color of sticky notes, you can make other configuration changes. Here's what to do.

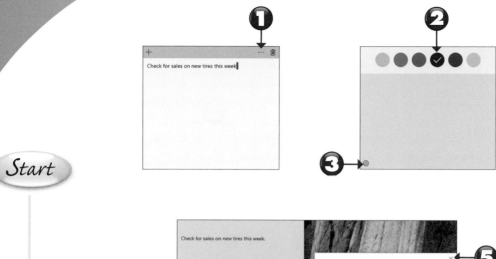

Start

① Click or tap the note's three-dot menu button.

② Choose a new note color if desired.

③ Click or tap the **Settings** (gear) icon.

④ If you want to create Cortana reminders using sticky notes, make sure **Enable insights** is turned on; click or press and drag the control to **On**.

⑤ Click or tap to close Settings.

End

TIP

Bold, Italic, Underlining, and More To add bold text to your sticky note, type the text, highlight it, and then press Ctrl+B. For italic, highlight the text and press Ctrl+I. For underlining, highlight the text and press Ctrl+U. You can also make highlighted text bigger with Ctrl+Shift+> and smaller with Ctrl+Shift+<. ■

GETTING STARTED WITH SKETCHPAD

Sketchpad is the second member of the Windows Ink Workspace team. It's designed to create simple sketches that you can save as PNG files for use with other apps. You can draw using ballpoint pen, pencil, or highlighter tools from the Sketchpad toolbar. The toolbar also offers features to help you as you draw and edit your sketches.

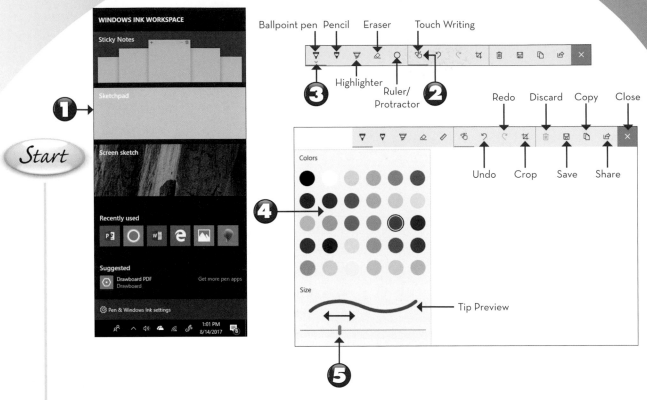

Start

1 From the Windows Ink Workspace menu, click or tap **Sketchpad**.

2 If **touch writing** is not already selected, click or tap this icon. Touch writing enables you to use your mouse, touch pad, touchscreen, or stylus to draw.

3 Click or tap to view colors and drawing tip size.

4 Click or tap to choose a drawing color.

5 Drag left to reduce the drawing tip size; drag right to increase it.

Continued

TIP

Clearing the Workspace If Sketchpad has an unneeded drawing in the workspace, click or tap **Discard**. It will be removed immediately.

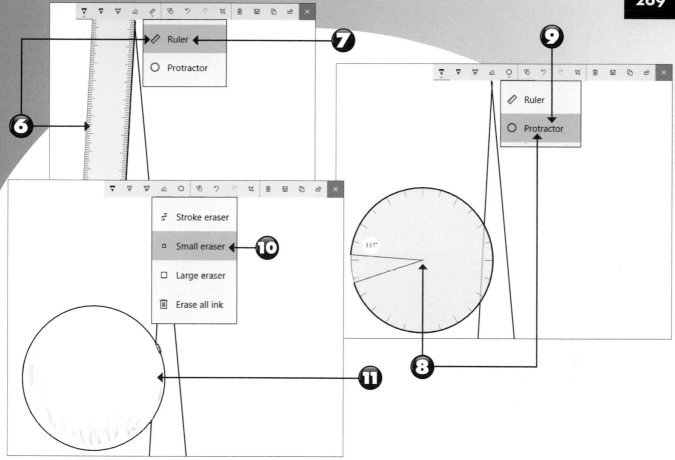

6 Open the Ruler/Protractor menu and click or tap the **Ruler** to help you draw straight lines.

7 When you are finished using the Ruler, open the Ruler menu and click or tap the **Ruler** icon again to remove it from the screen.

8 Open the Ruler/Protractor menu and click or tap the **Protractor** to help you draw curves.

9 When you are finished, open the menu and click or tap the **Protractor** icon again to remove it from the screen.

10 Open the Eraser menu and select an eraser.

11 Click or tap a shape or line to remove it.

End

TIP

Adjusting the Ruler and Protractor With any pointing device, you can drag the ruler and protractor wherever you need them. If you have a touchscreen or multi-touch touchpad, you can rotate the Ruler or resize the Protractor. If you have a scroll wheel mouse, click the Ruler or Protractor and use the scroll wheel to adjust the angle or size. ■

EDITING AND SAVING WITH SKETCHPAD

You can use Sketchpad to create drawings that work with many different apps. Here's how to make changes and save your work.

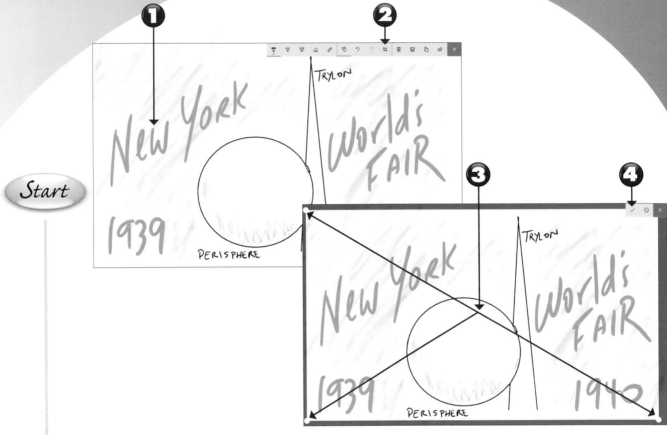

Start

1 Make additional changes as desired.

2 Click or tap the **Crop** tool to crop the picture.

3 Drag the corners to the desired crop size.

4 Click or tap the check mark to complete the crop.

Continued

TIP

Removing All Ink   To remove all the shapes and lines in a sketch without closing Sketchpad, click or tap the **Eraser** tool, and then click or tap the down arrow and select **Erase All Ink**. ■

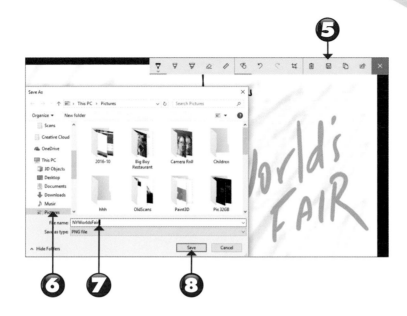

5 Click or tap the **Save** button to save your sketch.

6 Select the desired location.

7 Enter a filename. (Sketch is the default.)

8 Click or tap **Save**.

End

SHARING WITH SKETCHPAD

Sketchpad can also send sketches to other Windows 10 apps by using the Share option. This example shows you how to share a sketch with Mail.

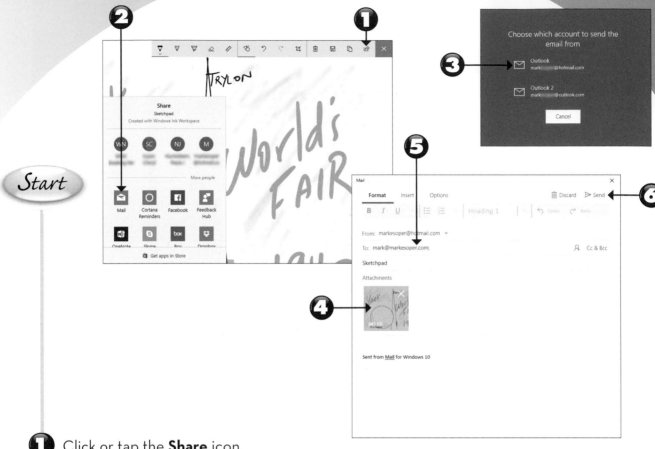

Start

1 Click or tap the **Share** icon.

2 Click or tap **Mail**.

3 If you use more than one account with Mail, click or tap the account to use.

4 Mail attaches the sketch to your message.

5 Enter the recipient and make any other changes.

6 Click or tap **Send**.

End

USING SCREEN SKETCH

Screen Sketch combines the features of Sketchpad with screen capture. Use it to sketch or make quick notes about whatever you have onscreen. This example shows you how to capture a File Manager window containing photos and use the Screen Sketch feature to annotate the pictures.

1 Open the app or apps you want to use with Screen Sketch.

2 When you have everything onscreen that you want to capture, click or tap the **Windows Ink Workspace** icon in the taskbar.

3 Click or tap **Screen sketch**.

Continued

4 Use the Sketchpad tools to mark up the screen.

5 Mark the screen as needed.

6 When you are finished, save or share the sketch using the same Save and Share tools as with Sketchpad.

End

TIP

Screen Capture, with or Without Ink   If you need to capture the screen but don't want to mark it up, skip steps 4–5 and click or tap **Save** in step 6. ■

USING WINDOWS INK WITH OTHER APPS

Windows 10 FCU enables Windows Ink to be used in other Windows apps. Here are a few of the ways you can put Windows Ink to work.

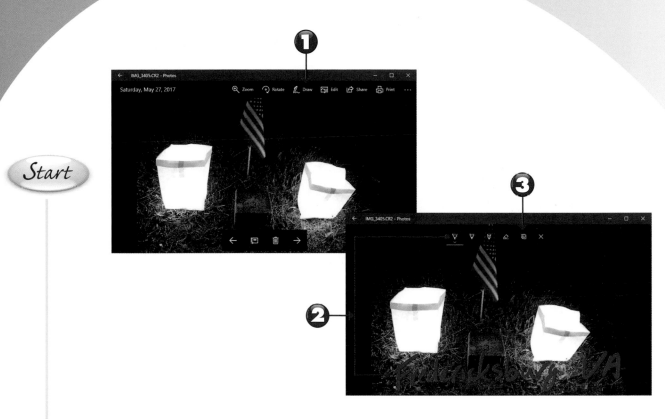

Start

1. In Photos, select a photo and click or tap **Draw**.

2. Use the Windows Ink tools to mark up the photo as desired.

3. When you click or tap **Save**, the edited photo is saved as a new file, preserving the original.

Continued

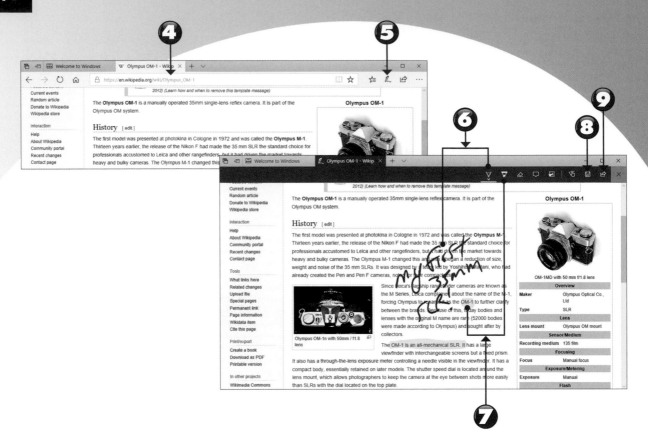

4 In Microsoft Edge, open a web page you want to annotate.

5 Click the **Draw** button to mark up the page.

6 You can see the pen tool in use.

7 Note the highlighter tool in use.

8 Click or tap to save the page.

9 Click or tap to share the page.

End

NOTE

Office 2016 and More Ink-Friendly Apps   To learn more about how you can use Microsoft Ink with Office 2016 and other apps, go to https://www.microsoft.com/en-us/windows/windows-ink. ■

Chapter 14

STORING AND FINDING YOUR FILES

Windows 10 FCU's File Explorer provides access to both local files and One-Drive cloud-based storage. File Explorer makes it easier than ever to locate folders and files and access recently used documents, photos, and other file types. In this chapter, you find out how to utilize File Explorer to learn more about your folders and files and find ways to make them more useful.

Using Details
pane

Configuring
OneDrive's
AutoSave features

Folders in
OneDrive (synced,
shared, and Files
On-Demand)

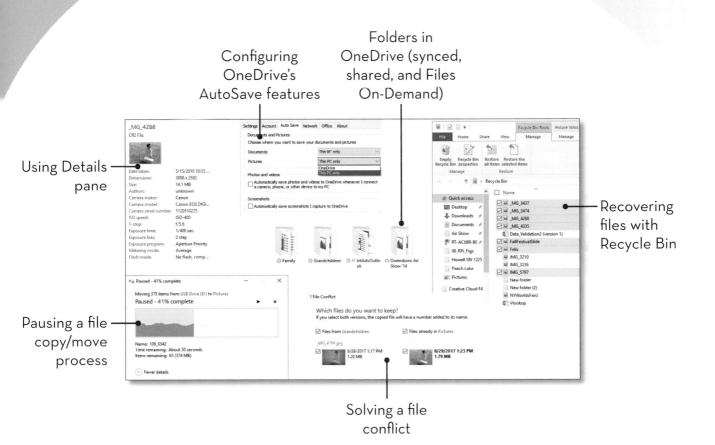

Recovering
files with
Recycle Bin

Pausing a file
copy/move
process

Solving a file
conflict

OPENING FILE EXPLORER

File Explorer is Windows 10 FCU's version of the venerable Windows Explorer file and drive management interface. Follow these steps to open File Explorer and view some of its features.

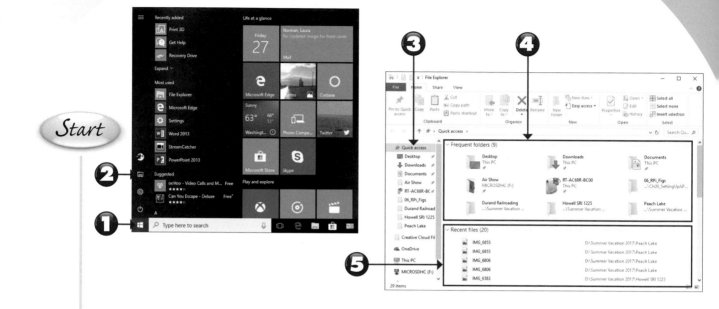

Start

1 Click or tap the **Start** button (Desktop Mode).

2 Click or tap **File Explorer**.

3 File Explorer opens to the default Quick access view.

4 Folders you open most often (Frequent folders) are at the top of the pane.

5 Files you've opened most recently (Recent files) are at the bottom of the pane.

Continued

NOTE

Using the Home Tab Click or tap the **Home** tab to view sections of tools for working with folders and files. The Clipboard section enables you to cut, copy, and paste files and folders and their locations (paths) to different locations. Use the Organize section to move, copy, delete, or rename selected files or folders. The New section's Easy Access tool lets you map a location to a drive letter or add a folder to a library. Use the Open section to see file or folder properties and history. Use the Select section to select or deselect files and folders. ■

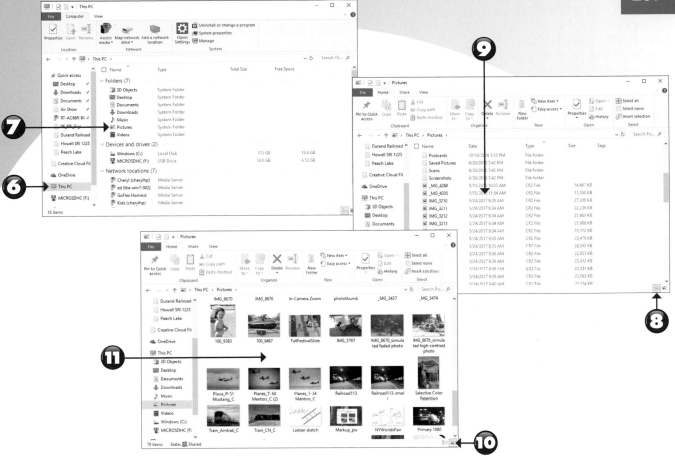

6 Click or tap **This PC** to see the folders and drives on your computer.

7 Double-click or double-tap the **Pictures** folder.

8 The Details view is active (if not, click or tap to view Details).

9 The Details view lists file/folder names, date created, size, type, and tags.

10 Click or tap to switch to the Large thumbnails view.

11 The Large thumbnails view shows a preview of each file.

End

TIP

Open File Explorer from the Keyboard To quickly open File Explorer from the keyboard, press the Windows key+E. ■

USING THE VIEW TAB

The File Explorer's View tab helps you select from a variety of settings so you can view drives, files, folders, and network locations in the most appropriate ways. Here are some examples of how to use the View tab.

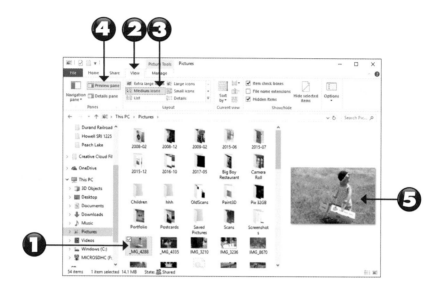

1 Click or tap a picture from your Pictures folder.

2 Click or tap the **View** tab.

3 Click or tap **Medium icons**.

4 Click or tap the **Preview pane** button.

5 A preview is shown of the selected file.

Continued

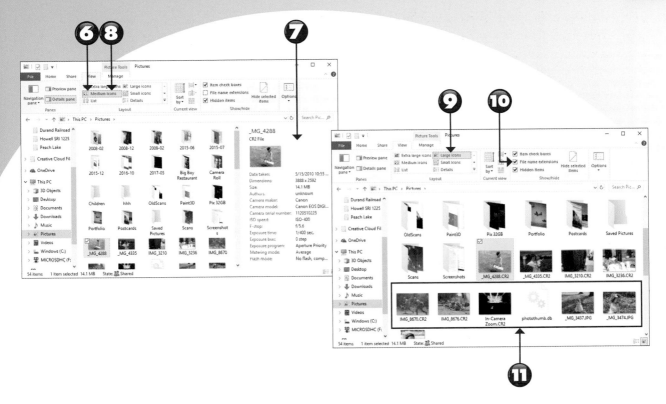

6 Click or tap the **Details pane** button.

7 Details appear about the selected file.

8 Click or tap the **Details pane** button again to close the pane.

9 Click or tap the **Large icons** button.

10 Click or tap the empty **File name extensions** check box.

11 Files with various filename extensions are shown.

End

NOTE

Filename Extensions Displaying filename extensions is useful when you have similar-looking files or want to find specific file types. For example, CR2 and other RAW files created by high-end digital cameras are very large and need special software to be viewed or edited, but JPG (JPEG) and PNG files use less disk space and can be viewed in web browsers and by email apps. TIF files are a good choice for publications. File extensions tell you what kind of file it is. To turn off filename extensions, simply uncheck the **File name extensions** check box. ■

USING COPY TO

In this exercise, you create a new folder in the Pictures folder and copy files to it. You can use these same steps to create other types of new folders in File Explorer and copy files.

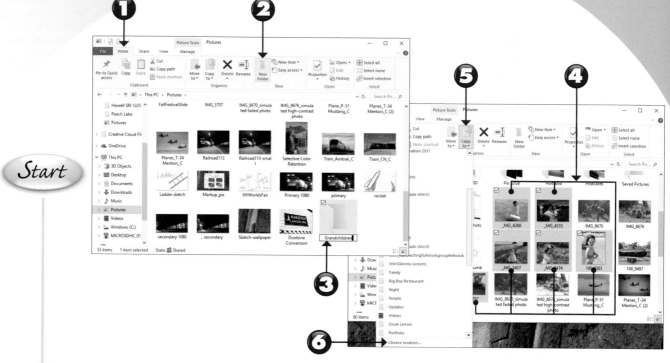

Start

1. Click or tap the **Home** tab.

2. Click or tap **New folder** to create a new folder.

3. Enter the name of the new folder. Press the **Enter** key or click outside the naming box when done.

4. Select the files you want to copy.

5. Click or tap **Copy to**.

6. Click or tap **Choose location**.

End

NOTE

Enabling Item Check Boxes Open the View tab and select the **Item check boxes** option (used in this chapter). You can then click or tap the check box for each item you want to select. ■

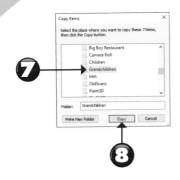

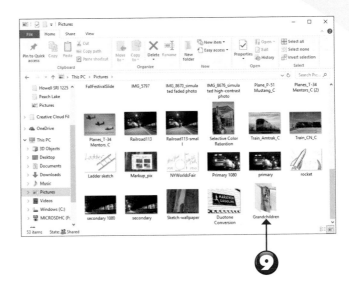

7 Navigate to and click or tap the folder you created in steps 2 and 3.

8 Click or tap **Copy**.

9 The files are copied into the folder; click or tap an empty section of the **File Explorer** window to unselect the highlighted files.

End

NOTE

Selecting Items Without Using Item Check Boxes Click the first item, and then hold down either the Ctrl key on the keyboard and click additional items or press and drag a box around items you want to select. ■

RENAMING FILES

You can easily rename files to better help you identify them and keep them organized. In this exercise, you rename a file you copied in the previous exercise.

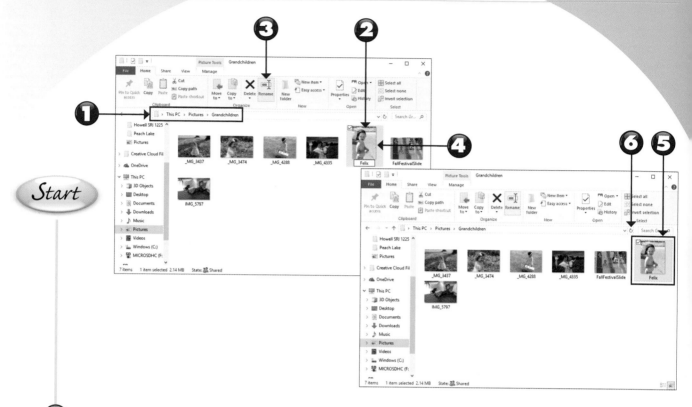

1 Open the folder where the file copies are located.

2 Click or tap a file.

3 Click or tap **Rename** on the Home tab.

4 Enter a new name for the file.

5 The file is renamed; click an empty part of the folder to unselect the file.

6 If the folder is not reordered alphabetically, click or tap **Refresh**.

NOTE

Renaming Multiple Files If you select more than one file in step 2, the files are renamed using the name you specified in step 4, followed by a sequential number (1, 2, 3, and so on). ■

SELECTING FILES

Although you can select a file simply by clicking or tapping its name, you can also activate other selection options in File Explorer. This exercise demonstrates how to select files using Invert Selection and deselect files.

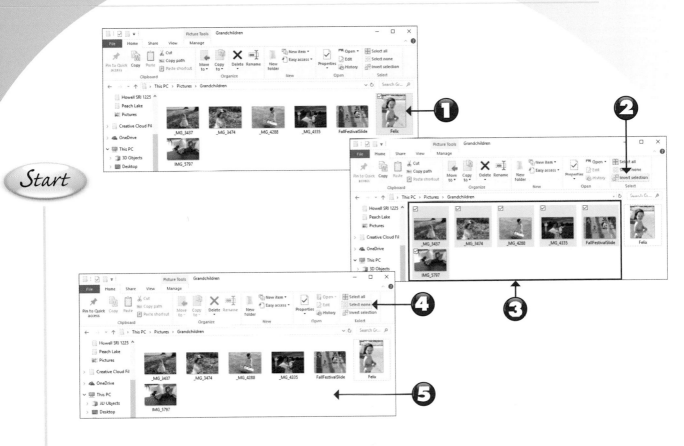

1 Click or tap the file you renamed in the previous exercise.

2 From the Home tab, click or tap **Invert selection**.

3 All files in the folder except the one selected in step 1 are selected.

4 Click or tap **Select none** on the Home tab.

5 None of the files are selected.

DELETING FILES

This exercise demonstrates how to select and delete all files in a location and remove them to the Recycle Bin, using the folder of copied files you created earlier in this chapter.

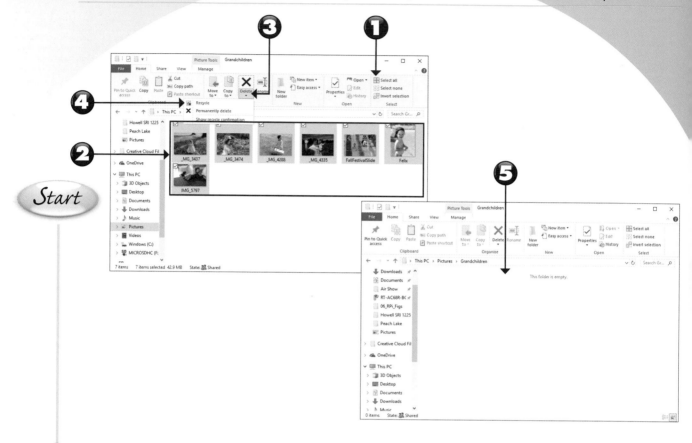

 Start

1. From the Home tab, click or tap **Select all**.

2. All the files are selected.

3. Open the **Delete** menu.

4. Click or tap **Recycle** to send files to the Recycle Bin.

5. The files are removed from the folder.

End

CAUTION

Permanently Delete Versus Recycle If you permanently delete files, the space they occupy on the drive can be reused by new files. If you decide you need to retrieve those files, you must use a third-party data-recovery utility. ■

RETRIEVING FILES FROM THE RECYCLE BIN

If you delete files you should have kept, the Recycle Bin is here to help. In this lesson, you learn how to restore files from the Recycle Bin to their original location.

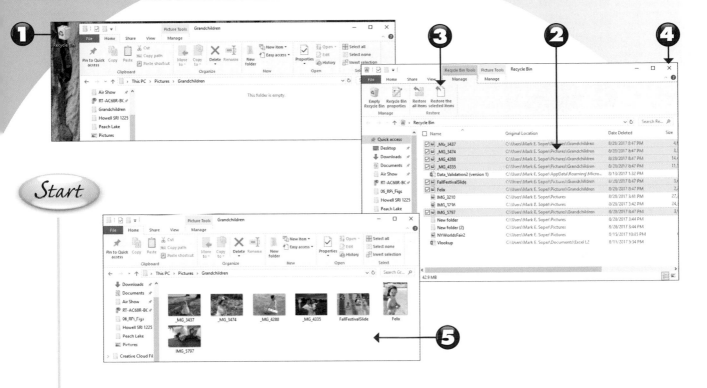

Start

1 Double-click or double-tap **Recycle Bin**.

2 Select the files you want to restore.

3 Click or tap **Restore the selected items**.

4 Click or tap to close the Recycle Bin.

5 The files are restored to their original location(s).

End

TIP

Recycle Bin Tips If you can't see the Recycle Bin on your desktop, right-click or press and hold an empty area on the desktop, select **View**, and click or tap **Show desktop icons**.
To remove all the files if you no longer need them, click or tap **Empty Recycle Bin**.
If you send more files to the Recycle Bin than it has room for, the oldest files in the bin are permanently deleted to make room for newer files. ■

MOVING FILES OR FOLDERS

The Move To command enables you to easily move files or folders to a different location. You can select from a listed destination (as in this example) or choose another location. With either Copy To or Move To, you might be able to pause and continue the process if the process takes more than a few seconds. In this example, you see how to move a folder containing many photos from an external drive to your Pictures folder.

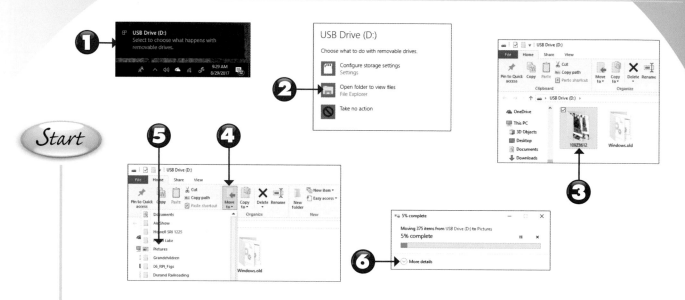

Start

1. Connect the external drive and click or tap the pop-up message.

2. Click or tap **Open folder to view files**.

3. Select the folder you want to move.

4. On File Manager's Home tab, open the **Move to** menu.

5. Click or tap **Pictures**.

6. To see more information about the process, click or tap the down arrow next to **More details**.

Continued

NOTE

Drive Already Connected? If the drive you want to move/copy folders from is already connected, start with step 3. ■

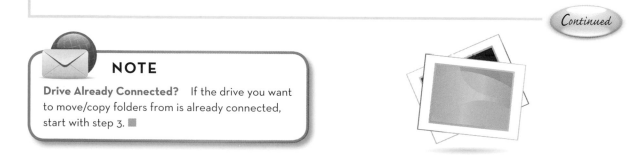

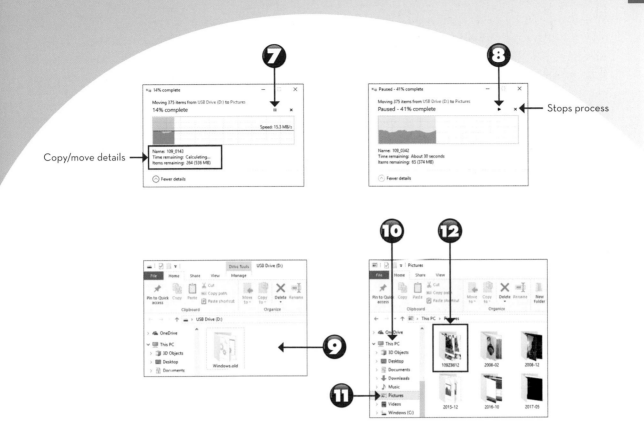

Copy/move details

Stops process

7 To pause the process, click or tap the **Pause** button.

8 To continue the process, click the **Resume** button.

9 The folder has been moved from its original location.

10 Click or tap **This PC** if the Pictures folder is not visible.

11 Click or tap **Pictures**.

12 The folder in its new location.

End

DEALING WITH FILENAME CONFLICTS

When you copy or move files with File Explorer, you might discover that some files being copied or moved have the same names as files already in the destination location. File Explorer can help you resolve duplicate naming issues. Using a photo file as an example in this task, here's what to do.

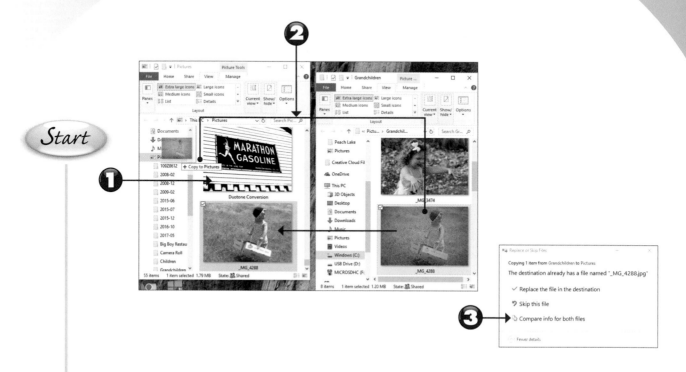

1 Note this photo in the Pictures folder.

2 Copy a different photo with the same name to that folder.

3 Click or tap **Compare info for both files**.

Continued

NOTE

Using Drag and Drop In step 2, the file is copied using drag and drop (you can also use the Copy and Paste or Copy to commands). If you use drag and drop with a file or folder on the same drive (as in step 2), the default is to move the file from the old to the new location. To copy the file instead, press and hold the **Ctrl** key while dragging the file. The text next to the file/folder thumbnail tells you whether you are copying or moving the file or folder.

If you use drag and drop with a file or folder from a different drive, the default is to copy the file. To move the file instead, press and hold the **Ctrl** key while dragging the file. ■

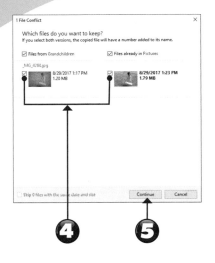

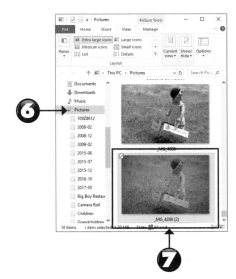

4 To keep both files, click or tap both check boxes.

5 Click or tap **Continue**.

6 Click or tap the destination folder.

7 The copied file with the name conflict is renamed to avoid replacing the original file.

End

NOTE

Dealing with Multiple Filename Conflicts If you copy or move more than one file or folder with a name conflict, choose **Let me decide for each** in step 3. You are then prompted to choose what to do with each file. ∎

CREATING ZIP FILES WITH THE SHARE TAB

Zip files are handy because you can store multiple files and folders into a single file that's usually smaller than the combined size of the original files. The resulting file is also easier to email or upload. You use the Share tab in File Explorer to create zip files.

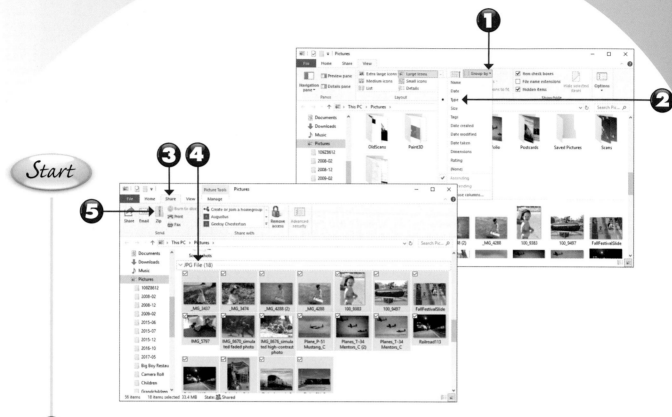

Start

1 From the View tab, open the **Group by** menu.

2 Click or tap **Type**.

3 Click or tap the **Share** tab.

4 Click or tap a group category to select all files.

5 Click or tap **Zip**.

Continued

NOTE

Easy File Selection with Grouped Files When files are grouped, you can select all the files in the group by clicking the group name, such as JPG File (as in step 4). ■

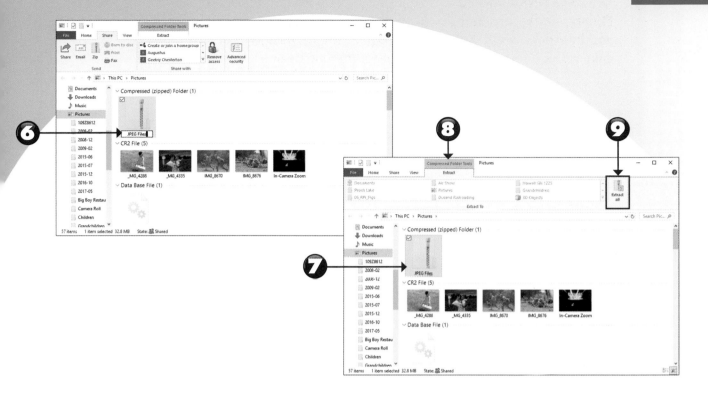

6 Enter a new name for the Zip file. Press **Enter** or click outside the name box when finished.

7 When you need to extract files from the Zip file, click or tap the Zip file.

8 Click or tap **Compressed Folder Tools**.

9 Click or tap the **Extract all** button.

End

NOTE

Extracting Files   You can use the **Extract all** button to copy all files from the Zip file to a folder named after the Zip file in the current location. You can also specify a different destination. ■

NOTE

Renaming the Zip File   You can rename a Zip file or any other type of file by using the **Rename** button on the **Home** tab. ■

SYNCING FILES WITH ONEDRIVE

Microsoft provides OneDrive cloud-based storage to everyone with a Microsoft account and Internet access. You can synchronize local files and folders with OneDrive so you can access them from other computers and mobile devices. Here's how.

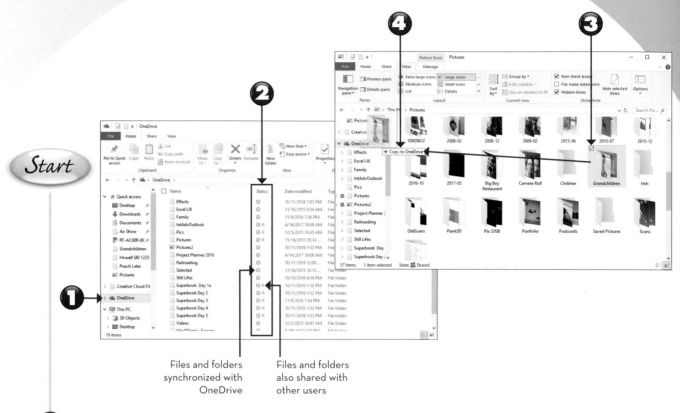

Files and folders
synchronized with
OneDrive

Files and folders
also shared with
other users

1 From File Explorer, click or tap the OneDrive folder in the left pane.

2 The current status of each folder or file is displayed.

3 Navigate to the folder you want to sync.

4 Drag and drop it to copy/move it to OneDrive.

Continued

NOTE

Drag and Drop, the Sequel   See the Note earlier in this chapter on using Drag and Drop. You can also use Copy To or Copy/Paste. ■

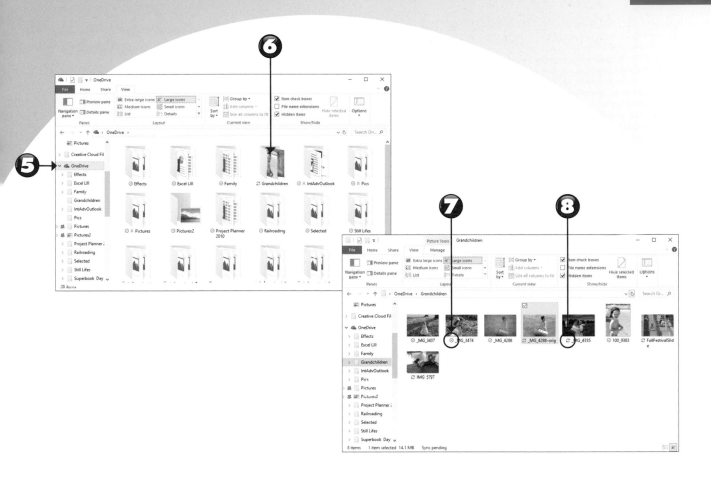

5 Click or tap **OneDrive** (if it is not already open).

6 Folder being synced to OneDrive. Click or tap this folder to see file status.

7 File that has finished syncing to OneDrive.

8 File still in the process of syncing to OneDrive.

End

USING ONEDRIVE FILES ON DEMAND

In Windows 10 FCU, OneDrive enables you to save space on your device by giving you quick access to online files whenever you are connected to the Internet with the new Files on Demand feature. In this exercise, we set a folder that has already been synced with One-Drive to be available only when online.

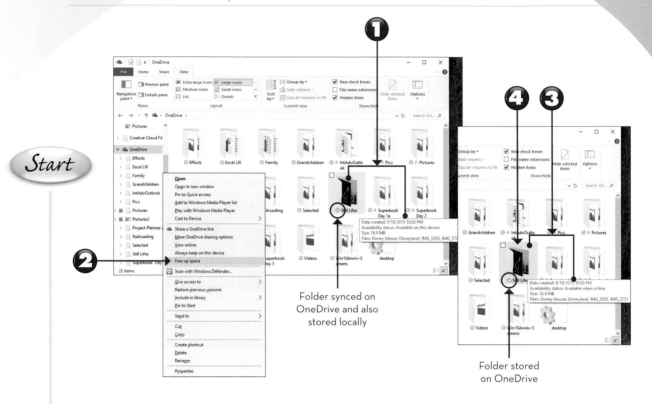

Folder synced on OneDrive and also stored locally

Folder stored on OneDrive

1 Hover the mouse over a folder in OneDrive to see its status (*Available on this device* in this example).

2 Right-click or press and hold it and select **Free up space**.

3 After a few moments, hover the mouse over the same folder to see the change in status (*Available when online*).

4 Double-click or double-tap the folder to open it.

Continued

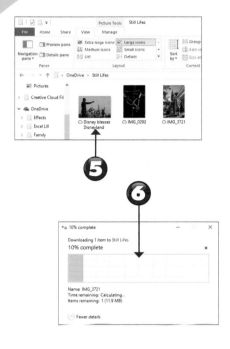

5 Double-click or double-tap a file in the folder.

6 Windows downloads the file to your system.

7 Windows opens the file with the default app for the file type.

End

CONFIGURING ONEDRIVE

The OneDrive Settings dialog shows you how much space your OneDrive storage has remaining and provides various options for using OneDrive on your system.

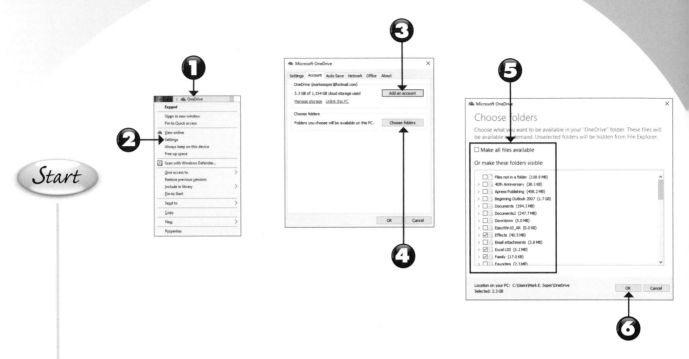

Start

1 From File Manager, right-click or press and hold the OneDrive icon.

2 Click or tap **Settings**.

3 The **Account** tab shows you the amount of space used and available. Click **Add an account** to share the drive with another user.

4 Click or tap the **Choose folders** button to view the folders stored in the cloud on OneDrive and select the ones you want to sync to this computer.

5 Check boxes for items you want to have access to in your computer's OneDrive folder; clear boxes you don't want to access.

6 Click or tap **OK** when finished.

Continued

NOTE

Accessing OneDrive Settings from the Notification Area   Click or tap the OneDrive icon and select the Settings (gear) icon. When you access OneDrive from the notification area, you also see recent activity and can go directly to the OneDrive folder. ■

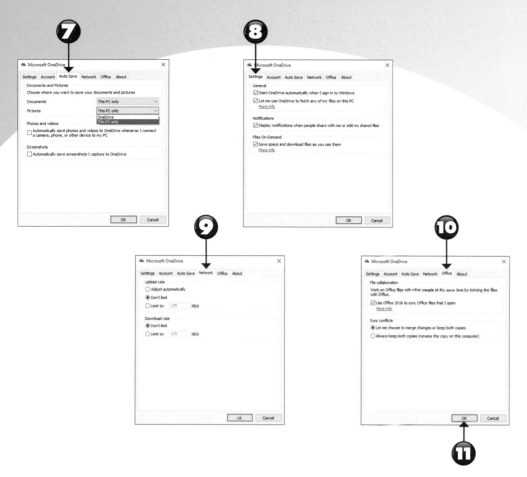

7 Click or tap the **Auto Save** tab to specify where to save documents, pictures, videos, and screenshots.

8 Click the **Settings** tab to configure automatic startup of OneDrive, Files On-Demand, and other features.

9 Click the **Network** tab to limit upload and download speeds.

10 Click or tap **Office** to configure how to handle file collaboration and sync issues.

11 Click or tap **OK** when you are finished configuring OneDrive.

End

NOTE

Viewing OneDrive Folders and Files in Your Browser and on Your Device   You can also use your web browser to view and download OneDrive files. Go to https://onedrive.live.com, log in if prompted, and your OneDrive folders and files appear in your browser window.

To install a OneDrive app for your device, log in to OneDrive from your browser and click or tap **Get the OneDrive apps**. You can also open the menu (three-line icon) and click or tap **Get the OneDrive apps** to learn more or start the process. ■

DISCOVERING AND USING WINDOWS 10 FCU'S TOOLS AND ACCESSORIES

Windows 10 FCU includes a variety of apps. Some apps, such as Money and Sports, are designed to perform several tasks and are covered in other chapters. This chapter focuses on the newest specialized Windows apps (Paint 3D, View 3D, and Print 3D) and others such as Calculator and Alarms & Clock. To learn more about older Windows tools such as Character Map and Notepad, see the online content for this book.

Creating a 3D scene
with Paint 3D

Setting up a new alarm
with Alarms & Clock

Using the
new Date
Calculation
feature in
Calculator

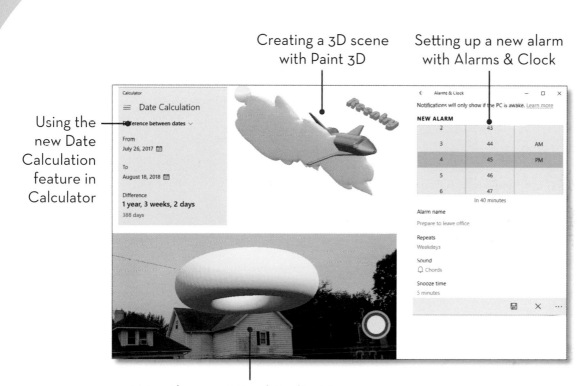

Using the new Mixed Reality Viewer
to add a 3D object to the real world

FINDING ACCESSORIES AND TOOLS IN TABLET MODE

To find Windows tools from the Start menu in Tablet mode, you must dig in to the All Apps menu. Here's what you'll find.

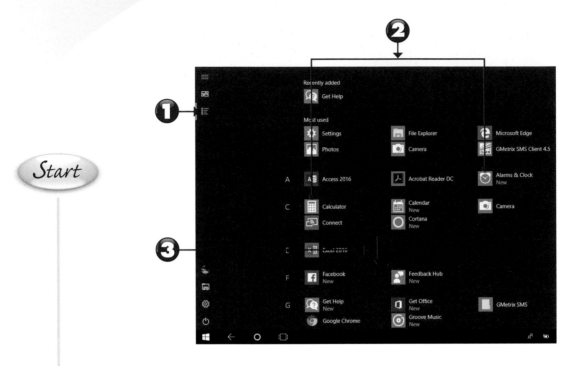

Start

1 Click or tap **All apps**.

2 Note the Alarms & Clock and Calculator apps.

3 Flick up or scroll down to see additional Windows apps covered in this chapter.

Continued

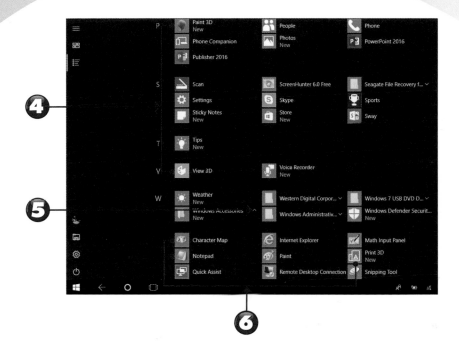

4 Note the Paint 3D and View 3D apps.

5 Click or tap the arrow for the **Windows Accessories** folder to see more Windows tools.

6 Note Character Map, Print 3D, Notepad, and others.

End

NOTE

Finding Windows Tools in Desktop Mode   Click or tap the **Start** button and then scroll down to find Alarms & Clock, Calculator, Paint 3D, and View 3D. Click or tap the **Windows Accessories** folder to find Character Map, Print 3D, Notepad, and other accessories. ■

SETTING ALARMS WITH THE ALARMS & CLOCK APP

You can use the Modern UI Alarms & Clock app as a stopwatch, an alarm clock, or a timer. Here's how to use it as an alarm clock to prepare to leave the office Monday through Friday.

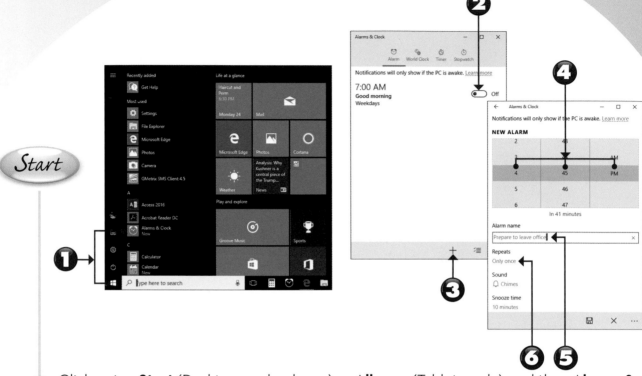

1 Click or tap **Start** (Desktop mode, shown) or **All apps** (Tablet mode), and then **Alarms & Clock**.

2 The Good Morning alarm is automatically set up. Click or press and drag the button to the right if you want to turn it on.

3 Click or tap the plus (+) sign to set up a new alarm.

4 Click or tap each column, and scroll with your finger or mouse to select hour, minute, and AM/PM settings.

5 Type in a unique name for the alarm.

6 Click or tap to select which day(s) of the week the alarm repeats.

Continued

NOTE

Modern/Universal UI Appearance Modern UI and Universal UI apps (apps that also run on Windows 10 Mobile) run full screen in Tablet mode. Illustrations in this chapter use desktop mode to save space. ■

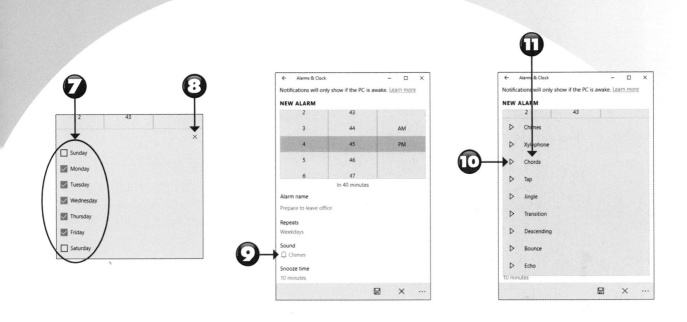

7 Click or tap the check box for each day of the week you want the alarm to be active.

8 Click or tap the **X** (Close) button to continue.

9 Click or tap to select a different alarm sound.

10 Click or tap to preview a sound.

11 Click or tap a sound to select it.

Continued

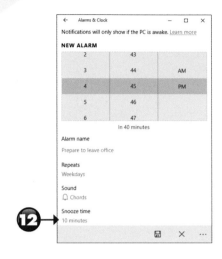

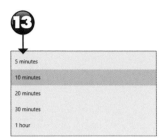

12 Click or tap to select a different snooze interval.

13 Tap the snooze interval desired.

Continued

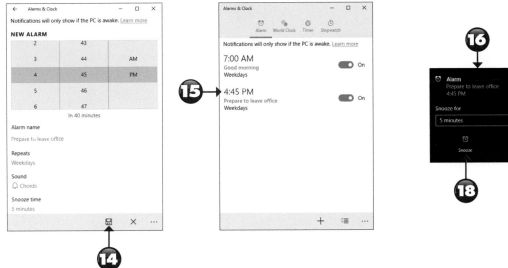

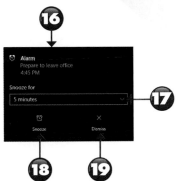

14 Click the **Save** icon to save the alarm.

15 The new alarm is added to the Alarms & Clock app screen.

16 The alarm is displayed in the Notification area when triggered.

17 Click or tap to change the snooze interval.

18 Click or tap to snooze the alarm.

19 Click or tap to shut off the alarm.

End

CALCULATING DATES WITH CALCULATOR

Windows 10's Calculator now includes a new date calculator as well as standard and scientific calculators and conversions. Here's how to use it to calculate dates.

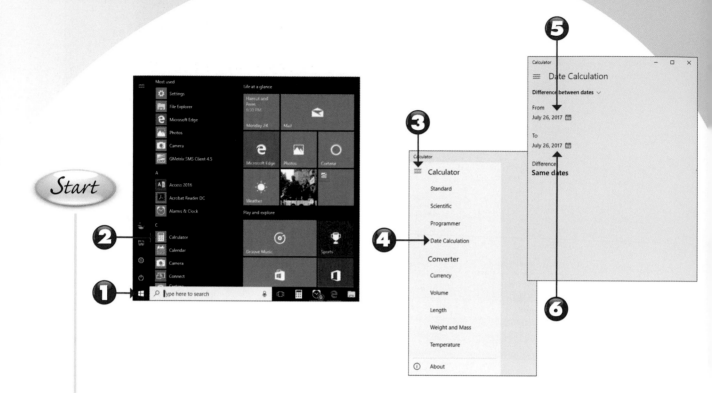

Start

1 Click or tap **Start**.

2 Click or tap **Calculator**.

3 Click or tap the **Menu** button.

4 Select **Date Calculation**.

5 The default From: and To: dates are the current date.

6 To change the default From or To: dates, click the calendar icon.

Continued

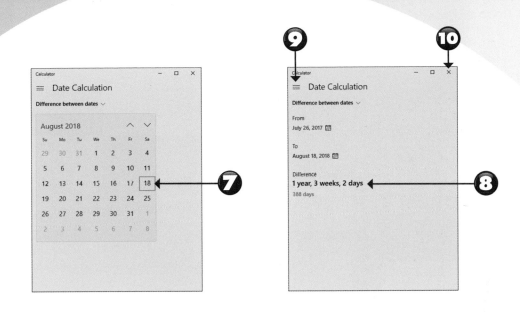

7 Select the dates desired.

8 After you select the dates desired, the answer appears.

9 Click the menu button to select a different calculator option.

10 Click to close the calculator.

End

USING PAINT 3D

The new Paint 3D app lets you create traditional graphics or work with 3D objects. Here's how to get started. In this example, you will download an existing 3D model and add additional 3D objects to it.

Start

1 Click or tap **Start**.

2 Click or tap **Paint 3D**.

3 To work with an existing 3D model, click or tap **Start**.

4 Enter a search term.

5 Select a model.

Continued

NOTE

Searching for Boards or People   Select **Boards** as the search type if you want to search for boards with matching terms. Select **People** to search for people with matching names. ▪

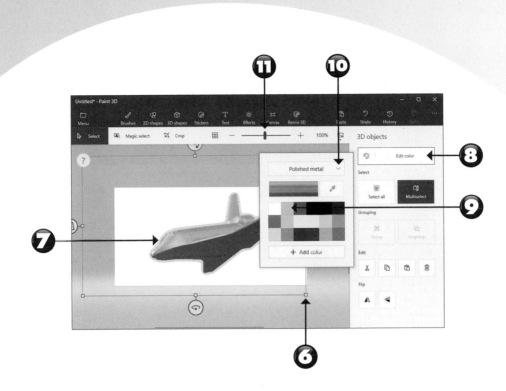

6 To change the size of the model, drag the adjustment handles.

7 The selected object has a contrasting-color halo around it.

8 Click or tap **Edit color** to change the object's color.

9 Click or tap a color.

10 Click or tap a surface type.

11 Use the slider to adjust the magnification of the workspace.

Continued

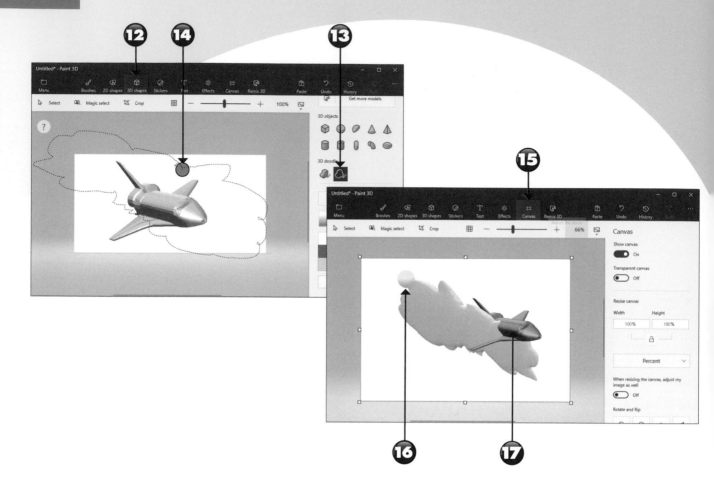

12 Click or tap **3D shapes** to add more objects.

13 Click or tap a 3D object or doodle.

14 If you select a doodle, click or press and drag to create the outline.

15 Click or tap **Canvas** and adjust the canvas size.

16 Move and add objects as desired.

17 Change the color and finish of existing objects as desired.

Continued

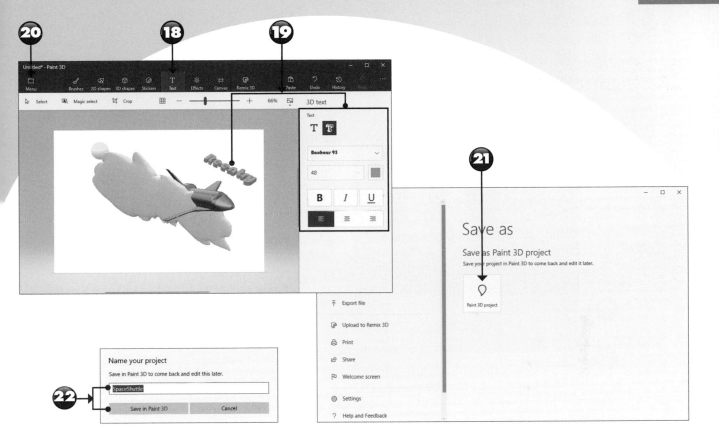

18 Click or tap **Text** to add text.

19 Choose the settings desired and enter the text on the page.

20 Click or tap **Menu** to save or export your creation.

21 Click or tap **Paint 3D project** to work on it in Paint 3D again.

22 Enter a name, and then click **Save in Paint 3D**.

End

NOTE

Export Options In step 21, click or tap **Export file** to save a painting as a finished 3D project or as a 2D PNG or JPG file. You cannot edit an exported file in Paint 3D, but you can edit a PNG or JPG file using Photos. ▪

USING MIXED REALITY VIEWER

The new Mixed Reality Viewer enables you to view the 3D objects provided with Windows 10 and the 3D illustrations you exported with Paint 3D. Plus, you can add them to the real world with your device's camera. Here's how it works.

1 Click or tap **Start**.

2 Click or tap **Mixed Reality Viewer**.

3 Click or tap to clear the check box.

4 Click or tap to close the welcome screen.

5 Click or tap **Menu**.

Continued

6 Click or tap **Open**.

7 Click or tap the object you want to view.

8 Click or tap **Open**.

9 To change object view settings, click or tap **Controls**.

10 Click or tap the input device you use to see controls.

11 Click or tap to close the Controls menu.

Continued

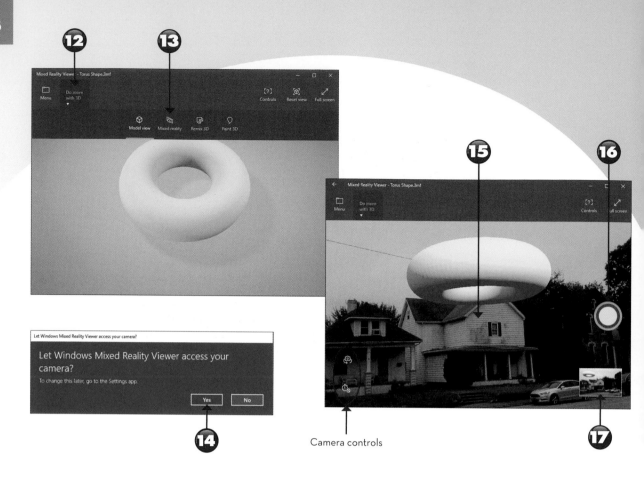

Camera controls

12 For additional options, click or tap **Do more with 3D**.

13 Click **Mixed reality**.

14 If prompted, click or tap **Yes** to use your device's camera.

15 After you position the object in your display, click or tap the screen.

16 Click or tap the button to take a mixed reality photo.

17 As you take additional pictures, the previous picture is shown in a small window.

Continued

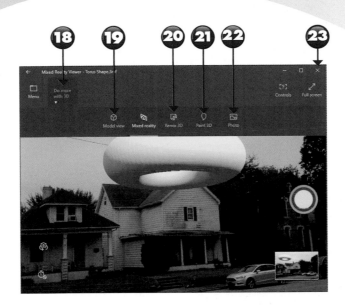

18 When you are done, click or tap **Do more with 3D**.

19 To return to the original view, click or tap **Model view**.

20 To upload your object to Remix 3D, click or tap **Remix 3D**.

21 To open your object in Paint 3D, click or tap **Paint 3D**.

22 To see your mixed-reality photos, click or tap **Photo**.

23 To close, click or tap the **X** (close) button.

End

NOTE

Remix 3D The Remix 3D website (www.remix3d.com) enables you to share your Paint 3D creations with other users and download other users' creations. To upload or download content, log in to the site with your Microsoft ID when prompted. ◼

USING PRINT 3D

Whether you have a 3D printer or need to use an online printing service, you can use Print 3D to turn your 3D creations (or the 3D models and objects included with Windows 10) into actual objects. Here's how to get started using an online printing service.

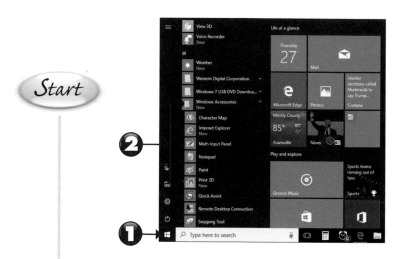

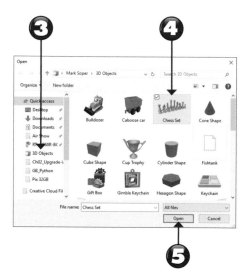

1 Click or tap **Start**.

2 Click or tap **Windows Accessories**, **Print 3D**.

3 Open the **3D Objects** folder.

4 Select an object to print.

5 Click or tap **Open**.

Continued

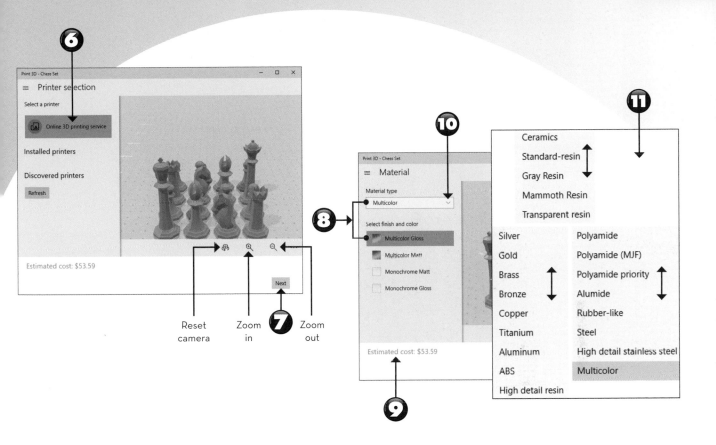

6 Select **Online 3D printing service**.

7 Click or tap **Next**.

8 Note the default material, color, and finish.

9 You see the estimated cost for the current object.

10 To change the material, click or tap **Material type**.

11 Scroll to find the material you want, and then click or tap it.

Continued

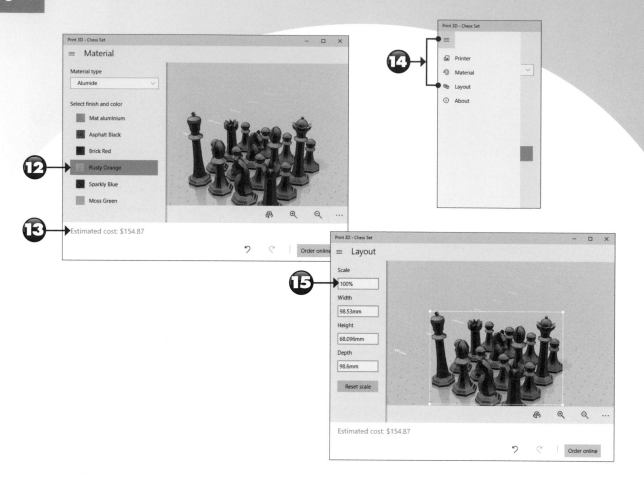

12 Select the desired color and finish.

13 Changing the material and color affects the estimated cost.

14 To print a larger or small object, open the menu and click **Layout**.

15 Adjust the scale to change the size of the project.

Continued

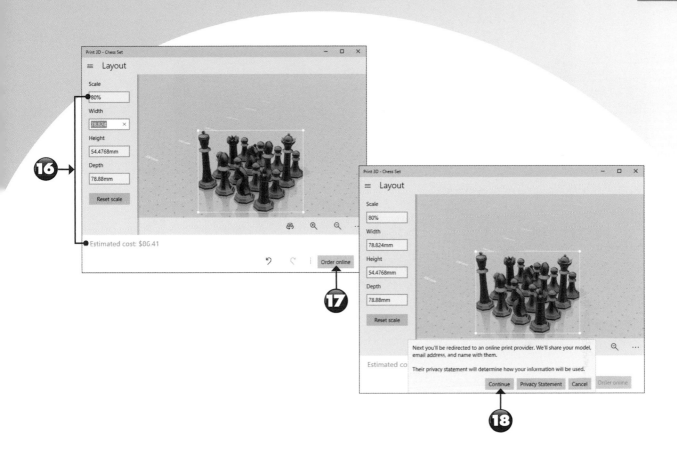

16 Reducing or increasing the scale changes the estimated cost of the project.

17 After making your final selection, click or tap **Order online**.

18 Click or tap **Continue**. You will complete your order at the 3D printing service's website.

End

USING THE MICROSOFT STORE

You can use the Microsoft Store (formerly Windows Store) app to shop online for more apps, games, and TV shows and movies. The Microsoft Store features a variety of apps and media content, for a variety of uses. You can find plenty of free apps, paid apps, and trial versions in the Store using the Search or Categories view. In this chapter, you learn how to navigate the Store to find just the right apps for you and your device. To shop for TV and movies, see Chapter 10. To shop for games, see Chapter 17.

Collections and categories
in the Microsoft Store

Reviewing an app

Searching
for an app

Filtering apps
by chart type
and category

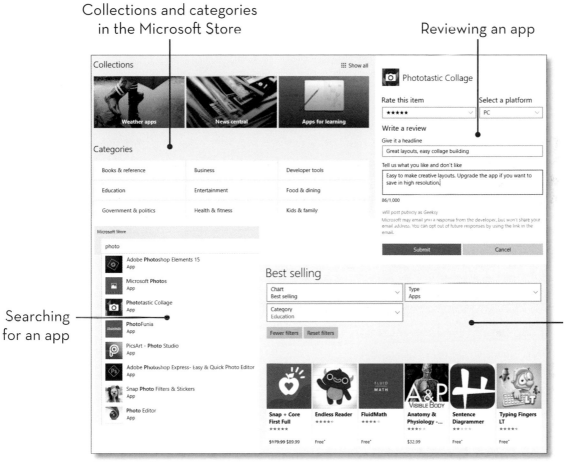

GOING TO THE STORE

When you initially open the Microsoft Store app, the first screen displays the currently featured app and links to the most popular apps and new releases. As you scroll through the Store, you can find new apps and the most popular paid and free apps.

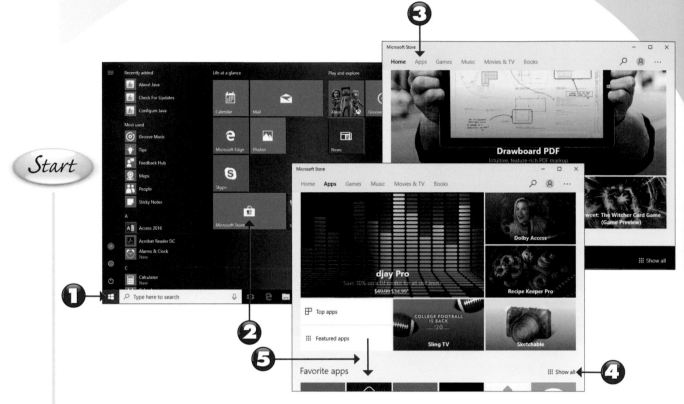

Start

1 Click or tap **Start** (Desktop mode; in Tablet Mode, tap **Start** if the Tiles are not visible, then **All apps**).

2 Click or tap **Microsoft Store**.

3 Click or tap to go to a category.

4 Click or tap to see all items in the category.

5 Scroll down or flick up to see more apps.

End

NOTE

Apps We Picked For You   After you visit the Store and download or purchase content, the next time you open the Store, you see an "Apps we picked for you" category when you scroll down. These choices are based on the apps you have downloaded or what people with similar interests are downloading or purchasing. ■

SEARCHING FOR APPS BY NAME

You can use the Microsoft Store Search window to search the Store for a specific app or type of app. Here's how to search for your favorite app.

Start

End

1 In the Microsoft Store, click or tap the **search** icon and type the search text.

2 Matches appear as you start typing the search text.

3 Press **Enter/Return** or click or tap the **Search** icon.

4 Click or tap to see all the matches in a category.

5 Scroll down or flick up as needed to see the results you want.

6 Click or tap an app you want to check out.

NOTE

Resize Your Window You might have to resize the Store window to view the Search field. ■

INSTALLING AN APP

When you find an app you want, you can easily install it in just a few clicks. Windows 10 FCU does most of the hard work for you. When you install an app, the app is added to the Windows All apps menu.

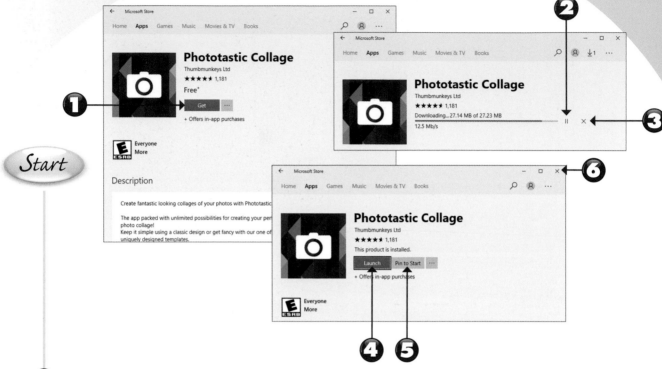

Start

1 From the app's details page, click or tap the **Buy/Get/Redeem a Code** button.

2 If needed, you can click or tap here to pause/continue downloading and installing.

3 If you need to cancel the procedure, click or tap **X**.

4 When the download and installation are complete, you can click or tap **Launch** to open the app immediately.

5 For faster access, click or tap **Pin to Start**.

6 Click or tap to close the Store window.

Continued

NOTE

Installing Paid Apps When you install a paid app, Windows 10 FCU directs you to a login screen where you can log in to your Microsoft account and choose a payment method. Windows might also prompt you to log in to your Microsoft account before continuing with the download.

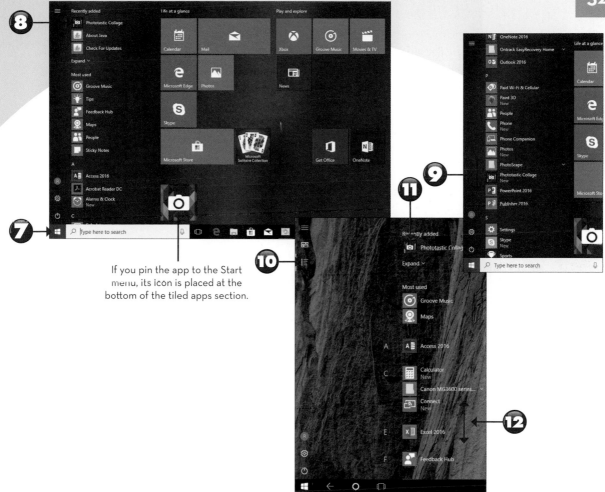

If you pin the app to the Start menu, its icon is placed at the bottom of the tiled apps section.

7 To locate the app later in Desktop mode, click or tap **Start**.

8 The most recently added apps are at the top of the menu, followed by most used.

9 The app can also be located by scrolling down or flicking up the alphabetic list.

10 In Tablet mode, click or tap **All apps** to find the app.

11 The most recently added apps are at the top of the menu, followed by the most used.

12 The app can also be located by scrolling down or flicking up the alphabetic list.

End

UNINSTALLING AN APP FROM THE START SCREEN

You can easily remove an app you no longer use or want. Uninstalling an app removes it from your computer and deletes the app from your Start menu. You can reinstall it at any time from the Microsoft Store.

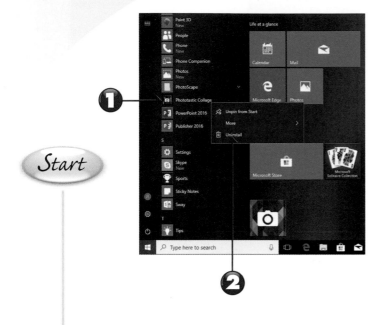

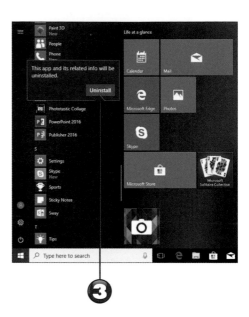

Start

1 From the Start or All Apps menu, right-click or press and hold the app you want to uninstall.

2 Click or tap **Uninstall**.

3 Click or tap **Uninstall**, and the app is removed.

End

TIP

Discovering the Largest Apps   If you're wondering which apps take up the most storage space on your system, use the Apps & Features dialog box in System settings. For details, see "Apps & Features" in Chapter 19, p. 414.

RATING AN APP

The Microsoft Store offers user reviews of apps. This information is helpful when you're deciding whether you want to try an app. By adding your rating to the app reviews, you can help other potential users know how it worked for you.

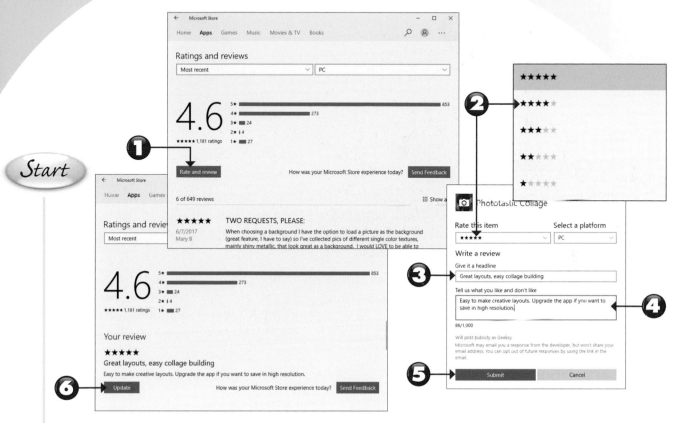

Start

From the app's page in the Store, click or tap **Rate and review**.

Click or tap, and select the number of stars for your review.

Enter a title for your review.

Enter review text.

Click or tap **Submit**.

Click or tap **Update** if you want to change your review at any time.

End

GAMING

Windows 10 Fall Creators Update and Xbox One work together better than ever before. You can download updated versions of classic Windows games from the Microsoft Store or buy the latest shooters, sports, or racing games for your PC or Xbox.

Xbox One users can use the Xbox app to play back shared game clips from either PC or Xbox games, connect with friends, and check out the latest news in the Xbox world. Xbox One SmartGlass puts you in control of your Xbox configuration. Xbox 360 SmartGlass provides the same features for Xbox 360.

Customizing a card deck in
Microsoft Solitaire Collection

Using the new
Game bar

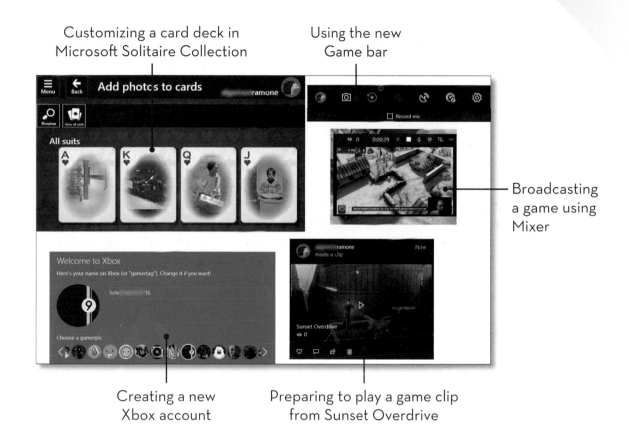

Broadcasting
a game using
Mixer

Creating a new
Xbox account

Preparing to play a game clip
from Sunset Overdrive

GETTING STARTED WITH MICROSOFT SOLITAIRE COLLECTION

Microsoft Solitaire Collection brings your favorite versions of Solitaire (Klondike, Spider, FreeCell, Pyramid, and TriPeaks) to Windows 10 and provides access to Microsoft Minesweeper and other favorites. Here's how to play.

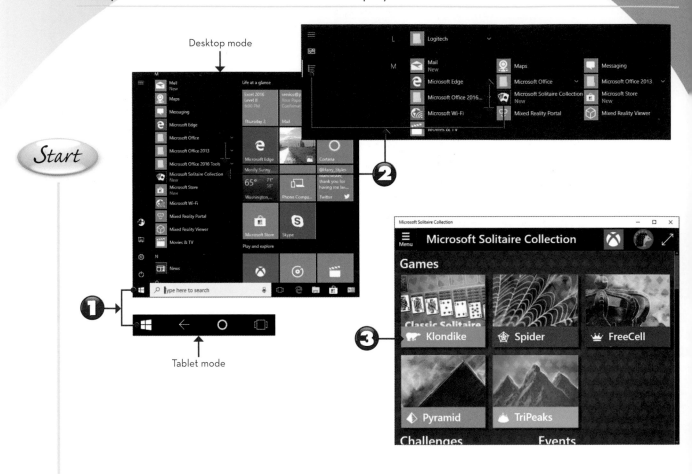

Desktop mode

Start

Tablet mode

1 Click or tap **Start.**

In Desktop mode, scroll down and click or tap **Microsoft Solitaire Collection**.
2 In Tablet mode, click or tap **All apps.**
Flick up/scroll down and click or tap **Microsoft Solitaire Collection**.

3 Click or tap the game you want to play.

Continued

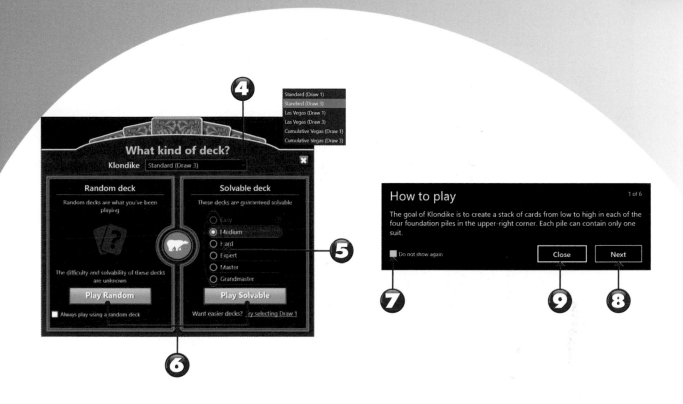

4 Change the draw type if desired.

5 Choose the difficulty level if you want to play a solvable deck.

6 Click or tap **Play Random** or **Play Solvable**.

7 Click or tap the **Do not show again** check box if you don't need instructions.

8 Click or tap **Next** to see the next set of instructions.

9 Click or tap **Close** to close the How to play window.

Continued

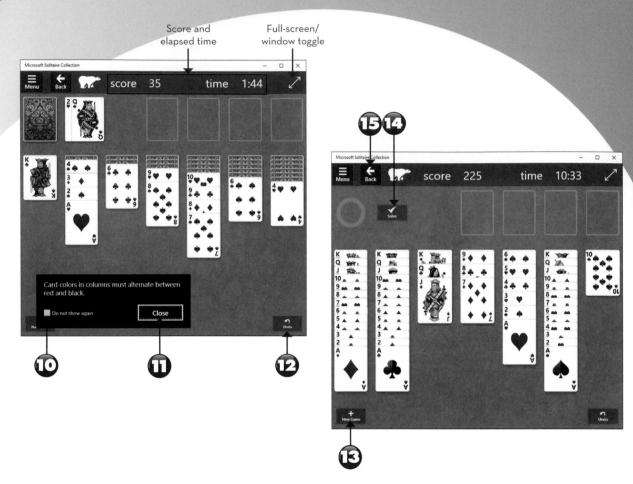

Score and elapsed time

Full-screen/ window toggle

10 As you play, hints are displayed if you make an error. Click the **Do not show again** check box to hide hints.

11 Click or tap **Close**.

12 Click or tap to undo the last play.

13 Click or tap to start a new game.

14 Click or tap to solve the game.

15 Click or tap to return to the opening screen.

Continued

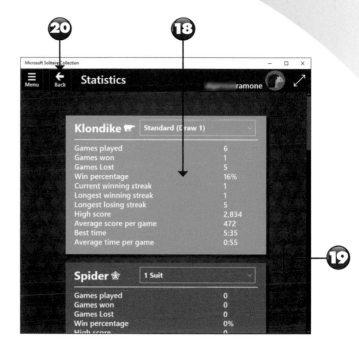

16 After you win a game, click or tap to start a new game.

17 Click or tap to show all statistics.

18 Klondike stats are shown first.

19 Scroll down or flick up to see stats for other games.

20 Click or tap to return to the opening screen.

End

CUSTOMIZING YOUR CARDS

Tired of standard solitaire decks and backgrounds? Here's how to play solitaire your way. You might be prompted to log in to your Xbox Live account (used for gaming) during this process.

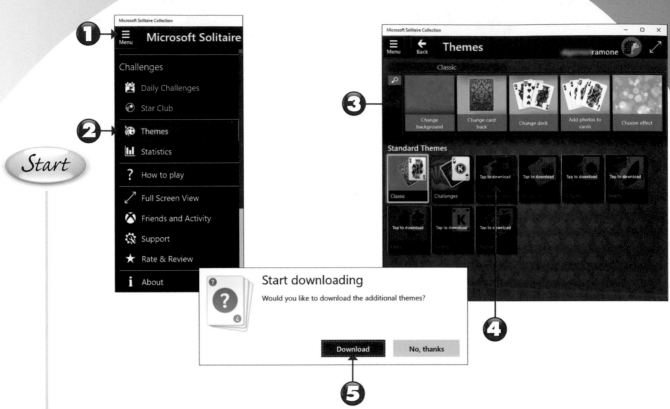

Start

1 Click or tap **Menu**.

2 Click or tap **Themes**.

3 Note the default theme settings.

4 Click or tap **Tap to download** to download additional themes.

5 Click or tap **Download** to continue.

Continued

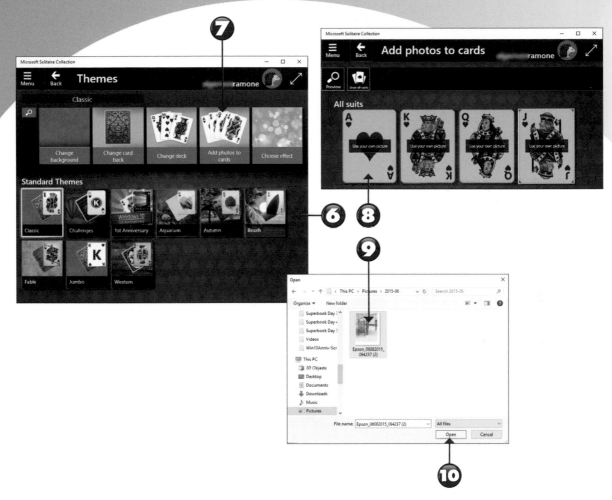

6 Click or tap a different theme to change the background, card back, and deck.

7 To create your own theme, click or tap what you want to change, such as **Add photos to cards**.

8 Click or tap a card to change.

9 Navigate to the photo you want to use and click or tap it.

10 Click or tap **Open**.

Continued

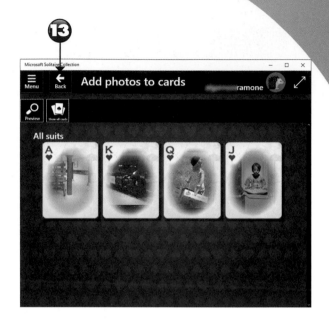

11 Adjust photo size and position with these controls.

12 Click or tap when finished.

13 After repeating steps 8 through 12 with other cards as desired, click or tap to return to the Themes menu.

Continued

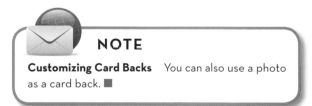

NOTE

Customizing Card Backs You can also use a photo as a card back. ∎

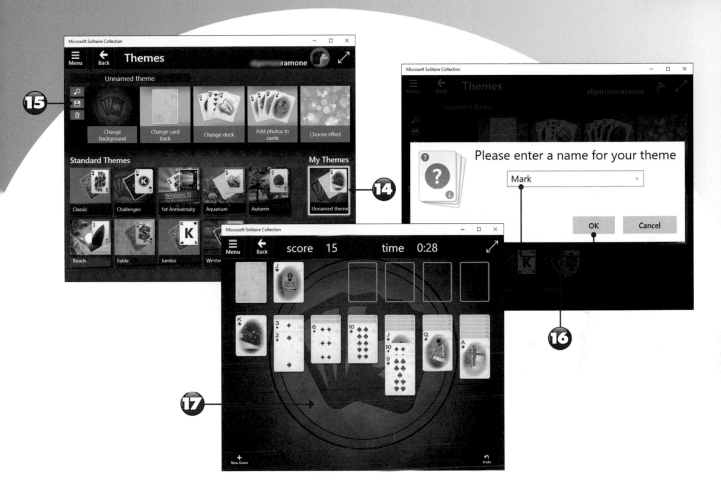

14 Preview your theme as you make other changes (background, card back, deck).

15 When satisfied, click or tap the **Save** button.

16 Enter a name for your new theme and click or tap **OK**.

17 When you continue a game or play a new game, your custom theme will be used until you choose a different theme or create a new one.

End

GETTING MORE GAMES, HAVING MORE FUN

The Microsoft Solitaire Collection offers more than just solitaire games. It also offers easy access to other popular games, including Minesweeper. Here's how to get them on your system.

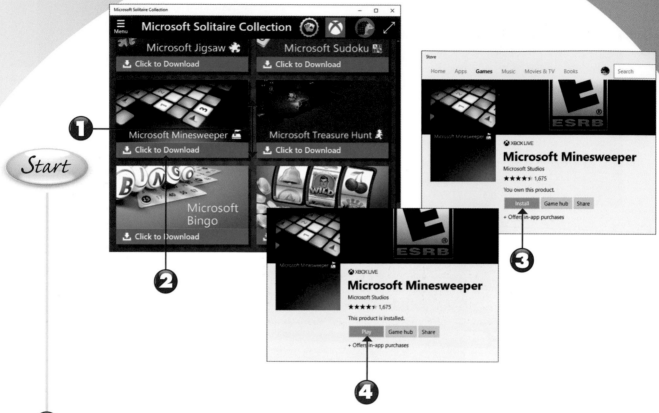

Start

1. From the opening screen, scroll down or flick up to locate the Other Games section.

2. Click or tap the **Click to download** button for the game you want.

3. Click or tap **Install**.

4. Click or tap **Play** to start your game.

Continued

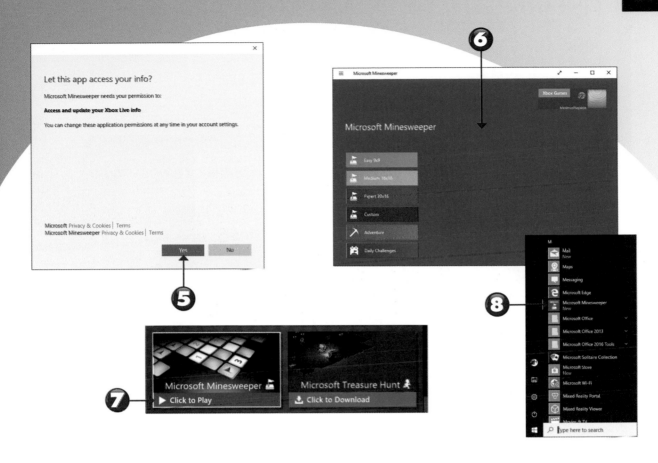

5 If prompted, click or tap **Yes** to allow your game to access your Xbox Live info.

6 The game opens in its own window.

7 To start the game from Microsoft Solitaire Collection, click or tap the **Click to Play** button.

8 You can also start the game from the Windows 10 Start or All Apps menu.

End

FINDING GAMES WITH THE STORE APP

Looking for games with more action? Visit the Microsoft Store. The Store offers all kinds of games you can download and buy.

If you know the name of the game, click or tap the Search tool and enter it in the Search window.

Start

1 Click or tap **Start**.

2 Click or tap **Microsoft Store**.

3 Click or tap the Menu (three-line) icon.

4 Click or tap **Games**.

5 Scroll down or flick up to see paid and free games or click a category.

6 Click or tap to see all games in a category.

Continued

TIP

Xbox Live Games Many games in the Xbox Live category can be played on both a Windows 10 device and an Xbox One console with a single license. Click or tap the game for details. ■

7 Click or tap a game you want to try.

8 Scroll down or flick up to learn more about the game.

9 After checking reviews and game hardware/requirements and recommendations, click or tap **Get** or **Buy** to download the game.

10 Windows 10 FCU installs the game automatically and adds it to the Apps/All apps list under **Recently added** items.

End

NOTE

Buying a Game? If you're buying a game, you see a price button instead of the Get button. You also go through some extra steps before downloading the game, such as logging in to your Microsoft account and choosing a payment option. ■

TIP

Xbox Gamers Click or tap **Game Hub** to open the Xbox app. You can also open the Xbox app from the Start menu. ■

USING THE GAME BAR

Windows 10 FCU includes the Game bar, which can be used to optimize Windows for gaming and enables you to capture game screens and videos and to broadcast your videos via your Xbox Live account. Here's how to use it.

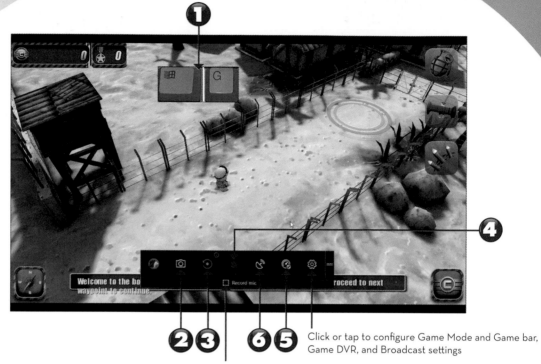

Start

Click or tap to configure Game Mode and Game bar, Game DVR, and Broadcast settings

Click or tap to record narration

1 Start a game and press Windows key+G to open the Game bar.

2 Click or tap to capture the screen image.

3 Click or tap to enable background recording (Game DVR).

4 Click or tap to record gameplay (Game DVR).

5 Click or tap to turn on/off Game mode.

6 Click or tap to broadcast your game to your Xbox Live account.

Continued

TIP

The Game Settings Dialog The Game Settings dialog has three tabs: the General tab is used to enable Game Mode (optimizes gameplay on Windows 10) and to configure the Game bar. The Broadcast tab is used to configure broadcasts to your Xbox Live account. The Game DVR tab is used to configure Game DVR settings. ■

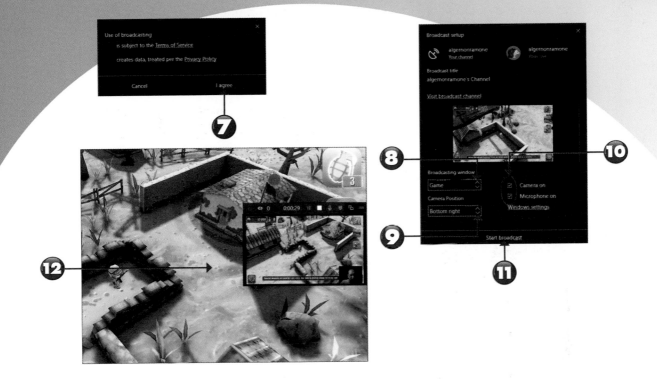

7 Click or tap **I agree** to begin broadcasting.

8 Click or tap to choose between showing your game or desktop.

9 Click or tap to select the camera position.

10 Make sure the camera and microphone are enabled.

11 Click or tap to start the broadcast.

12 The game window shows what is being broadcast.

End

TIP

More About Broadcasts To view live broadcasts, use your Xbox app (discussed later in this chapter) or go to Mixer.com. To learn more about Mixer, go to www.xbox.com/en-us/mixer. To enable Mixer broadcasts to be saved as Video on Demand (VoD), enable **Keep recordings (VoDs) of my streams**. See https://blogs.windows.com/windowsexperience/2017/07/10/windows-10-tip-get-started-viewing-streaming-mixer/ to learn more. ■

CREATING A NEW XBOX ACCOUNT

Whether you have an Xbox console or play Xbox Live games, you need an Xbox Live account if you want to keep track of game achievements or compare your game stats to your friends. An Xbox account is free, and you can sign up through the Xbox app. If you already have an Xbox account, go to the next tutorial.

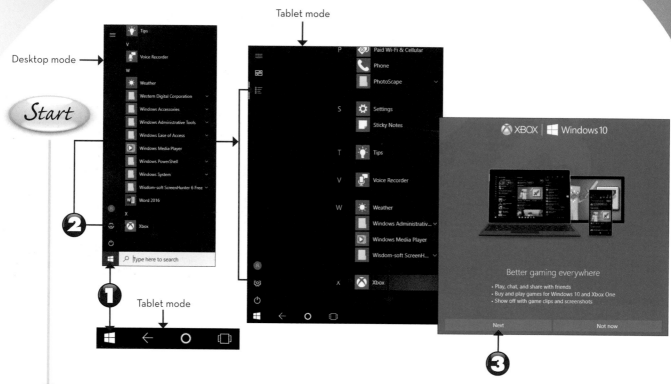

Desktop mode

Tablet mode

Start

Tablet mode

1 Click or tap **Start**.

2 In Desktop mode, scroll down and click or tap **Xbox**. In Tablet mode, click or tap **All apps** (Tablet mode), and then flick up/scroll down and click or tap **Xbox**.

3 Click or tap **Next**.

Continued

TIP

No Xbox App? Here's How to Get It   If the Xbox app isn't showing in your list of apps, open the Store app, search for Xbox, and download it. Click **Play** to start it, or close the Store and run it from the Windows 10 Start/All Apps menu. ∎

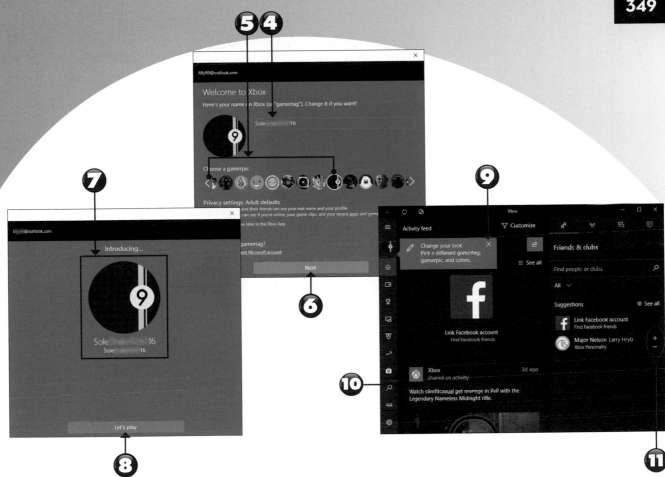

4 The app generates a gamertag for you. To choose a different gamertag, type one.

5 The app chooses a gamerpic for you, but you can scroll and click or tap a different one.

6 Click or tap **Next** to continue.

7 View your gamerpic (avatar) and gamertag.

8 Click or tap **Let's play**.

9 Click or tap to close this prompt.

10 Click or tap to watch a featured video.

11 Click or tap to scroll through Xbox personalities.

End

STARTING THE XBOX APP

The Xbox app is your gaming headquarters for all things Xbox. You can use the app to log in to your gaming account, chat with friends, play games, track your achievements, and more. This task shows you how to use the app's major features.

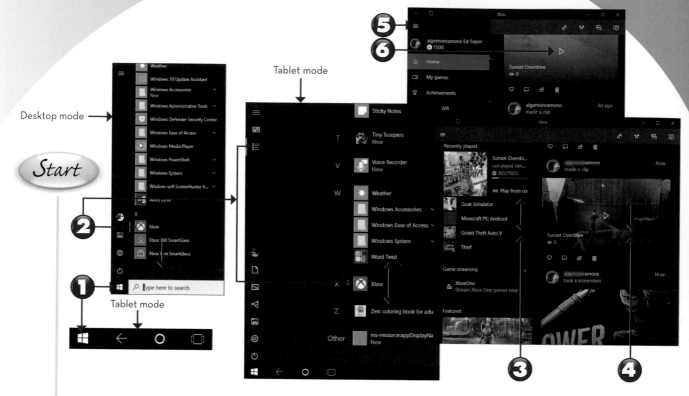

Desktop mode →

Tablet mode →

Tablet mode

Start

① Click or tap Start (Desktop or Tablet modes).

② In Tablet mode, click or tap **All apps**, and then click or tap Xbox (Desktop and Tablet modes).

③ Scroll down or flick up the left menu to see game activity.

④ Scroll down or flick up the right menu to see game clips, screenshots, and social notifications.

⑤ Click or tap to expand the menu.

⑥ Click or tap to play a game clip.

End

TIP

Full-Screen View for Easier Use To save space, I am running the Xbox app in a small window. However, if you use a larger window or run the app in full screen, you will be able to see the menu icons without clicking the menu button. See "Viewing Gaming Clips," this chapter, p. 352, for an example. ∎

CONNECTING TO XBOX ONE

Any Xbox One (the original Xbox One, Xbox One S, and Xbox One X) is designed to work with Windows 10 FCU. To use these features, you must connect your Windows 10 FCU device with the Xbox One device on your network from within the Xbox app and make sure you have installed the latest updates to your Xbox One. After you connect to your Xbox One, you can stream compatible games from your Xbox One to your Windows 10 FCU device or use your Windows 10 FCU device as a controller for the game.

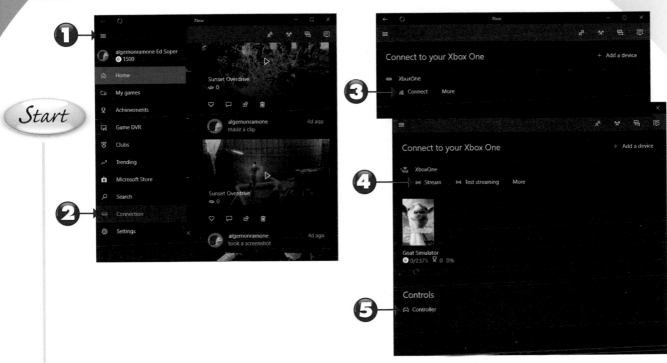

Start

End

1 From the Xbox app, click or tap the **Menu** button.

2 Click or tap **Connection**.

3 Click or tap **Connect** or **Turn on**, and then click or tap **Connect**.

4 Click or tap to stream gameplay from your Xbox One to your device.

5 Click or tap to play the game using an Xbox One controller (connected to your PC or to the Xbox One).

TIP

Dealing with a "Missing" Console   If your console isn't visible in step 3, enter its IP (Internet) address into the box at the bottom of the dialog box. To find your console's IP address, start your console and go to **Settings, Network, Advanced settings**. ■

VIEWING GAMING CLIPS

Any Xbox One can capture gaming clips, which are video files of the game recorded while you're playing. Want to show friends your marksmanship or amazing luck? Share your video clips. You can also capture gaming clips or screenshots from games you play in Windows 10 FCU. Here's how to view gaming clips from either source with the Xbox app.

Video clip duration   Screenshot

1 From the Xbox menu, click or tap **Game DVR**.

2 Click or tap the source you want to use for clips. To choose by date/game or to choose game clips or screenshots only, select options from the drop-down menus.

3 Scroll down and click or tap a clip.

4 Click or tap **Play**.

5 Click or tap to rename the clip.

6 Click or tap to play it full screen.

End

TIP

Choosing a Clip Source   Click or tap **On this PC** to view clips you created on your PC. Click or tap **On Xbox Live** to view clips created with your own or others' Xbox devices. ∎

WORKING WITH ACHIEVEMENTS, FRIENDS, AND MORE

To see what you've been up to, and to see how your activity compares with your friends, view your profile information.

1 Click or tap your gamerpic.

2 Scroll the headings as needed.

3 Click or tap **Info** to customize your account.

4 Click or tap **Activity feed** to see clips or other activity.

5 Click or tap **Achievements** to see the leaders in activity among your friends.

6 Click or tap **Following** to find out who's online.

End

CONTROLLING XBOX ONE AND XBOX 360 WITH XBOX SMARTGLASS

Thanks to the new Xbox SmartGlass apps for Xbox One and Xbox 360, you can remotely control your Xbox. This lesson shows you how to use Xbox One SmartGlass. For SmartGlass to work, your Xbox must be turned on and connected to the same network as your Windows 10 device. If the Xbox One SmartGlass apps are not installed on your system, get them from the Microsoft Store.

Desktop mode

Tablet mode

Tablet mode

1 Click or tap **Start**.

2 Scroll down or flick up and then click or tap **Xbox One SmartGlass** (Desktop or Tablet mode).

3 When prompted, click or tap **Sign in**.

4 Enter your username.

5 Click or tap **Next**.

Continued

6 Click or tap the empty **Connect automatically** check box.

7 Click **Connect** to connect to your Xbox One console.

8 Scroll horizontally with your mouse wheel or by flicking to the left or right.

9 Click or tap to record the current game.

10 Click or tap to display the Xbox remote.

11 Click or tap to display the menu.

12 Use the menu to go more quickly to different parts of the SmartGlass interface.

End

VIEWING GAME SCREEN CAPTURES AND RECORDINGS

To enjoy your greatest moments in gaming over again, take a look at your screen captures and recordings. Here's where to find them.

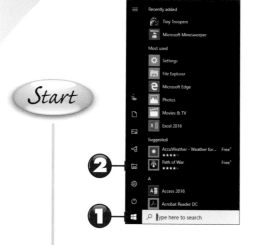

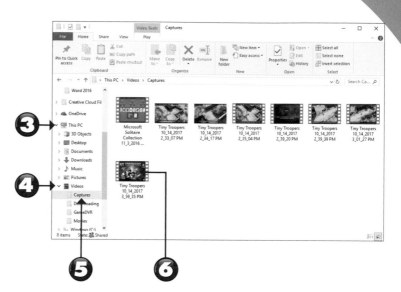

Start

1 Click or tap **Start**.

2 Click or tap **File Manager**.

3 Click or tap **This PC**.

4 Click or tap **Videos**.

5 Click or tap **Captures**.

6 You see video and screen captures from your gameplay.

End

PRINTING AND SCANNING

Windows 10 FCU can work with most existing printers, scanners, and all-in-one units. This chapter covers how to use these various devices with Windows 10 FCU's built-in apps and features.

Selecting the paper type

Configuring Scan for a grayscale scan

Preparing to print a photo

Renaming a scanned photo with File Explorer

PRINTING A DOCUMENT

Windows 10 FCU includes virtual printers that can create PDF (Adobe Reader) or XPS (Microsoft XPS) files. You can also install printers through Settings (see Chapter 19, "Managing Windows 10 Fall Creators Update," for details), or you can use the printer's own setup program. After your printer is installed, you can change the normal settings as needed, depending on the print job. Here's how to print a document from a typical Windows app. Depending on the app, the Print command might be found in a different location.

1. Depending on the app, click or tap the app's **File** or three-dot menu button.

2. Click or tap **Print**.

3. With some apps, such as the Directions feature in Maps, the print job is started from a submenu.

4. The Print dialog box usually opens with the preview area showing what the printout will look like when printed.

5. Click or tap **Print** to print the document.

Start

End

TIP

How to Print Photos in Email   Before you can print photos attached to email, you need to save them to a folder or open them in a graphics app such as Paint. Then you can print each photo separately. ■

PRINTER SETTINGS AVAILABLE FROM THE PRINTER MENU

Basic printer settings, such as number of copies, which pages to print, paper size, and whether to use duplex printing, are available from the normal Windows print dialog. Here's how to select the options you want.

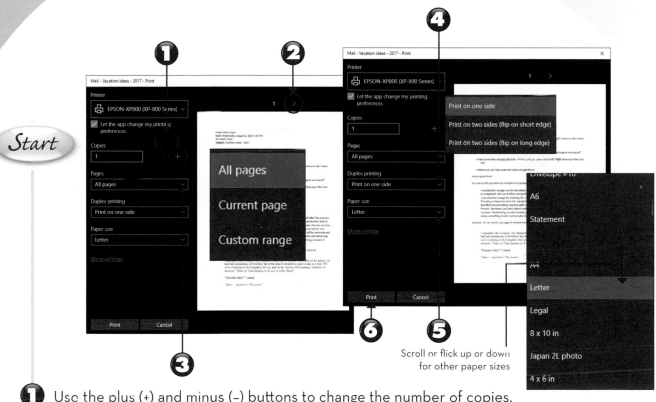

Scroll or flick up or down for other paper sizes

① Use the plus (+) and minus (–) buttons to change the number of copies.

② Click or tap to preview other pages in the document, if applicable.

③ Select the pages to print.

④ Select whether to print on both or one side of the paper with a duplex (two-sided) printer.

⑤ Click or tap to change paper size.

⑥ Click or tap **Print** to print the document.

TIP

Different Printer Options   Don't expect to see the same print options when you select a different printer. The options vary from printer to printer and because of the app you use to print a document or photo. ■

SELECTING A DIFFERENT PRINTER

Even before you install a physical printer, Windows 10 FCU includes virtual printer apps that can create an Adobe Reader (PDF file extension) or Microsoft XPS (Open XML Paper Specification, XPS file extension) file. These files can be viewed or printed to any printer. Use this lesson to learn how to choose the physical printer or app from those installed.

1 With the Print dialog box open, click or tap to open the printer selection menu.

2 Notice the software (virtual) printers included in Windows 10 FCU.

3 You see here the software (virtual) printer installed by Microsoft OneNote.

4 Note the user-installed local and network printers.

5 Click or tap to install an additional printer.

6 Click or tap a printer name to choose that printer.

End

TIP

Set a Default Printer You can designate a printer as the default. When you do, the apps that allow printing list the chosen printer without needing to specify a printer every time. Conduct a Windows search for Devices and Printers (found in the Control Panel). Locate your printer, and right-click or press and hold the printer name, and choose **Set as default printer**. ∎

PAPER AND PRINT QUALITY SETTINGS

The basic printer settings are all you need for document printing. However, if you need to use a different type of paper, such as printing for photos, or adjust how your printer prints, you must use the **More settings** link. Here's what to expect with a typical inkjet printer.

Scroll or flick up or down
for other paper/media types

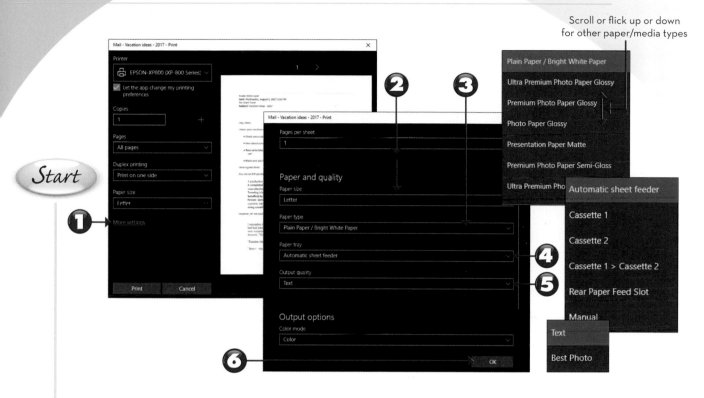

1 From the Printer dialog box or menu, click or tap **More settings**.

2 Scroll down or flick up to the Paper and quality section.

3 Click or tap **Paper type** to use matte or photo paper instead of plain paper.

4 Click or tap **Paper tray** to select the paper tray used for your paper or media.

5 Click or tap **Output quality** to change the print quality.

6 Click or tap **OK** to return to the main print menu.

End

NOTE

More About Printer Options **Color mode:** color/monochrome/grayscale. **Document binding:** left edge, right edge, top edge. **Orientation:** portrait (long side to left/right), landscape (long edge to top/bottom). **Borderless printing:** yes, no. ■

PHOTO PRINTING SETTINGS

If you want to print a photo on photo paper, you can choose from several print settings to achieve the desired printout results. You can select these options in any order, and some printers offer slightly different options or wording.

Start

1 Open a picture in the Photos app.

2 Click or tap **Print**.

3 Click or tap **Paper tray** to select the location for the photo paper you are using.

4 Click or tap the **Paper size** menu and select **4 × 6 in** or another appropriate paper size for your photo printout.

5 Click or tap **Paper type** to change the paper type. Most photo paper is glossy or ultra glossy.

6 Click or tap **More settings**.

Continued

7 Click or tap the **Output quality** menu and select **Best Photo** or a similar setting.

8 If you want borderless printing, turn the setting to **On**.

9 Click **OK** to return to the main print options.

10 To utilize borderless printing, you might also need to change the setting in the **Fit** menu.

11 Review the preview image here.

12 Click or tap **Print**.

End

USING SCAN

If you have a flatbed scanner or multifunction device, you can use Windows 10 FCU's simple scanning utility, called Scan, to convert prints or documents into electronic form. If the Scan app is not installed on your system, install it from the Microsoft Store. (It's free.) In most cases, you must also install the vendor's own driver software to enable Windows to use the scanning functions. In this exercise, we will use the flatbed scan option.

1 Click or tap **Start**.

2 Scroll down or flick up, and click or tap **Scan**. (In Tablet mode, click or tap **All apps** first.)

3 If you have more than one scanner available, select the one you want to use.

4 If necessary, select **Flatbed** as the source.

5 After placing a photo or document face down on the scanner glass, click or tap **Preview**.

Continued

NOTE

Scan Versus Vendor-Supplied Tools   The Scan app performs basic scanning with flatbed scanners or all-in-one units. However, if you need to adjust exposure or contrast, restore color to faded originals, use a sheet feeder, use a transparency unit to scan slides or negatives, or use dust- or scratch-removal tools, you must use software provided by the scanner vendor or third-party scanning software. Note that vendor-supplied apps available in the Store are typically much more limited than the drivers you can obtain directly from the vendors' websites. If a Windows 10 version is not available, you can usually install and use the Windows 8.1 version. ■

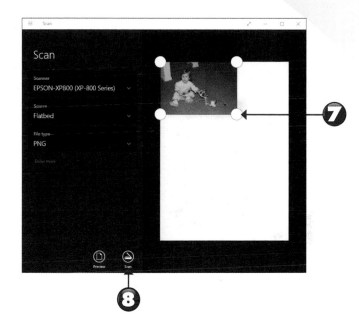

(6) The preview scans the entire flatbed area.

(7) Drag the crop dots as desired around the photo. The area inside the dot boundary will be scanned.

(8) Click or tap **Scan**.

Continued

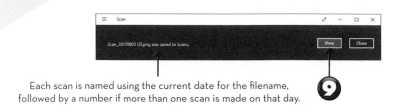

Each scan is named using the current date for the filename,
followed by a number if more than one scan is made on that day.

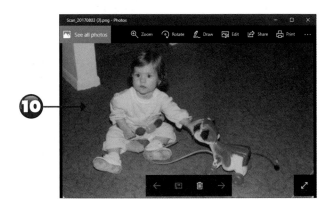

9 Click or tap **View**.

10 Your scan is opened by the default app for the file type.

End

NOTE

What Scan Uses to View Your Scans If you use
only the apps included in Windows 10 FCU, Scan
uses the Photos app for most file types. For XPS
and OpenXPS files, Scan uses the Reader app. For
PDF files, Scan uses Reader or Microsoft Edge. If
you install third-party apps that use these file types,
your results might vary. ■

ADJUSTING SCAN SETTINGS

By default, Scan assigns the PNG file type. However, you can select other file types if they are more suitable for your needs. Some scanners use a default resolution of 100dpi (dots per inch). This is sufficient for scanning images that you plan to view or email. However, if you want to print a scanned photo or document, you should use a resolution of 300dpi. To print a scan at a larger size than the original, use a resolution of 600dpi. In this lesson, you learn how to use these features.

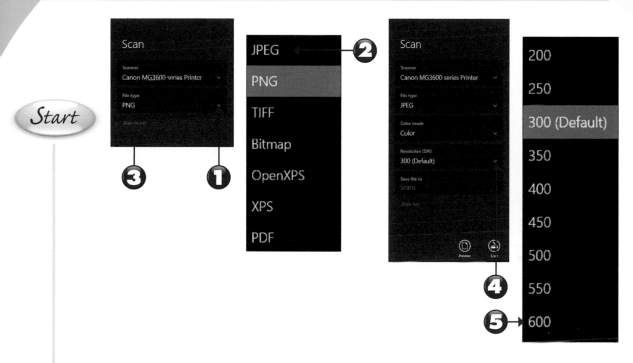

① Click or tap to change the file type.

② Choose a file type. This example uses JPEG because it is compatible with online photo-printing services and photo-editing programs.

③ Click or tap **Show more**.

④ Click or tap to change the resolution.

⑤ Select 600 dpi (if available). Continue the scanning process as outlined in a previous section.

End

NOTE

Choose a Folder By default, all scans are saved to the Scans folder. Click or tap the **Save File To** link if you want to specify another folder in which to save the scanned image. ■

SELECTING COLOR, GRAYSCALE, OR BLACK-AND-WHITE MODES

Normally, you use the default color mode to scan color photos or documents. However, you can apply grayscale or black-and-white mode to create a colorless version of a color photo. These modes are primarily intended for scanning printed or typed documents, but as you learn in this lesson, you can turn ordinary photos into graphic designs with these colorless effects. For this example, we compare grayscale and black-and-white modes.

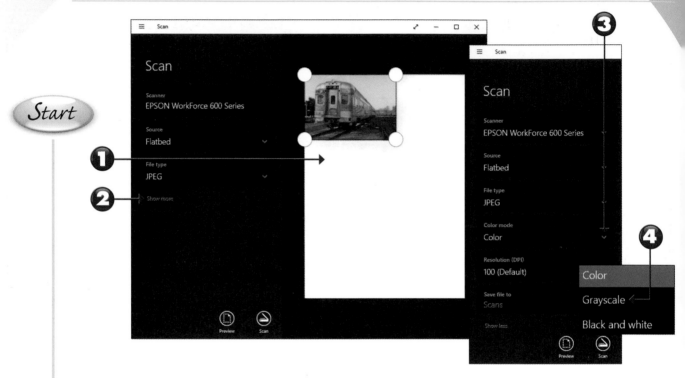

Start

1. With the Scan app open, preview the image and adjust the cropping as needed.

2. Click or tap **Show more** (if the additional settings are not already displayed).

3. Click or tap **Color mode**.

4. Click or tap **Grayscale**.

Continued

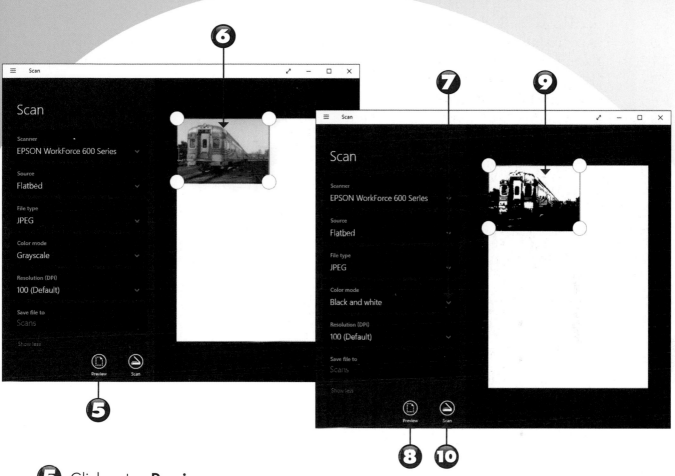

5 Click or tap **Preview**.

6 The image appears in grayscale in the preview area.

7 Change the Color mode to **Black and white**.

8 Click or tap **Preview**.

9 The black-and-white image appears in the preview area.

10 You can scan the image using the selected color mode, or reset it to a preferred color mode before scanning.

End

OPENING THE SCANS FOLDER

Unless you change the default setting for Scan, all scans are stored in the Scans folder by default. You can view all your scans by opening this folder with File Manager.

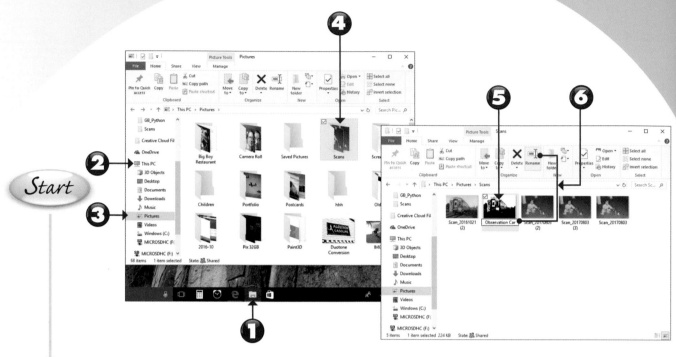

1 Click or tap **File Manager**.

2 Click or tap **This PC**.

3 Click or tap **Pictures**.

4 Double-click or double-tap **Scans**.

5 Click or tap a file you want to rename.

6 Click or tap **Rename** and type a more descriptive name.

Continued

NOTE

How Scans Are Named Scans are named with the date of the scan. If more than one file of the same type is scanned, each additional file is numbered (2), (3), and so on. ■

373

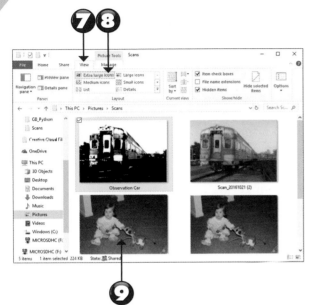

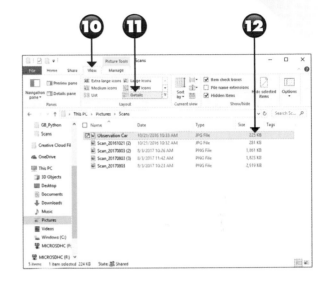

7 Click or tap **View**.

8 Click or tap a layout mode, such as **Extra large icons**.

9 File Manager adjusts the view layout.

10 To view your scans with detailed information, click or tap **View** again.

11 Click or tap **Details**.

12 The detailed information includes the date and time the image scan was created, the file type, and the file size.

End

NOTE

More About File Manager and Working with Scanned Photos To learn more about organizing, copying, moving, and deleting scans, see Chapter 14, "Storing and Finding Your Files." To learn more about editing your scanned photos, see Chapter 9, "Taking, Editing, and Sharing Photos and Videos." ■

Chapter 19

MANAGING WINDOWS 10 FALL CREATORS UPDATE

The Settings dialog box in Windows 10 FCU is where to go to change basic settings of all types. This chapter focuses on configuring system and privacy options as well as settings for volume and microphone control, screen resolution, battery saver options, and more.

Location
settings by app

Configuring
display settings

Viewing data types
stored in cloud

Preparing
to move or
uninstall an
app

Some settings
categories

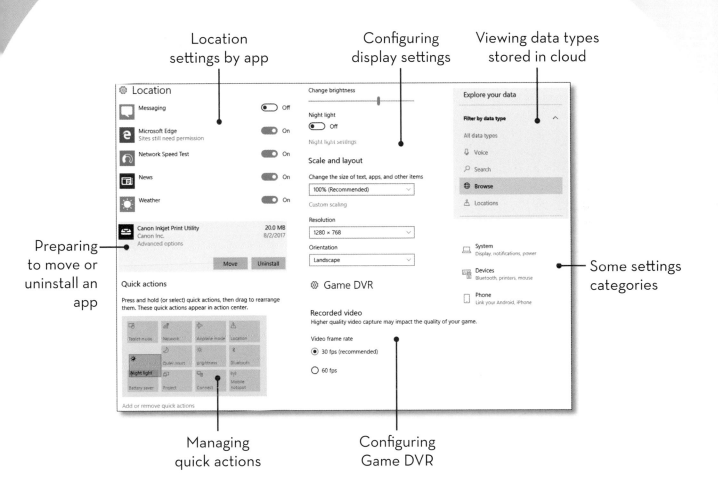

Managing
quick actions

Configuring
Game DVR

ADJUSTING SPEAKER/HEADSET VOLUME

If your music is too loud or you can't hear the audio in the YouTube video you're playing, it's time to adjust the volume. Here's how.

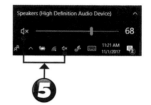

1 Click or tap the **Speaker** icon on the taskbar.

2 Drag the slider to adjust the volume.

3 This shows the current volume.

4 To mute the audio, click or tap the **Speaker** icon.

5 Note that the audio is muted.

6 To unmute the audio, click or tap the **Speaker** icon again.

TIP

Changing Speaker Settings   If you have just connected speakers to a different jack, or if you have connected a new display via HDMI or DisplayPort, you might not hear audio. To select the audio source to use, see the tip in "Advanced Audio Options," (p. 377). ■

ADVANCED AUDIO OPTIONS

From the Speaker icon in the taskbar, you can adjust the volume of specific apps, switch between default audio output and input sources, and select system sounds. Here's how.

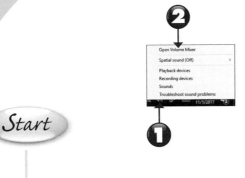

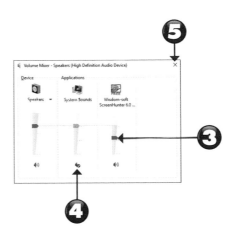

Start

1 Right-click or press and hold the **Speaker** icon in the Notification area.

2 Click or tap **Open Volume Mixer**.

3 To adjust the volume separately for audio, system sounds, or individual apps, drag the control up (louder) or down (softer).

4 To mute the volume for speaker, system sounds, or individual apps, click or tap the appropriate **Speaker** icon.

5 Click or tap to close the dialog box.

End

TIP

Changing Playback Devices   You can click or tap **Playback devices** in step 2 to select and configure default speakers or other playback devices. ∎

ADJUSTING MICROPHONE VOLUME

If you are having problems using Cortana's voice control or using Skype chat, it's time to increase the recording level on your microphone. Here's how.

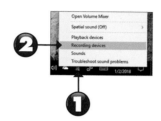

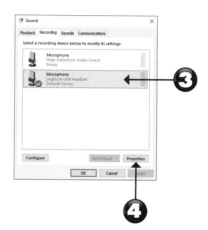

1 Right-click or press and hold the **Speaker** icon in the Notification area.

2 Click or tap **Recording devices**.

3 Click or tap the microphone you use.

4 Click or tap the **Properties** button.

Continued

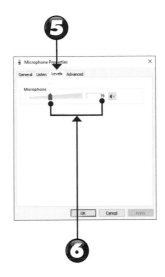

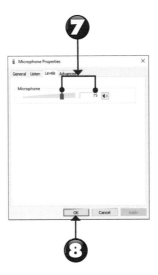

5 Click or tap the **Levels** tab.

6 Drag the slider to the right (increase volume).

7 Adjust the levels to around 55–75 for good volume without distortion.

8 Click or tap **OK**. Retry your app to verify better operation of your microphone.

End

NOTE

Better Microphone Choices   If you are using the built-in microphone in a laptop or tablet and are not happy with the volume or sound quality, consider getting a headset microphone. Most late-model laptops and tablets don't have microphone jacks, so choose a USB headset microphone. ■

ACCESSING THE SETTINGS DIALOG BOX

You use the Settings dialog box to make most of the adjustments discussed in this chapter. Here's how to open Windows Settings.

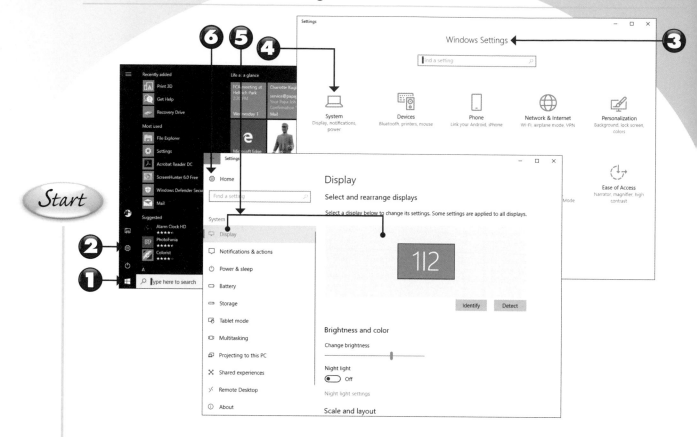

In Desktop mode, click or tap the **Start** button. In Tablet mode, click or tap **Start** if the Start menu is not visible.

Click or tap **Settings**.

The Settings dialog box appears (default size shown).

Tap a category.

The category options appear in the left pane; the selected option appears in the right pane.

Tap **Home** to return to the main Settings dialog.

Continued

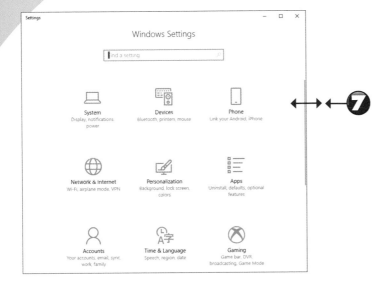

7 To reduce the size of the box, move the mouse pointer over the right side, and when it becomes a double-headed arrow, drag it to the left.

8 The Settings dialog box uses small icons when reduced to minimum size.

End

NOTE

Resizing Settings To make most efficient use of space, this book primarily shows windowed versions of Settings dialog boxes (as demonstrated in step 8), which can be resized as desired. You might need to scroll vertically or swipe to see all categories or specific settings. In Tablet mode, Settings opens full screen.

SETTINGS OVERVIEW

The Settings dialog box provides a useful way to access the settings you're most likely to change. Let's look at some of the categories covered in this chapter and learn how to search for a particular setting. When you use the Settings Search box, some matches point to portions of the Control Panel, which is still present in Windows 10 FCU (for example, **Sound** in step 5).

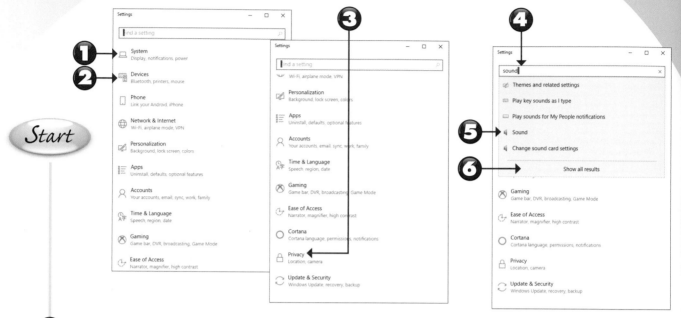

1. Use System settings to configure your computer's display, notifications, and power settings.

2. Use Devices settings to configure your add-on hardware (printers, mouse, keyboard, and more).

3. Use Privacy settings to protect your confidentiality.

4. To locate specific settings, enter text in the Search box. Matching settings are displayed.

5. Click or tap a setting to open its dialog box.

6. Click or tap **Show all results** for additional settings.

NOTE

Other Menus See Chapter 20, "Networking Your Home," for more information on using Network & Internet. See Chapter 21, "Customizing Windows," for more information on using Personalization, and Time & Language. See Chapter 22, "Adding and Managing Users," for more information on using Accounts. See Chapter 23, "Protecting Your System," and Chapter 24, "System Maintenance and Performance," for more information on using Windows Update, backup, and recovery options. Ease of Access is covered in this book's online content.

ADJUSTING DISPLAY BRIGHTNESS AND ROTATION

You can change many display settings in Windows 10 FCU. Adjusting brightness on built-in displays and rotation on tablets is easy, as this exercise points out. (In this exercise, no additional display is connected.)

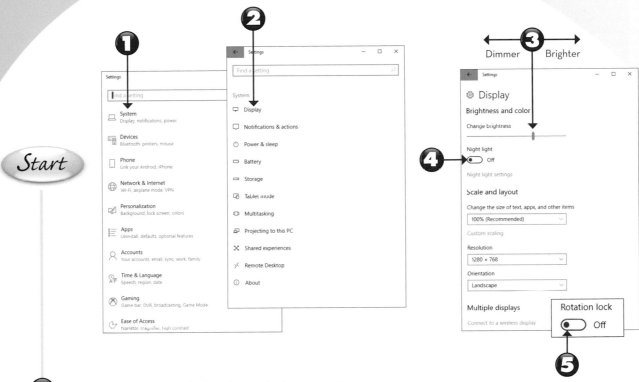

1 From the Settings dialog box, click or tap **System**.

2 Click or tap **Display**.

3 Click or tap and drag the screen brightness control as desired.

4 To turn on warmer screen colors at night, drag **Night light** to **On**.

5 If you use a tablet but don't want it to rotate the display, set **Rotation lock** to **On**. (This setting is not visible on laptops or convertible tablets in laptop mode.)

End

NOTE

Lock Rotation Off Pros and Cons   Leaving Rotation lock off enables you to rotate your tablet from portrait (vertical) to landscape (horizontal) to view different types of content at the largest possible size. However, leaving rotation lock off could use up battery power faster. ■

ADJUSTING SCREEN RESOLUTION

If your display is not using the recommended resolution (horizontal and vertical pixel settings), you might need to scroll more when using some apps to see all of the menus. With some older displays, visual quality might also be lower. Follow this procedure to change your display's resolution for optimal screen viewing. If you use two or more displays, click or tap the icon for the display you want to change.

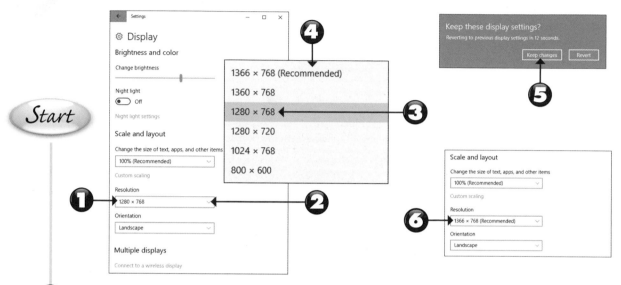

Start

1. Review the current resolution setting.

2. To change it, click or tap the down-arrow to display other resolutions.

3. The current resolution is shown (available resolutions vary by display characteristics).

4. Click or tap the recommended resolution.

5. Click or tap **Keep changes**.

6. The new resolution is now in use.

End

NOTE

Recommended = Optimal Windows 10 FCU refers to the optimal resolution for your display as "Recommended." However, if you find the size of text, apps, and other items are too small or too large onscreen, use the **Scale and Layout** menu to choose the best scaling factor for you. If you need to use two displays in duplicate mode (next lesson), you can use the highest resolution supported by both displays (which might not be the recommended one).

ADDING A SECOND DISPLAY

You can get more done more quickly and have more fun with media if you add a second display to your desktop or laptop computer. Here's how it works.

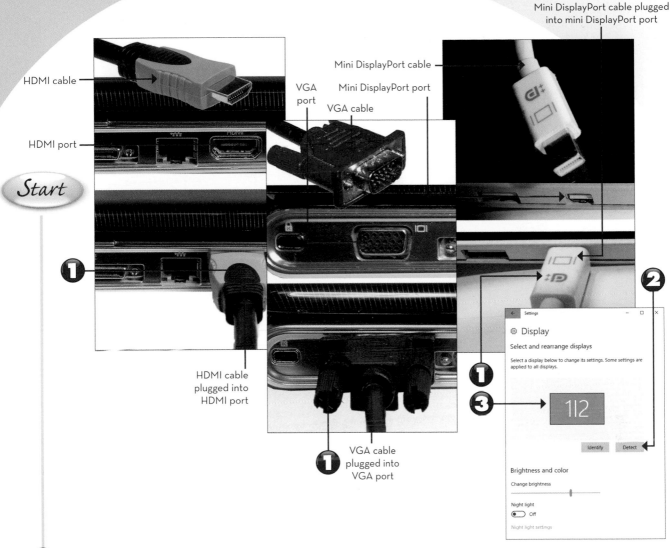

Mini DisplayPort cable plugged into mini DisplayPort port

Mini DisplayPort cable

HDMI cable

VGA port

Mini DisplayPort port

VGA cable

HDMI port

Start

HDMI cable plugged into HDMI port

VGA cable plugged into VGA port

1 Plug in a display to the video port on your computer and turn it on.

2 If the second display is not detected automatically, click or tap **Detect**.

3 When detected, both displays appear at the top of the Display dialog.

End

NOTE

Duplicate Versus Extend Desktop   When you add a second display, it is normally configured to duplicate the first display (step 3). If you want to run different apps on each display, extend the desktop (see the next exercise). ■

EXTENDING YOUR DESKTOP

In most cases, if you add an additional display it's because you want more onscreen space for apps. Here's how to configure your additional display as an extended desktop.

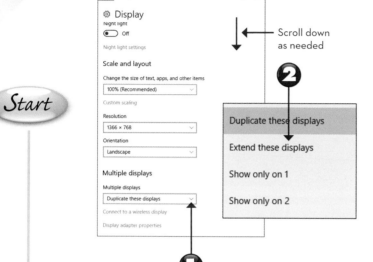

Scroll down as needed

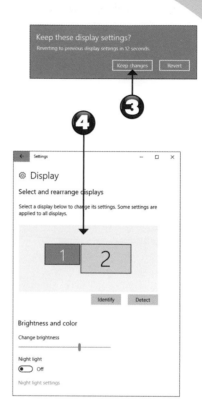

1 From the Display dialog, scroll down and open the **Multiple displays** menu.

2 Select **Extend these displays**.

3 Click or tap **Keep changes**.

4 The different icon sizes indicate relative resolutions (larger icon = higher resolution setting).

End

NOTE

Using the Extended Desktop Drag a program window to the second display, and when you close that program, Windows remembers which display was last used for the program. When you open the program again, it opens in that display. ■

ADJUSTING SCREEN POSITION

When you add a second display, Windows 10 FCU assumes that it is located to the right of your original display by default. If your additional display is in some other relative position, you should move the display icon accordingly so moving the mouse pointer between displays work properly. In this example, the additional display is placed above the original.

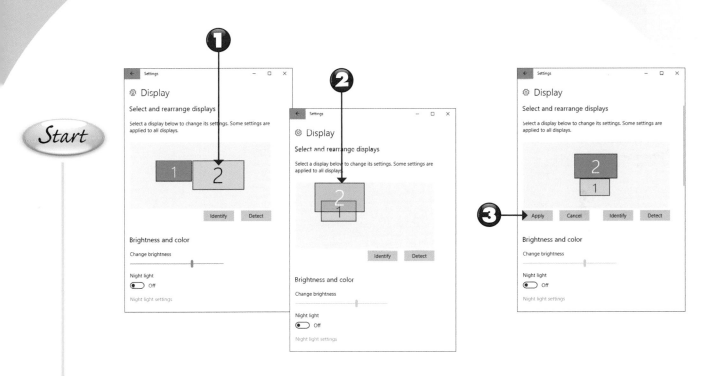

1 Click or press and drag the additional display icon.

2 Release the icon when it is in the correct position relative to the original display.

3 Click or tap **Apply**.

CHANGING QUICK ACTIONS

You use the Action Center on the taskbar to get access to features you use frequently. By default, the Action Center includes icons such as network or screen brightness. Use the Notifications & Actions settings to customize the icons you prefer to display as quick actions.

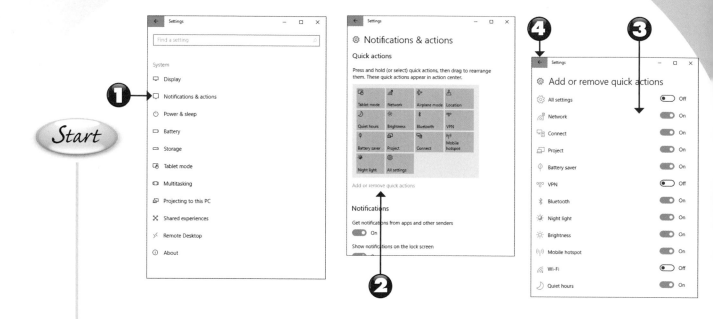

1 From System settings, click or tap **Notifications & actions**.

2 Click or tap **Add or remove quick actions**.

3 Use sliders to turn quick actions on or off.

4 Click to return to Notifications & actions settings.

Continued

This row is displayed first when you click or tap the Action Center button. Put the quick actions you use most here.

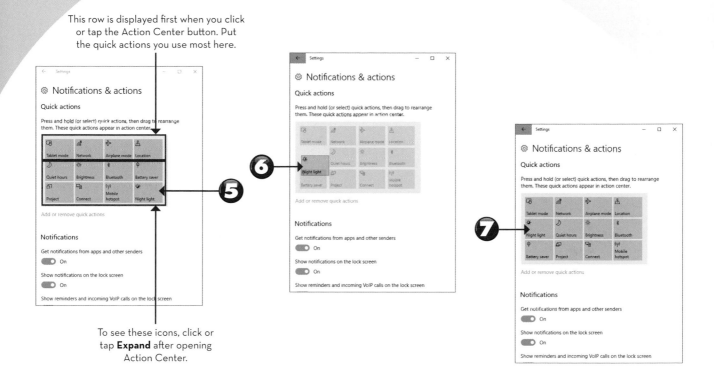

To see these icons, click or tap **Expand** after opening Action Center.

5 To move an icon to a different position, press and hold or click and hold it.

6 Drag it to the desired position. Other icons move to make room for it.

7 Release it.

End

CONFIGURING APP-SPECIFIC NOTIFICATIONS

Many of the apps included in Windows 10 FCU (and some you can install) can display notifications. In this exercise, you learn how to turn off notifications you do not need.

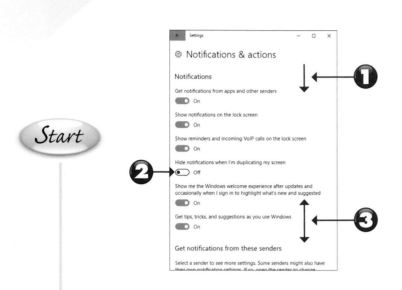

 Start

1 From the Notifications & actions settings, scroll down or flick up to the Notifications section.

2 If you want to turn off app notifications while your display is duplicated (useful when running a presentation), make sure this setting is turned **Off**.

3 Scroll down or flick up to see all apps with notification options.

4 To turn off notifications for an app, click or tap to turn the switch **Off**.

5 Click or tap to return to System settings.

End

NOTE

Notifications Where You Want Them By default, notifications occur on the Lock screen as well as from the Windows Desktop or Start menu (Notifications). Use the sliders shown in the Notifications section of the Notifications & actions settings to limit where notifications appear. ■

CONFIGURING SNAP

Windows 10 FCU's Multitasking settings enable you to configure how your screen functions when you are using two or more apps. In this exercise, you learn how to configure the Snap feature, which controls how app windows behave.

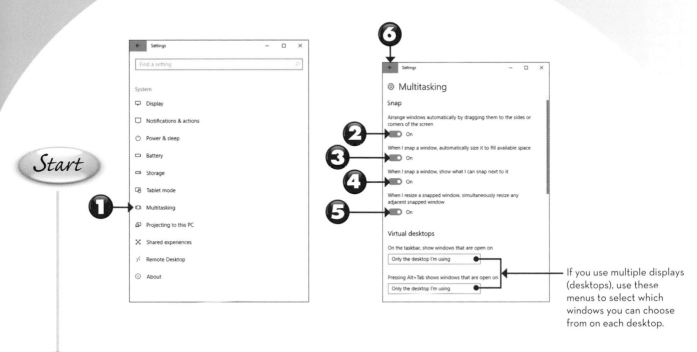

If you use multiple displays (desktops), use these menus to select which windows you can choose from on each desktop.

1 From System settings, click or tap **Multitasking**.

2 If you don't want a window that you drag to the top of the screen to expand to full screen, click or press and drag to **Off**.

3 If you prefer to arrange window sizes manually, click or press and drag to **Off**.

4 If you don't want to see additional running apps you can snap when you snap a window to one side, click or press and drag to **Off**.

5 If you don't want other windows to automatically resize when you resize a snapped window, click or press and drag to **Off**.

6 Click or tap to return to System settings.

End

CONFIGURING TABLET MODE

If you use a tablet or a device that switches between laptop and tablet designs (such as a 2-in-1 device or convertible tablet/laptop device with a quick-release keyboard), the Tablet mode dialog box helps you optimize your device for touch use.

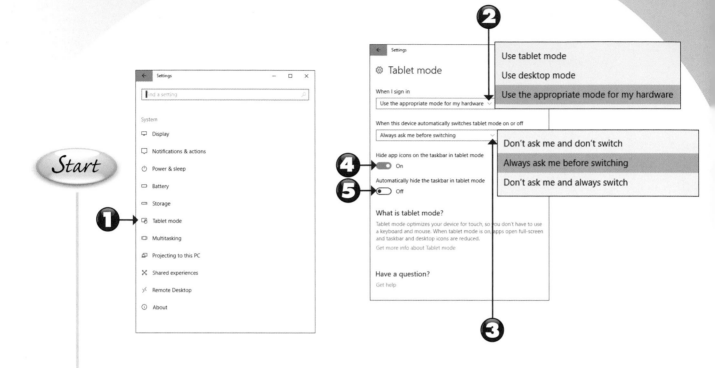

1 From System settings, click or tap **Tablet mode**.

2 By default, Windows 10 FCU uses the appropriate mode for your hardware. Click or tap to change.

3 By default, Windows 10 FCU asks before switching to or from Tablet mode. Click or tap to change.

4 To hide app icons in Tablet mode, press and drag or click and drag to **On**.

5 To hide the taskbar in Tablet mode, press and drag or click and drag to **On**.

Continued

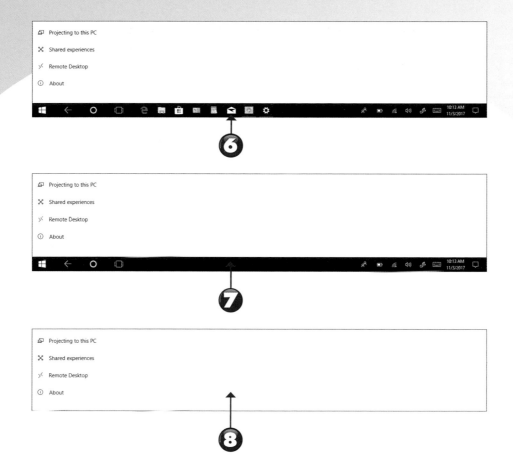

⑥ Tablet mode desktop with taskbar and app icons visible.

⑦ Tablet mode desktop with taskbar but without app icons.

⑧ Tablet mode desktop without taskbar or app icons.

End

NOTE

Switching Apps in Tablet Mode To learn how to switch between apps in Tablet mode, see Chapter 6, "Running Apps." ◼

NOTE

Start Menu in Tablet Mode To see how the Start menu looks in Tablet mode, see Chapter 3. ◼

USING BATTERY SAVER

If you use Windows 10 FCU on a laptop or a tablet, Battery settings shows you how your system uses battery power. Here's how to apply battery saving settings.

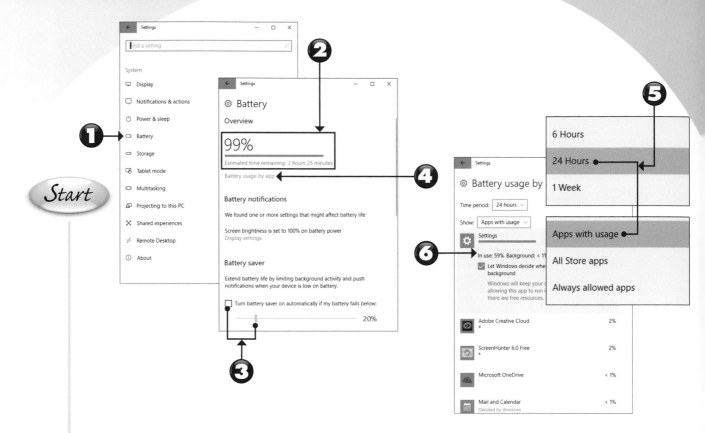

Start

End

1 From Settings, click or tap **Battery**.

2 View the remaining charge here (and runtime, if you are using battery power).

3 Click the empty battery saver check box to enable it, and drag the slider to adjust when the feature turns on.

4 Click or tap to see battery use by app.

5 Select the amount of elapsed time and the type of apps to view.

6 Click an app to view details.

POWER & SLEEP

Use the Power & sleep settings to adjust how long your device stays on when idle.

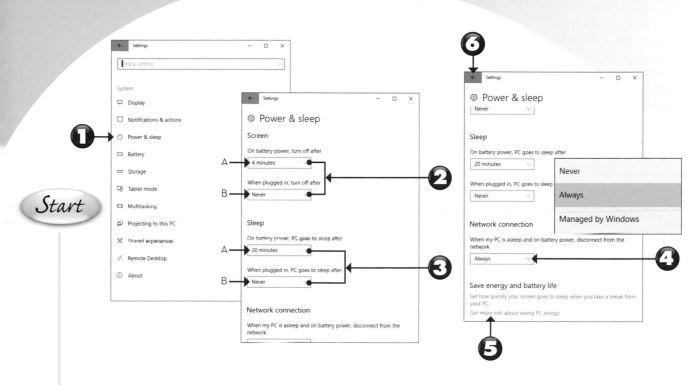

From Settings, click or tap **Power & sleep**.

Click or tap to select when to turn off the screen when on battery power (A) or AC power (B).

Click or tap to select when to sleep on battery power (A) or AC power (B).

Click or tap to select whether a sleeping battery powered system should disconnect from the network.

Click or tap to open the Power Plan menu. (See Chapter 24 for details.)

Click or tap to return to System settings.

NOTE

Power Settings Vary Between Systems   Some systems lack the Network Connection drop-down menu shown in step 4, and some might not have Managed by Windows as an option.

CHECKING DRIVE CAPACITY WITH STORAGE

Use Storage settings to find out how much and what type of information is stored on the drives connected to your system.

Start

1 From System settings, click or tap **Storage**.

2 Click or tap a storage location for more information.

3 Click or tap a category to see the details.

4 Click or tap a folder you want to manage. The folder opens in File Manager.

Continued

TIP

Configuring Storage Sense Click or tap the **Change how we free up space** link shown in step 2 if you want to learn how Storage Sense can save space or to configure it. ■

5 In this example, a folder containing unneeded photos is deleted to free up space.

6 After deleting, copying, or moving files, close the window.

7 Click or tap **Refresh** to update storage usage. (You might need to scroll down.)

8 Review the current storage usage for the category you chose in step 3. (You might need to scroll up.)

9 Click or tap to return to Storage settings.

End

NOTE

Copying, Moving, and Deleting Files and Folders To learn more about working with files and folders, see Chapter 14, "Storing and Finding Your Files."

CHANGING FILE LOCATIONS WITH STORAGE

Storage settings can also help you use other drives, such as additional drive letters on your internal hard drive, flash memory, or external hard disks for new apps and files. Here's how.

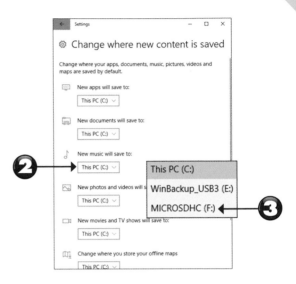

Start

1 From Storage settings, scroll down or flick up to **Change where new content is saved**.

2 Choose a location you want to change.

3 Select a new location for the file category.

Continued

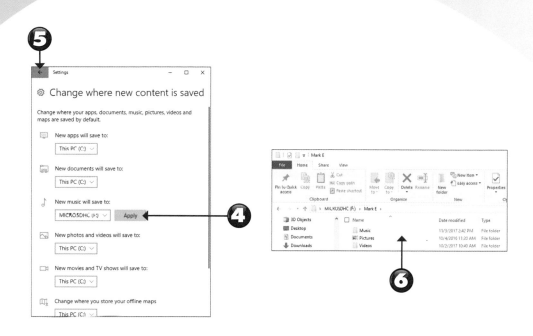

4 Click or tap **Apply**. New music files will be stored at the new location.

5 Click or tap as needed to return to System settings.

6 If you choose a different drive for your files, you can view it in File Manager. Open the drive you selected in step 3 with File Manager, and click or tap your name to see the new folder.

End

CAUTION

Changed Storage Location? Don't Disconnect That Drive! If you disconnect or remove a drive that you set up for new apps or files with Storage, Windows 10 FCU can't find new apps or files until you reconnect or insert the drive. ■

ABOUT YOUR SYSTEM

In Windows 10 FCU, the About page provides you with more information than ever before about your computer, your version of Windows, and the health of your system. Here's how to see it.

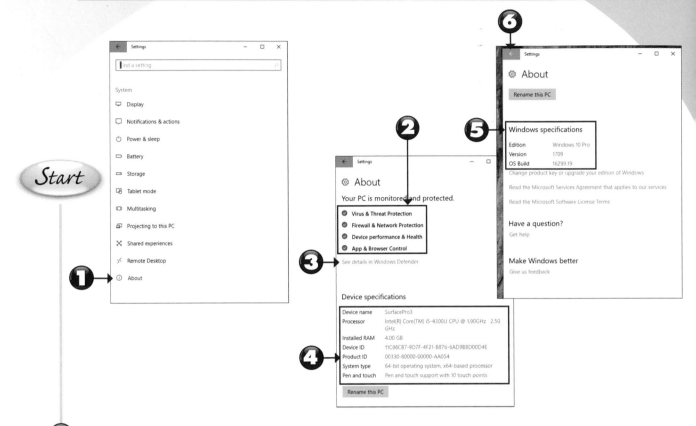

1 From System settings, click or tap **About**.

2 View the security and system health information.

3 For details, click or tap the link to **Windows Defender**.

4 Note the processor, RAM, system type, and pen/touch support information.

5 Scroll down to see the Windows version installed.

6 Click or tap to return to System settings.

Start

End

VIEWING DEVICE STATUS

USB devices that you plug into your computer or tablet are normally installed automatically. The Devices category is used to view and add external components such as Bluetooth devices, printers, and scanners that are not automatically installed. You can also manage mouse, keyboard, pen, and AutoPlay settings in the appropriate submenus. Here's how to see the status of devices that are already connected.

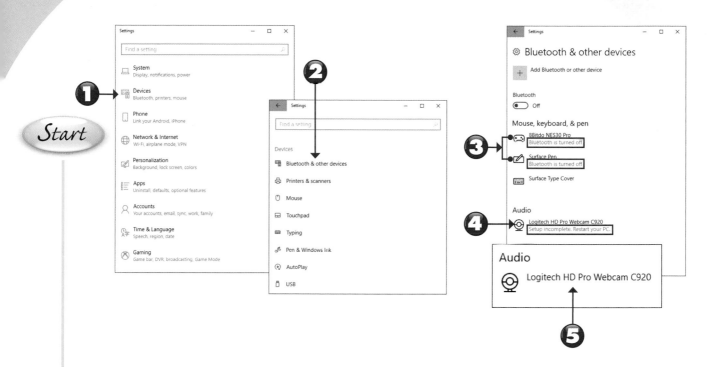

Start

1 From Settings, click or tap **Devices**.

2 Click or tap **Bluetooth & other devices**.

3 To enable these devices to work, turn on Bluetooth.

4 To enable this device to work, restart your computer or tablet.

5 After restart, this device is now ready to use.

End

INSTALLING BLUETOOTH DEVICES

To install Bluetooth devices such as keyboards or mice, you must enable Bluetooth and then open the **Add a device** dialog. This example demonstrates connecting a Bluetooth mouse to a tablet.

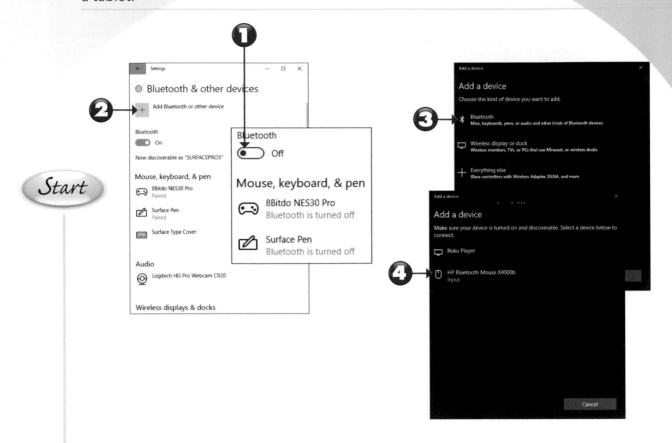

Start

1 If Bluetooth is turned off, click or press and drag to turn it on.

2 Click or tap **Add Bluetooth or other device**.

3 Click or tap **Bluetooth**.

4 Click or tap the device you want to pair (connect to).

Continued

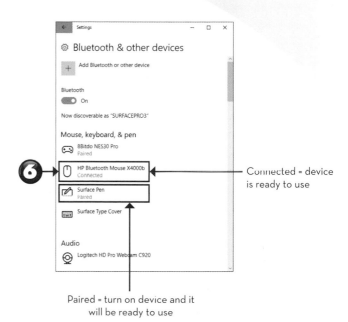

Connected = device
is ready to use

Paired = turn on device and it
will be ready to use

 After the connection is finished, click **Done**.

 The device is listed and ready to use.

End

TIP

Preparing to Connect a Device Before you can connect a Bluetooth device, you might need to press a **Connect** button on the device. This is common with mice, keyboards, and headsets. ▪

NOTE

Pairing a Keyboard When you pair a keyboard, you might need to enter a code displayed on-screen. ▪

INSTALLING A PRINTER OR SCANNER

If you connect a local or networked printer, scanner, or multifunction device to your computer, use the **Printers & scanners** dialog to install it. Here's a typical situation.

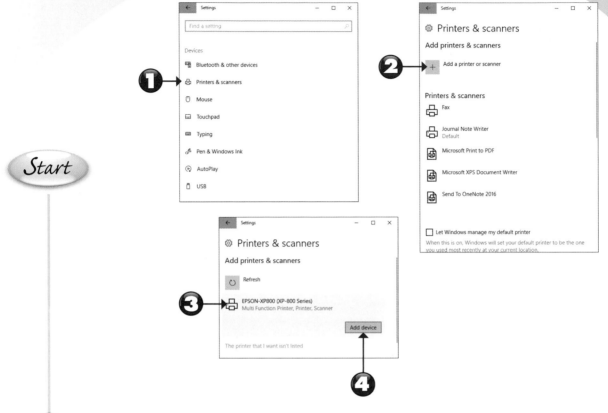

Start

1 From the Devices dialog, click or tap **Printers & scanners**.

2 Click or tap **Add a printer or scanner**.

3 Click or tap the printer, scanner, or multifunction device you want to install.

4 Click or tap **Add device**.

Continued

NOTE

The Printer That I Want Isn't Listed Click or tap this link to open a dialog with other methods of installing a printer (network name, TCP/IP address, Bluetooth or wireless, local printer with manual settings). ■

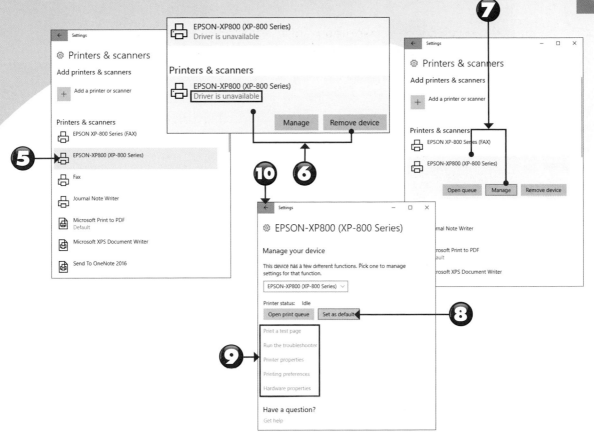

5 If your device is installed, it appears in the list of printers and scanners.

6 If your device doesn't have a driver installed, click or tap its listing; and click or tap **Remove device**. Download and install a driver from the device vendor, and start the process again with step 2.

7 To set your printer as the default printer, click or tap its listing, then click or tap **Manage**.

8 Click or tap **Set as default**. If this option is not listed, uncheck the **Let Windows manage my default printer** (see step 2).

9 Use other options to configure and manage your printer. Some printers use additional apps for configuration.

10 Click or tap to return to the Devices menu.

End

NOTE

Downloading Over Metered Connections Driver software will not be downloaded over a metered connection (such as a cellular connection) unless you enable the **Downloading over metered connections** option. (Scroll down from the list of printers and scanners to see it.) ■

CONFIGURING TOUCHPAD

With the increasing popularity of laptops and 2-in-1 devices, touchpads are now the primary pointing device for a lot of users. Windows 10 FCU makes it easy to configure touchpads with their own menu. Here's how to use it.

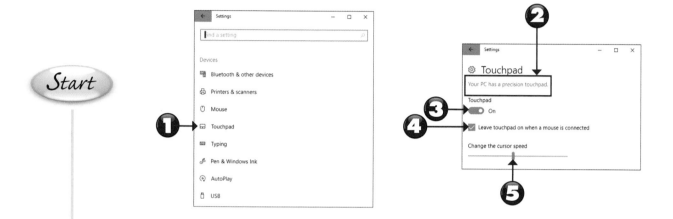

1 From the Devices settings, click or tap **Touchpad**.

2 If your device has a precision touchpad (as the example does), you can use three or four-finger gestures.

3 Hate using a touchpad? Disable it by dragging this to **Off**.

4 To disable your touchpad only when a mouse is connected, clear the check box.

5 Adjust the cursor speed by dragging the control to the left (slower) or right (faster).

Continued

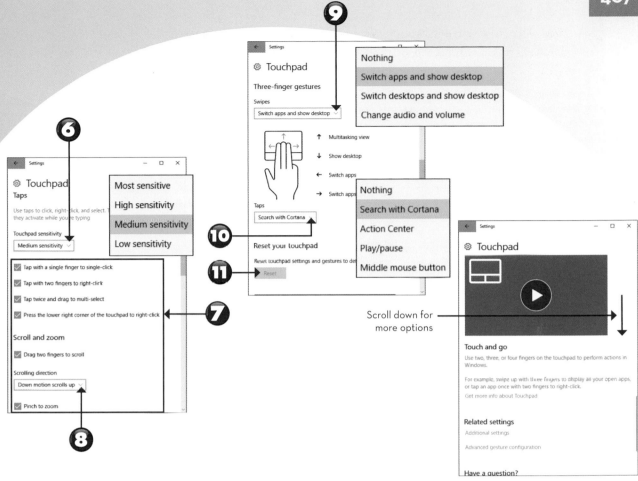

Scroll down for more options

6 If you find yourself engaging your touchpad accidentally while typing, change the sensitivity.

7 Use these settings to configure one-finger and two-finger touchpad operations.

8 Open to change the scrolling direction.

9 To change what a three-finger swipe does, click or tap here.

10 To change what a three-finger tap does, click or tap here.

11 To reset touchpad gestures and settings to defaults, click or tap here.

End

CHANGING AUTOPLAY SETTINGS

Use AutoPlay settings to determine what happens when you connect a removable-media drive or flash memory card.

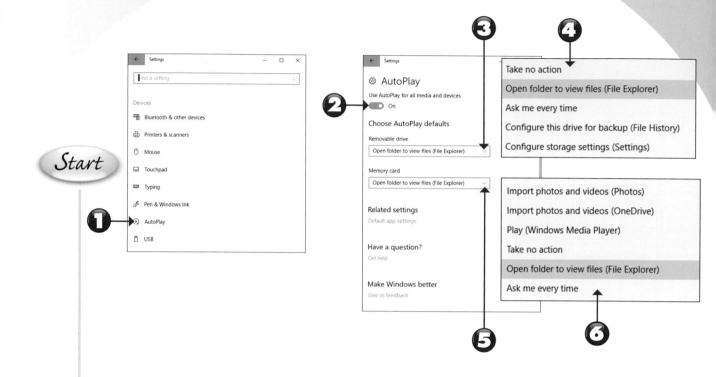

1 In Devices, click or tap **AutoPlay**.

2 To disable AutoPlay, set to **Off**.

3 Click or tap to select an action for removable drives.

4 Click or tap if you want to connect the drive without starting an app or being prompted.

5 Click or tap to select an action for memory cards.

6 Click or tap to be prompted for an action each time a memory card is connected.

Continued

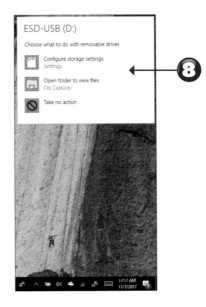

7 Click or tap the prompt to choose what happens when a removable drive is connected.

8 Choose from the available actions.

End

TIP

Dealing with Various File Types If you typically use removable drives or memory cards that contain more than one type of file, I recommend selecting **Open folder to view files** (File Explorer) or **Ask me every time**. ■

PHONE

You can now link your Android or iOS phone to Windows 10 to make it easier to share information. Here's how to use this new feature to continue opening a web page. This example uses an Android (Samsung) phone.

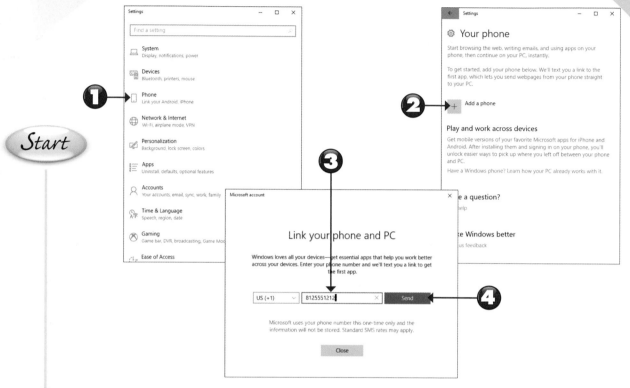

1 In Settings, click or tap **Phone**.

2 Click or tap **Add a phone**.

3 Enter the number for your mobile phone.

4 Click or tap **Send** to send an app link to your phone.

Continued

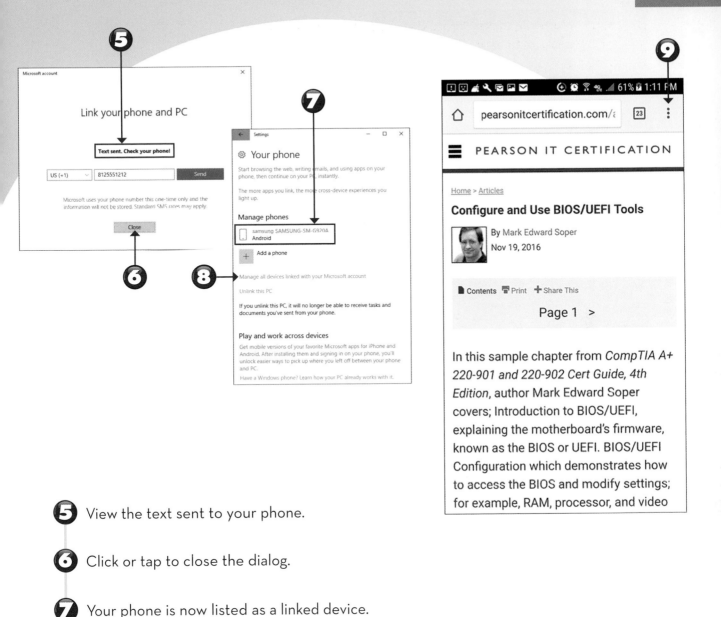

5 View the text sent to your phone.

6 Click or tap to close the dialog.

7 Your phone is now listed as a linked device.

8 If you want to manage all of your linked devices, click or tap **Manage all devices**.

9 Use the link sent to your phone to install and open Microsoft Apps. Then, open your phone's web browser, go to a page you want to share with your Windows 10 device, and open the menu.

Continued

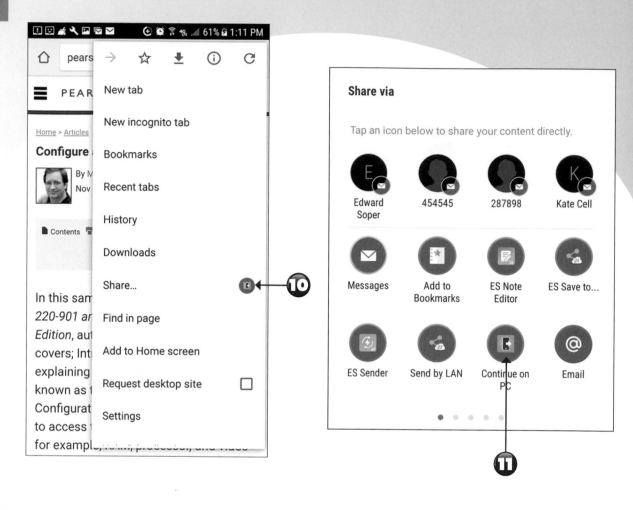

10 Tap **Share**.

11 Tap **Continue on PC**.

Continued

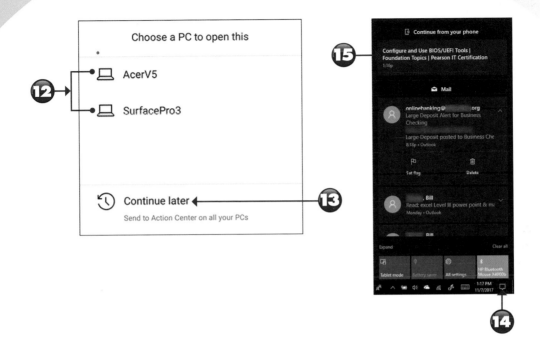

12 To open the web page on a PC immediately, click or tap the PC name.

13 To open it later, click or tap **Continue later**.

14 If you selected **Continue later**, open the Action Center on your Windows 10 PC.

15 Click or tap the link in the **Continue from your phone** section to open the page in your browser.

End

APPS & FEATURES

Particularly with Ultrabooks and tablets, both of which use small-capacity SSD storage, knowing how much space an app uses can be very helpful, especially if you also have the ability to uninstall apps that you don't need anymore. The Apps & features dialog box provides you with both capabilities.

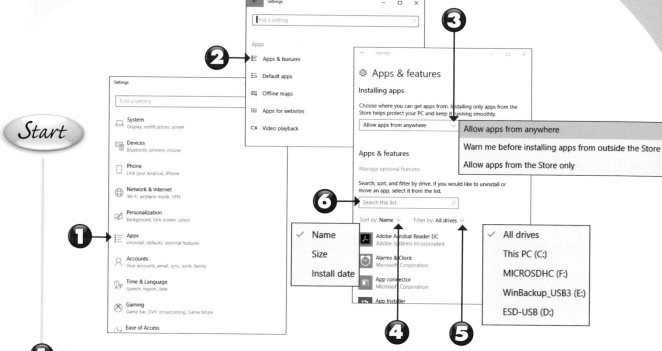

1 From Settings, click or tap **Apps**.

2 Click or tap **Apps & features**.

3 To restrict where to get apps for this computer, open this menu.

4 To change the sort order, click or tap **Sort by**.

5 To view only apps installed on a specific drive, click or tap **Filter by**.

6 To search for an app, click or tap **Search this list** and enter the name.

Continued

NOTE

Managing Optional Windows Features   Use the **Manage optional features** link under the Apps & features heading to add or remove Windows 10 FCU features. ■

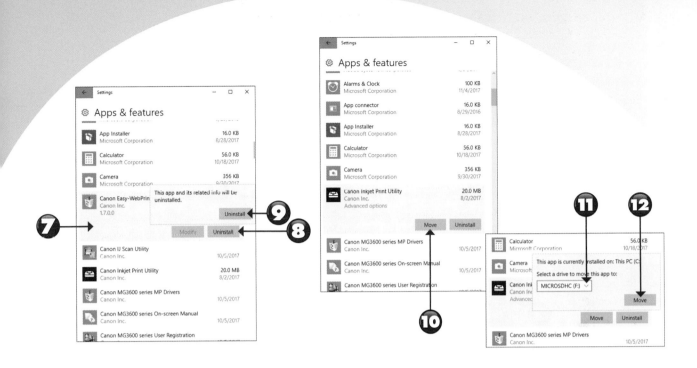

7 To uninstall an app or make other changes, click or tap it.

8 Click or tap **Uninstall**.

9 Click or tap **Uninstall** and follow the prompts to complete the process.

10 Some apps can be moved to another drive. Click or tap **Move** to start the process.

11 Select the drive you want to use.

12 Click or tap **Move** to move the app.

End

NOTE

Other Options Use the **Advanced options** link shown in step 10 to reset a malfunctioning app or to manage its add-ons. Use the **Modify** button (steps 7-9) to reinstall an app with different options. Available options vary by app. ■

CHANGING DEFAULT APPS

If you have more than one app that can be used for a particular task or to open a particular type of file, use the Default Apps settings to specify which app is the one you prefer.

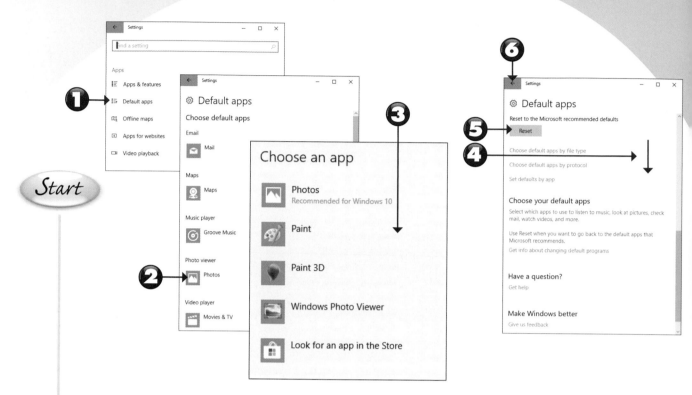

Start

1 From Apps, click or tap **Default apps**.

2 Click or tap an app. (In this example, Photos is used as the default photo viewer.)

3 Click or tap the app you want to use.

4 Scroll down or flick up for other file types and advanced settings.

5 Click or tap **Reset** to go back to the Windows 10 default app settings.

6 Click or tap to return to the Apps menu.

End

NOTE

Available Apps Vary   The exact list of default apps you can choose from depends on the file or app type you choose and the apps installed on your device. ■

VIDEO PLAYBACK

Video playback is an exciting way to use your Windows 10 FCU PC or tablet, but it can also run down your battery more quickly. Use the Video Playback menu to optimize video quality and improve battery life while enjoying video content.

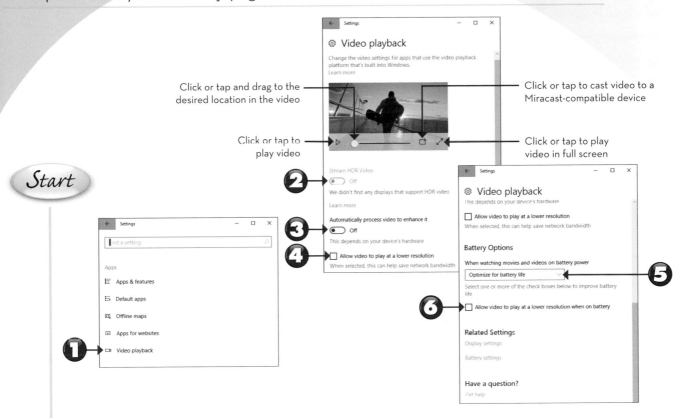

Click or tap and drag to the desired location in the video

Click or tap to cast video to a Miracast-compatible device

Click or tap to play video

Click or tap to play video in full screen

Start

1 From Apps, click or tap **Video playback**.

2 If you have a display or projector with HDR video, you can enable the feature.

3 To enhance video automatically, turn the **Automatically process** feature **On**.

4 To play video at a lower resolution, click or tap the empty **Allow video** check box.

5 Click or tap to change optimization (quality or battery life) when on battery.

6 To play video at a lower resolution on battery power, click or tap the empty **Allow video** check box.

End

MAKING MAPS AVAILABLE OFFLINE

Thanks to GPS units in smartphones, tablets, and cars, real-time navigation is a great way to get around—unless you don't have a signal. If you want to use your device to navigate no matter your location or signal availability, use Windows 10 FCU's downloadable offline maps feature. You can select maps for most regions of the world.

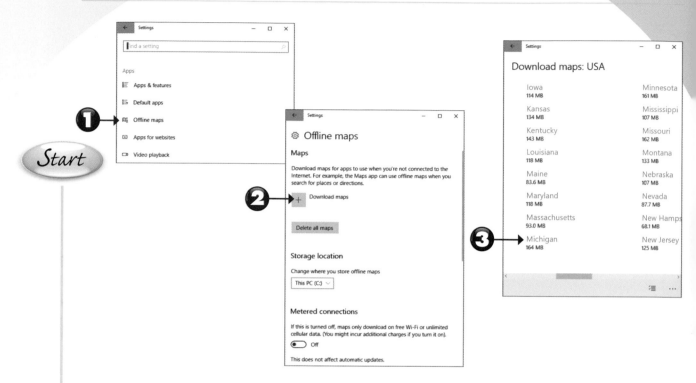

1 From Apps, click or tap **Offline maps**.

2 Click or tap + to select a map (region, country, state, or province as listed).

3 Select a map, and it starts downloading to your system.

Continued

NOTE

Maps Download in the Background Maps continue to download while you use your computer, so as soon as you start the download (step 3), you can make other changes in Settings as needed. ■

4 After you download a map, Windows 10 FCU's Maps app can use it even when you're not connected to the Internet.

5 Map updates are automatic if **Automatically update maps** is **On**.

6 If you prefer to check for updates manually, click or tap **Check now**.

7 To delete all maps, click or tap the **Delete all maps** button.

8 To delete a specific map, click or tap the map, and then click or tap **Delete**.

9 Click or tap to return to Apps.

End

GAMING AND GAME BAR

The new and improved Gaming section of Settings helps you optimize your system for gaming and use Windows 10's many gaming features. In this exercise, you open the Gaming dialog and check out Game bar's many keyboard shortcuts.

1 In Settings, click or tap **Gaming**.

2 Click or tap **Game bar**.

3 Game bar can record and broadcast unless you turn **Record** to **Off**.

4 Game bar opens from your controller unless you clear this check box.

5 Game bar is available in full-screen games unless you clear this check box.

6 Scroll down or flick up to see all default shortcuts for Game bar features.

Continued

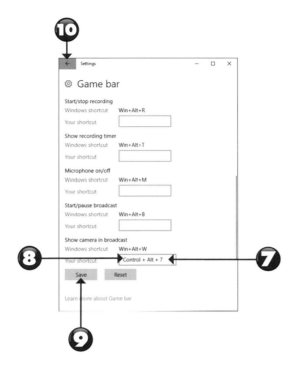

7 To change a shortcut, click or tap the box.

8 Press the keys for your own shortcut, such as Control-Alt-*letter*.

9 Click **Save**.

10 Click or tap to return to the Gaming menu.

End

CAUTION

Avoiding Keyboard Combinations Already In Use You cannot use Windows+Alt key combinations, but almost any other key combination will work, including keys that are already assigned to Windows tasks such as Paste (Ctrl+V). To avoid conflicts, check the Keyboard Shortcuts in Windows page at https://support.microsoft.com/en-us/help/12445/windows-keyboard-shortcuts and specify **Windows 10**. ▪

GAME DVR

Game DVR lets you record your greatest triumphs (or anything else you want to record). Use the Game DVR page to help customize how Game DVR works. Keep in mind that higher frame rates, higher audio quality, and higher video quality can provide a better recording but might slow down your game.

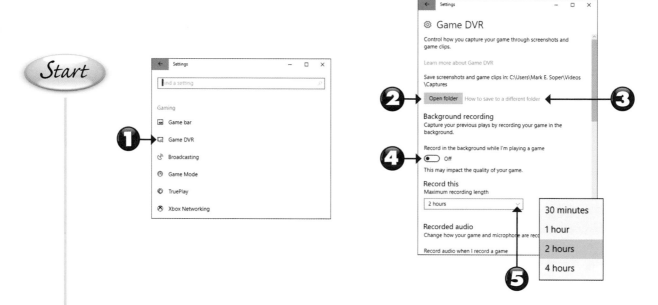

1 In Gaming, click or tap **Game DVR**.

2 To see your game captures (videos or stills), click or tap **Open folder**.

3 To change where you save game captures, click or tap the **How to save** link.

4 To enable background recording, drag the Record slider to **On**.

5 To change maximum recording time, open the **Record this** menu and choose the value desired.

Continued

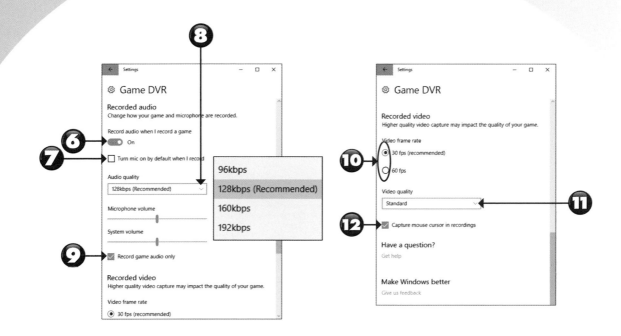

6 The game audio is recorded when this is **On**.

7 To turn on your mic automatically when recording a game, click the empty check box.

8 To change audio recording quality, open the **Audio recording** menu and choose your preferred recording rate.

9 Clear the **Record game audio only** check box if you want to record your comments as you play.

10 A higher frame rate increases video quality but might reduce game performance.

11 Click or tap and select High quality to improve video quality.

12 Clear this check box to omit the cursor from your recording.

End

BROADCASTING

The new Broadcasting feature enables you to broadcast your gameplay via the Mixer online service. Use the Broadcasting page in Apps to configure it.

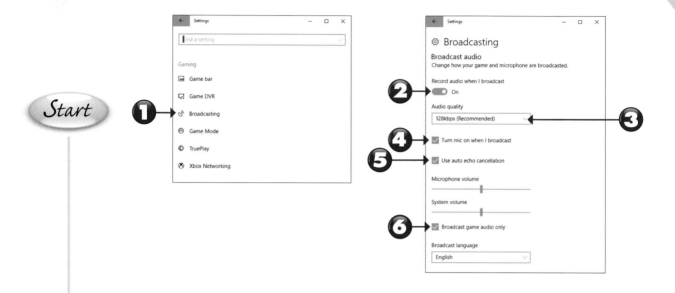

1 In Gaming, click or tap **Broadcasting**.

2 Game audio is recorded when this is **On**.

3 To change audio recording quality, open the **Audio recording** menu and choose your preferred recording rate.

4 When this box is checked, your mic is automatically turned on when broadcasting a game.

5 To use auto echo cancellation (prevents game audio from being recorded by your mic), check this box.

6 To broadcast game audio only, check this box.

Continued

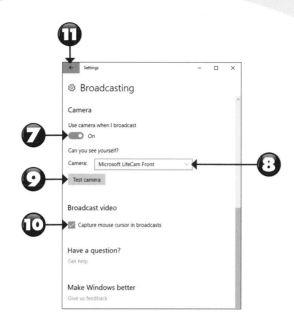

7 To turn off your device's camera during broadcast, drag to **Off**.

8 If you want to use the camera and have a front and rear-facing camera, select the camera to use. (The front-facing camera is the one facing you.)

9 Click or tap **Test camera** to make sure the camera is working and properly positioned to record yourself.

10 Don't want the mouse cursor in your broadcast? Clear this check box.

11 Click or tap to return to the Gaming menu.

End

GAME MODE AND TRUEPLAY

Use the Game Mode dialog to determine if your system supports Game Mode. Use True-Play to help stop game cheaters.

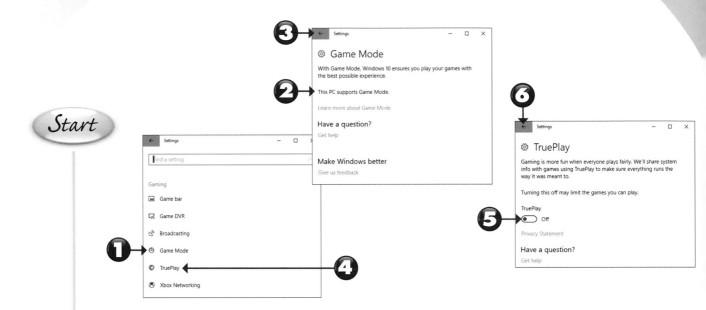

Start

End

1 In Gaming, click or tap **Game Mode**.

2 This computer supports Game Mode.

3 Click or tap to return to Gaming.

4 In Gaming, click or tap **TruePlay**.

5 To enable TruePlay, drag to **On**.

6 Click or tap to return to Gaming.

XBOX NETWORKING

Use the Xbox Networking dialog to check the performance of your network connection to your Xbox console and, if necessary, fix it. Here's how it works.

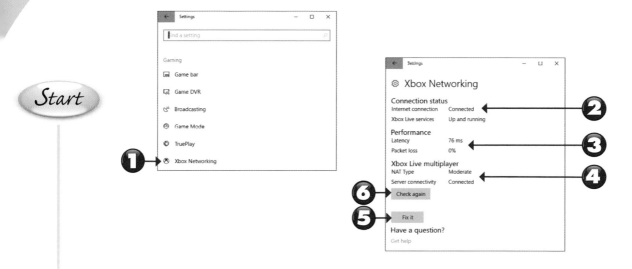

Start

1. In Gaming, click or tap **Xbox Networking**.

2. Note that the Internet and Xbox live services are working properly.

3. Be aware that packet loss above 0% could indicate network problems.

4. You can see that Xbox Live multiplayer is working properly.

5. If there are connection problems, click or tap **Fix it**.

6. After fixing problems, click or tap **Check again** to rerun the tests on this page.

End

PRIVACY OVERVIEW

Windows 10 FCU is designed to be even more helpful to users than previous editions. To accomplish this, it stores a lot of information about you. The more information Windows knows about you, the more targeted the information it provides, but the less privacy you have. Use the Privacy section of Settings to customize your privacy settings for apps included with Windows 10 FCU or available from the Microsoft Store. Let's start with an overview of privacy settings.

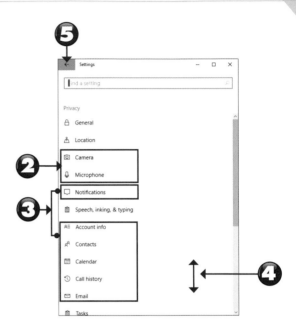

1 In Settings, scroll down or flick up and then click or tap **Privacy**.

2 These dialogs enable you to specify which apps can use the specified hardware.

3 These dialogs enable you to specify which apps can use the specified services.

4 Scroll down or flick up for more options.

5 Click or tap to return to the Settings dialog.

Continued

NOTE

Privacy Settings in More Detail Highlighted privacy settings are covered as a group because they work similarly. Privacy settings that are not highlighted in this exercise are covered separately. ■

GENERAL PRIVACY SETTINGS

Use the General dialog in Privacy for settings that affect all parts of Windows.

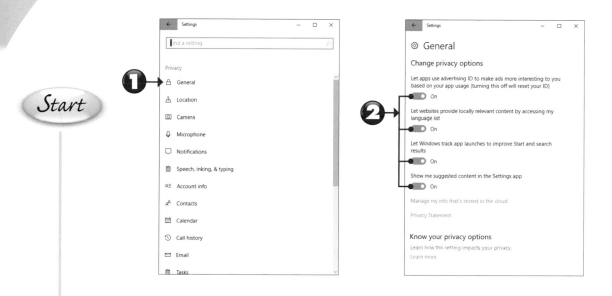

① From the Privacy dialog, click or tap **General**.

② Leaving these options enabled reduces your privacy while making searches, typing, and shopping easier.

Start

End

NOTE

More Management In the Cloud   In Windows 10 FCU, more information about you is stored online. See "Managing Privacy Information in the Cloud," this chapter, p. 436, for details. ▪

CONFIGURING LOCATION SETTINGS

Many apps are designed to use your location to provide you with more relevant information. If you need to change these settings, use the Location dialog box in the Privacy section of Settings.

Start

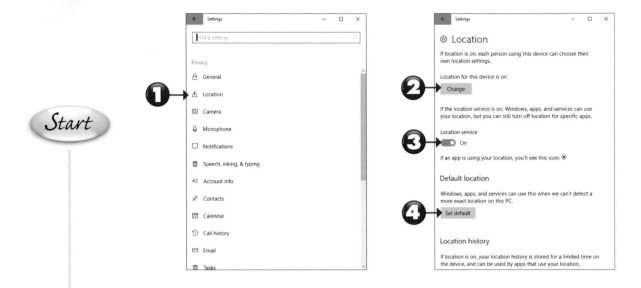

1 From the Privacy settings page, click or tap **Location**.

2 If you don't want each user to set individual location settings, click or tap **Change** and select **Off** in the pop-up window.

3 To disable location service for your account, click or press and drag to **Off**.

4 To set a default location, click or tap **Set default**.

Continued

5 Click or tap to clear location history on this device.

6 Scroll down or flick up to view or change location settings by app.

7 Turning on notification (off by default) for News and Weather can help keep you better informed.

8 Click or tap to return to Privacy settings.

End

CHANGING PRIVACY SETTINGS FOR MOST CATEGORIES

The process of setting privacy settings is very similar for the following: Camera, Microphone, Notifications, Account info, Contacts, Calendar, Call history, Email, Tasks, Messaging, Radios, Background apps, and App diagnostics. With these dialogs, you change privacy settings for all apps in a category or for individual apps in each category. This task demonstrates how privacy settings work for Camera. Similar methods are used with the other apps listed.

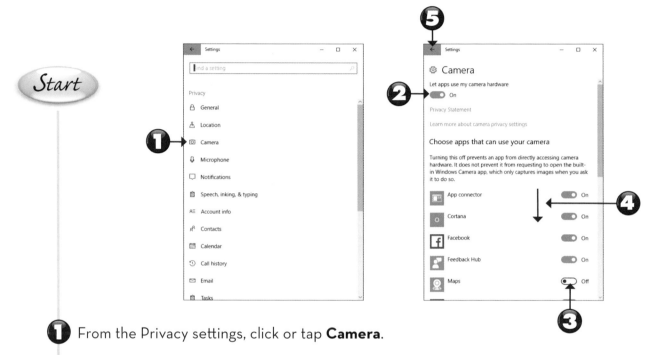

1 From the Privacy settings, click or tap **Camera**.

2 When this setting is **On** (the default), all listed apps can use your device's camera.

3 You can click or press and drag to turn specific app's access on or off; Maps' access to Camera has been turned off.

4 Scroll down to see more apps that use Camera.

5 Click or tap to return to Privacy settings.

End

CAUTION

Privacy, Cameras, and Microphones   Even if you block listed apps from using your camera or microphone, it's possible for malware to use these hardware devices. If you're concerned about this potential privacy risk, unplug your camera or microphone when you're not using it, and cover up the lens and microphone of your device's built-in camera. ■

CHANGING PRIVACY SETTINGS FOR OTHER DEVICES

The Other devices category lists all the other hardware with privacy settings, such as removable-media drives, media playback devices such as Roku set-top boxes, and others. In this task, you learn how to control privacy issues for these types of hardware. Keep in mind that the list of hardware varies from computer to computer, and some computers or tablets might not have any devices in this category.

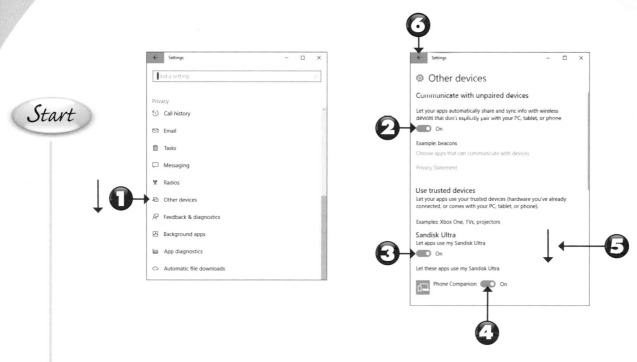

1. Scroll down the Privacy menu and click or tap **Other devices**.

2. When **Communicate with unpaired devices** is **On**, devices such as beacons that are not explicitly paired with your PC or tablet can be used.

3. For each trusted device, choose whether or not the device can be used.

4. Choose which apps can use the device.

5. Scroll down for more devices.

6. Click or tap to return to the Privacy menu.

CHANGING SPEECH, INK, AND TYPING PRIVACY SETTINGS

The Cortana search assistant in Windows 10 FCU works by learning your voice and your writing, and it collects information to serve your search and dictation needs better. If you're not interested, use the Speech, Inking, & Typing dialog box to stop the information gathering. If you change your mind later, you can restart the process. Here's how.

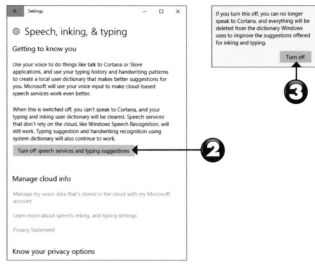

1 From the Privacy settings page, click or tap **Speech, inking, & typing**.

2 Click or tap **Turn off speech services and typing suggestions**.

3 Click or tap **Turn off**, and you turn off dictation and clear out the information on your device that Cortana uses.

NOTE

Turning on Speech Services and Typing Suggestions In step 2, click or tap **Turn on speech services and typing suggestions**. In step 3, click or tap **Turn on**.

FEEDBACK AND DIAGNOSTICS PRIVACY SETTINGS

Microsoft wants to know how well Windows is working for you and wants to improve the product based on feedback from users. Use the Feedback & diagnostics page to configure these settings.

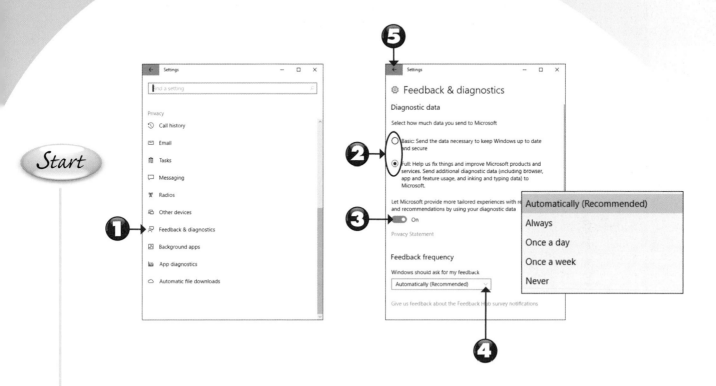

1 From Privacy, click or tap **Feedback & diagnostics**.

2 Select the level of diagnostic data to send to Microsoft.

3 To disable tailored experiences, drag to **Off**.

4 To change the frequency of feedback or to disable feedback, open the **Feedback frequency** menu and select the desired option.

5 Click or tap to return to the Privacy menu.

MANAGING PRIVACY INFORMATION IN THE CLOUD

In Windows 10 FCU, a lot of the data that Windows uses to provide personalized results is stored in the cloud. By doing this, Windows can provide you with the same level of personalization on any device you use with the same Microsoft Account. If this is a little too helpful, you can remove this information. Here's how.

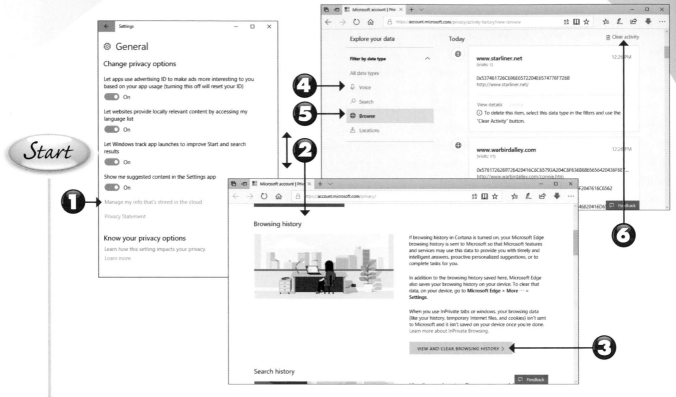

1 From the General dialog, click or tap **Manage my info that's stored in the cloud**.

2 The Privacy dashboard opens. Scroll down or flick up to Browsing history.

3 To view and clear browsing, search, location, or voice activity, click or tap **View and clear browsing history**.

4 Scroll down to the **Filter by data type** menu.

5 The browsing history (Browse) is already selected.

6 To clear your browsing history, click or tap the **Clear activity** button.

Continued

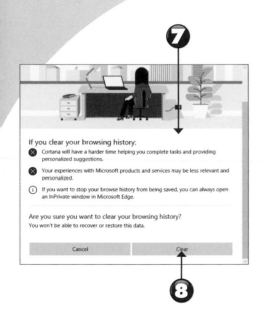

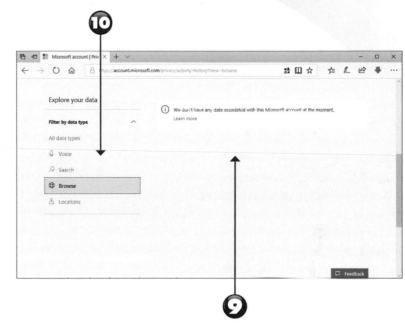

7 This dialog shows what changes if you delete your browsing history.

8 Click or tap **Clear** to remove the browsing history.

9 You can see there is no data available after you remove the browsing history.

10 To view or remove data from a different category, select the data type. Then repeat steps 6 through 8 for that category.

End

NOTE

Finishing the Job If you don't change privacy settings on your computer or tablet, Windows continues to gather information. To prevent information from being gathered, open the relevant Privacy dialogs and make the changes needed. ■

Chapter 20

NETWORKING YOUR HOME

Wireless networking (or Wi-Fi) and HomeGroup secure networking make it easy to connect your Windows 10 FCU device with the rest of the world. This chapter explains how to connect to and leave a wireless network, create a mobile hotspot, and use HomeGroup secure home networking.

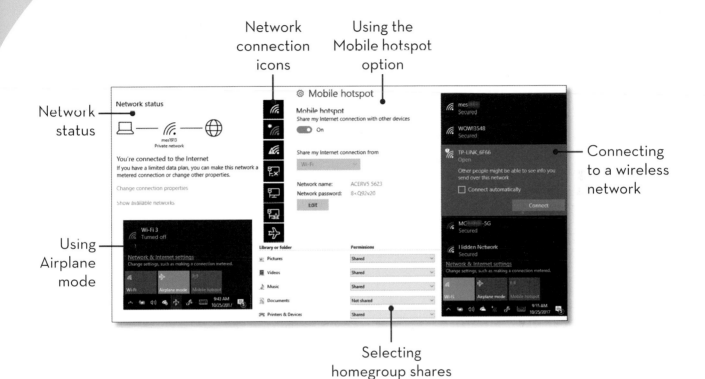

Network connection icons

Using the Mobile hotspot option

Network status

Connecting to a wireless network

Using Airplane mode

Selecting homegroup shares

CHECKING YOUR NETWORK CONNECTION STATUS

Windows 10 FCU makes it easy to tell if you're already connected to a wireless or wired network. Here's what to look for on the taskbar.

Start

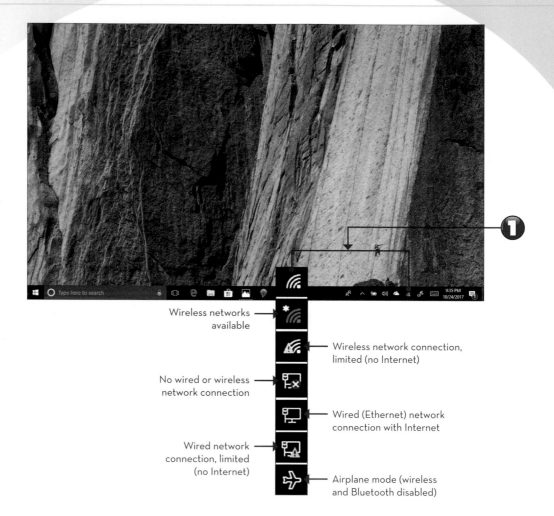

Wireless networks available

Wireless network connection, limited (no Internet)

No wired or wireless network connection

Wired (Ethernet) network connection with Internet

Wired network connection, limited (no Internet)

Airplane mode (wireless and Bluetooth disabled)

1 This system has a wireless connection to the Internet.

End

STARTING THE WIRELESS NETWORK CONNECTION PROCESS

To connect to a wireless network, use the Wireless Network button in the taskbar. Here's how.

Start

Secure networks

Unsecured (open) network

Hidden (and secured) network

Turns off Wi-Fi and Bluetooth

Network-related quick actions

Wi-Fi enabled

Turns on Mobile hotspot

1 Click the wireless network button in the taskbar.

2 The Network Connections dialog appears. Choose one of the listed networks for your connection.

End

NOTE

Secure, Unsecure, and Suggested Network Icons Secure networks use the signal strength icon. Unsecure networks add a shield marked with an exclamation point (!) to the icon, indicating they are not secure (see step 2). Suggested networks (not shown) are those recommended by your ISP. ■

NOTE

Finishing Your Connection To complete the process, see "Connecting to an Unsecured Wireless Network," p. 442 and "Connecting to a Secured Private Network," p. 444 (both in this chapter). ■

CONNECTING TO AN UNSECURED WIRELESS NETWORK

Your home and office networks should be secure networks (in other words, you should use a password when you set up your home Wi-Fi network; your work network is probably already secure); however, wireless networks in locations such as coffee shops, libraries, restaurants, and hotels often are unsecured. Here's how to connect to these networks using Windows 10 FCU.

① Click or tap the unsecured network's name (SSID) to connect to it.

② Check **Connect automatically** if you think you'll connect to this network at some point in the future.

③ Click or tap **Connect**.

④ Your new network connection is listed first in the wireless network list and is marked "Connected, Open."

Start

End

CONNECTING TO A NETWORK WITH TERMS AND CONDITIONS

Some unsecured wireless networks require you to use your web browser to accept the Wi-Fi service's terms before you can finish your connection. Here's a typical example.

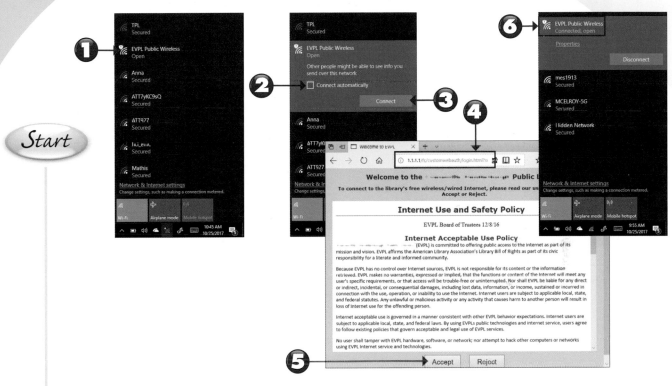

Start

1 Click or tap the unsecured network's name (SSID) to connect to it.

2 Check **Connect automatically** if you think you'll connect to this network at some point in the future.

3 Click or tap **Connect**.

4 If the network requires you to accept terms and conditions, your browser opens the agreement page.

5 Read and agree to the terms and conditions, and click or tap the **Accept** or **Get Connected** button to complete the connection.

6 Your new network connection is listed first in the wireless network list and is marked "Connected, Open."

End

CONNECTING TO A SECURED PRIVATE NETWORK

A secured network uses a network security key, also known as an *encryption key*. The first time you connect to a secured network, you must enter the network security key. Windows 10 FCU can remember your network security key and the rest of your connection details for you. Here's how this process works.

1 Click or tap a secure network.

2 If you want to connect to this network automatically in the future, check the **Connect automatically** box.

3 Click or tap **Connect**.

Continued

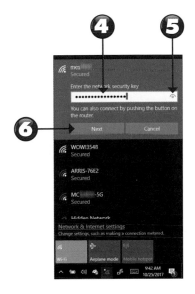

4 Enter the network security key.

5 To see the hidden characters as you type, click or tap the eye icon.

6 Click or tap **Next**.

7 Your network connection is listed first in the wireless network list.

End

DISCONNECTING A WIRELESS CONNECTION

If you decide that you need to connect to a stronger signal or want to disconnect from Wi-Fi altogether, follow these steps to disconnect from your current Wi-Fi network.

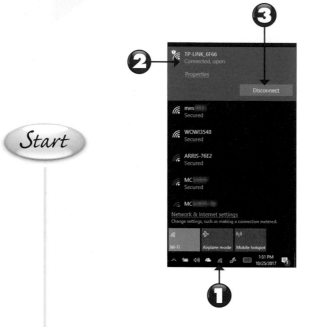

1 Click the network button in the taskbar.

2 Click or tap the current connection.

3 Click or tap **Disconnect**.

4 Your device disconnects from Wi-Fi.

NOTE

Disabling Automatic Reconnection In step 4, if you disconnect from a Wi-Fi network that is configured for automatic connections, the Connect button appears (as in this example). Click or tap it if you want to reconnect, click or tap a different network, or click or tap an empty part of the desktop if you don't want to connect right now. ■

USING AIRPLANE MODE

When Wi-Fi access is not needed, you can quickly turn off Wi-Fi (and Bluetooth) to save power. You can use the Airplane mode setting (named for air travel policies regarding radio signal frequency transmission) to quickly disable wireless transmission in Windows 10 FCU. Here's how.

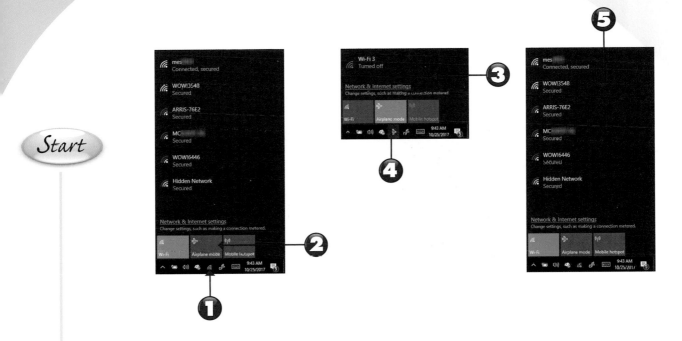

Start

1. Click or tap the **Wireless Network** button in the taskbar.

2. Click or tap the **Airplane mode** button.

3. Wi-Fi functionality is turned off; no wireless connections are available.

4. To reenable wireless access, click or tap **Airplane mode**.

5. Wireless connections are again available.

End

CAUTION

Selecting Wi-Fi Only Using the Airplane mode quick setting is a fast way to disable Wi-Fi, but it also disables Bluetooth. If you use Bluetooth devices and want to disable only Wi-Fi, you can turn off Wi-Fi without changing Bluetooth settings. For details, see "Disabling and Enabling Wi-Fi," p. 450 (this chapter). ∎

ACCESSING NETWORK & INTERNET SETTINGS

The Network & Internet dialog in Settings is used for many tasks, including creating a mobile hotspot, disabling and enabling Wi-Fi, and managing wireless connections. Here's how to get there.

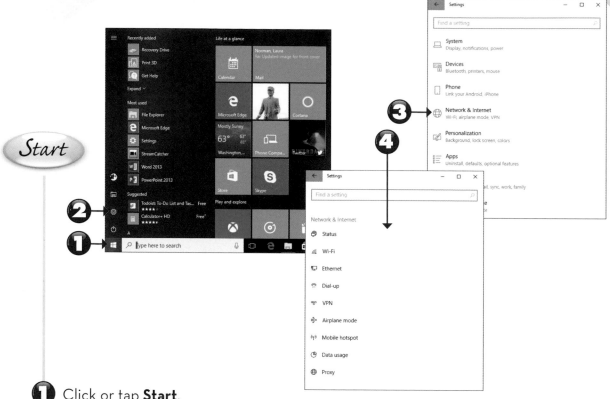

1 Click or tap **Start**.

2 Click or tap **Settings**.

3 Click or tap **Network & Internet**.

4 The Network & Internet settings page.

End

NOTE

Other Network & Internet Topics   This chapter focuses on the Mobile hotspot, Wi-Fi, Status, and Airplane mode dialogs. Use Ethernet to manage wired network connections. Use Data usage settings if you use metered connections, such as satellite. Use VPN settings to help set up or manage a virtual private network (typically used to connect to corporate networks). Use Dial-up settings to help set up or manage a modem that dials in to a telephone number for Internet connections. Use Proxy settings if you need to set up or manage a proxy connection (typically used in corporate networks). ■

CREATING A MOBILE HOTSPOT

If the only device you have that can make a network connection is your Windows 10 device, but other devices need a wireless connection, use Windows 10 FCU's mobile hotspot support to turn your Windows 10 device into a wireless gateway. Here's what to do after you open Internet & Network in Settings.

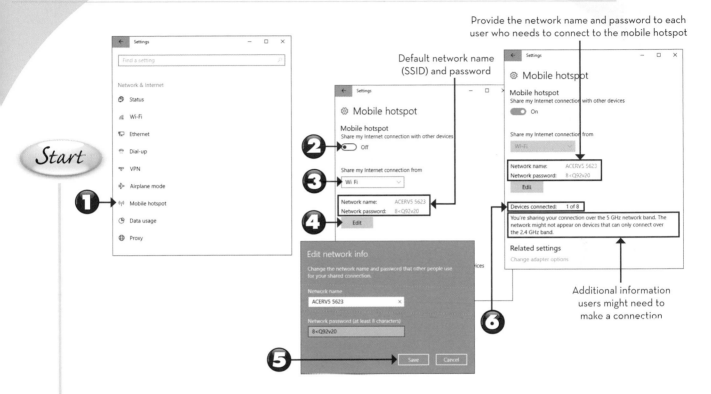

Provide the network name and password to each user who needs to connect to the mobile hotspot

Default network name (SSID) and password

Additional information users might need to make a connection

1 Click or tap **Mobile hotspot**.

2 Drag to **On** to enable the mobile hotspot.

3 If you have more than one network connection, click or tap **Share my Internet connection from** and select the connection.

4 Click or tap **Edit** to change the default network name (SSID) or password.

5 If you make changes, click **Save** to use them.

6 Note that up to eight users can connect to the mobile hotspot.

End

DISABLING AND ENABLING WI-FI

You can disable and enable Wi-Fi by using the Wi-Fi settings dialog. By using this menu, your Bluetooth settings are unaffected.

1 With Settings open to the Network & Internet settings dialog, click or tap **Wi-Fi**.

2 To disable Wi-Fi, drag the Wi-Fi switch to **Off**.

3 To enable Wi-Fi again, drag the Wi-Fi switch to **On**.

MANAGING WIRELESS CONNECTIONS

Windows 10 FCU stores information about each Wi-Fi connection you create. If you travel and use different Wi-Fi networks, the list can become very long. Here's how to remove ("forget") networks you won't be using again.

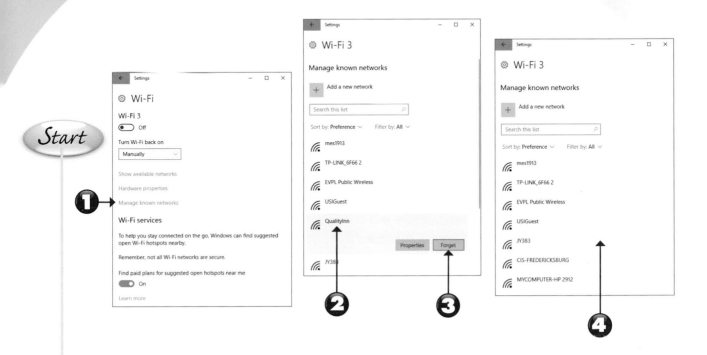

1. From the Wi-Fi page, click or tap **Manage known networks**.

2. Click or tap a network you want to forget.

3. Click or tap **Forget**.

4. The network is removed from the list of known networks.

End

NOTE

Reconnecting to a Forgotten Network   If you want to reconnect to a wireless network you forgot, you must reenter the SSID (if the network is hidden) and its encryption key (password) if it is secure. ■

CREATING A HOMEGROUP

Windows 10 FCU supports an easy-to-use, yet secure, type of home and small-business networking feature called a homegroup (also available in Windows 7, 8, and 8.1). Homegroup networking enables home network users to share libraries and printers—you can specify which libraries to share and whether to share printers and devices on a particular system. All users of a homegroup use the same password but don't need to worry about specifying particular folders to share. Here's how to start the process from the Status dialog.

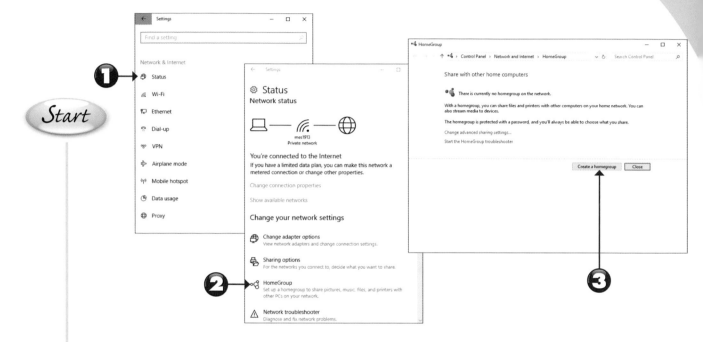

1 From the Network & Internet page, click or tap **Status**.

2 Click or tap **HomeGroup** to open the HomeGroup dialog in a new window.

3 If there is no homegroup, click or tap **Create a homegroup**.

Continued

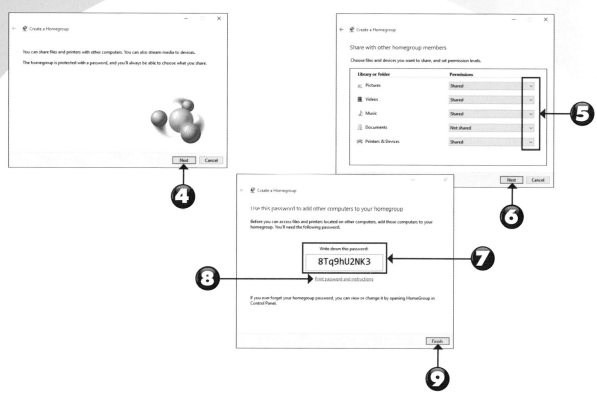

4 Click or tap **Next**.

5 Select **Shared** or **Not shared** as desired for the folders and devices on your system (defaults shown here).

6 Click or tap **Next**.

7 Provide this password to others who need to connect to the homegroup.

8 Click or tap to print the password and instructions.

9 Click or tap **Finish** to close the dialog box.

End

NOTE

Accessing Homegroup Files   To access files from other homegroup members, use File Manager and scroll down to Homegroup in the left pane. Open the homegroup user to access that user's files. ■

JOINING A HOMEGROUP

Microsoft introduced homegroups in Windows 7, so if you have one or more Windows 7, Windows 8/8.1, or Windows 10 computers in your home or small office, you might already have a homegroup. Here's how to add your Windows 10 FCU computer to an existing homegroup.

1 From the Status dialog, click or tap **HomeGroup**.

2 If there is an existing homegroup, click or tap **Join now**.

3 Click or tap **Next**.

Continued

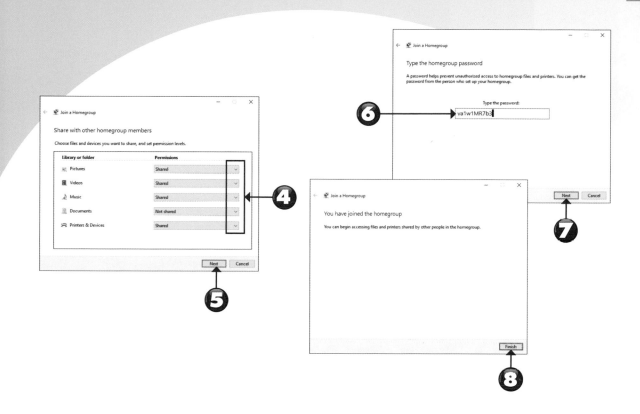

Select **Shared** or **Not shared** as desired for the folders and devices on your system (defaults shown here).

Click or tap **Next**.

Enter the password for the homegroup.

Click or tap **Next**.

Click or tap **Finish** to close the dialog box.

End

NOTE

Leaving a Homegroup If you want to leave a homegroup you've joined, open the HomeGroup dialog and select the link for **Leave the homegroup**. ■

CUSTOMIZING WINDOWS

From tweaking the Start menu and the taskbar to adjusting the desktop and personalizing the Lock screen, Windows 10 FCU provides many ways to make your account uniquely yours.

Using a custom picture on the Lock screen

Choosing the icons for the taskbar

Selecting a custom color for the taskbar and Start menu

Choosing the folders that appear on the Start menu

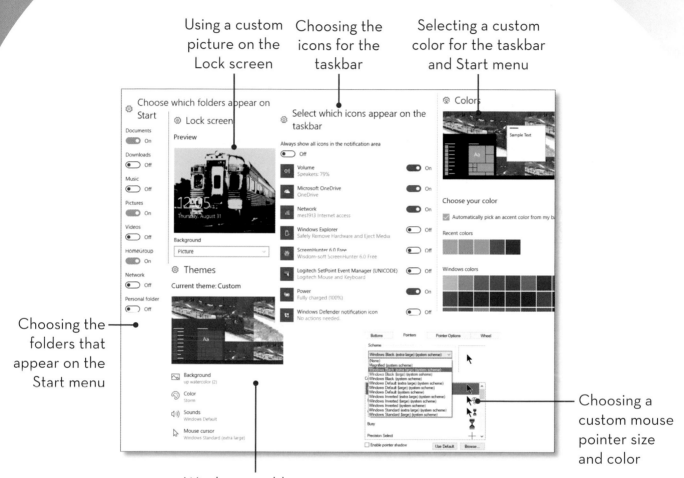

Choosing a custom mouse pointer size and color

Windows enables you to save your settings as a theme

USING PERSONALIZATION SETTINGS

The Personalization settings enable you to change your desktop background, colors, Lock screen, and themes. Here's how to start the process.

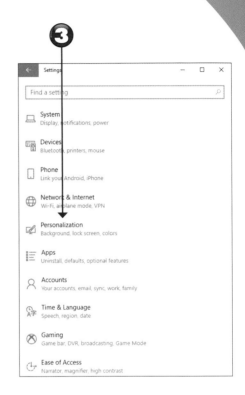

① Click or tap the **Start** button.

② Click or tap **Settings**.

③ Click or tap **Personalization**.

Continued

TIP

Opening Settings from Quick Actions Click or tap the **Notifications/Quick Actions** button in the taskbar (far right side of taskbar), and then click or tap **All settings** to open the Settings dialog box. ■

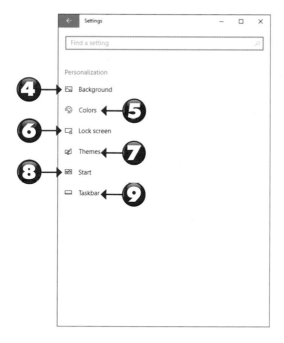

4 Click or tap to change the screen background.

5 Click or tap to change the taskbar and Start menu colors.

6 Click or tap to change the Lock screen.

7 Click or tap to change settings for sounds, mouse pointers, desktop icons, and themes.

8 Click or tap to change Start menu settings.

9 Click or tap to change taskbar settings.

End

CHANGING THE SCREEN BACKGROUND

Changing the screen background (or "wallpaper" for Windows veterans) is one of the most popular ways to personalize your system. In this exercise, you learn how to customize it, Windows 10 FCU style.

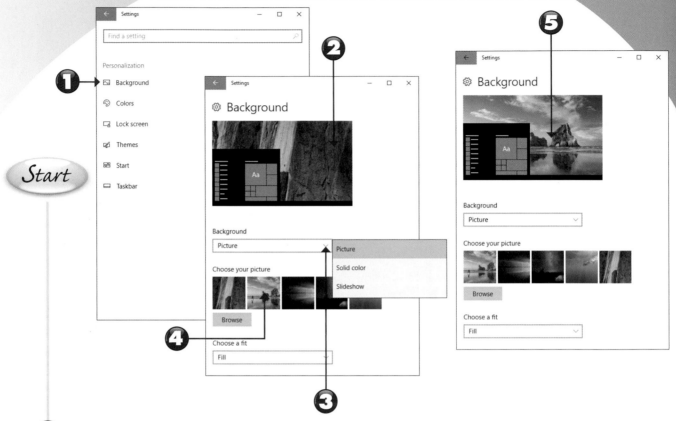

1 From the Personalization settings, click or tap **Background**.

2 This shows the preview of the current background.

3 Picture is the default background type; click or tap to select from other backgrounds, including solid colors and a slide show.

4 Click or tap a different picture.

5 Note the preview of the new selection.

End

CHOOSING YOUR OWN BACKGROUND PICTURE

Choosing one of Windows 10 FCU's spectacular nature photos adds pizazz to your desktop. But if you really want to say, "This is my computer," there's nothing like adding your own photo. Here's how to do that.

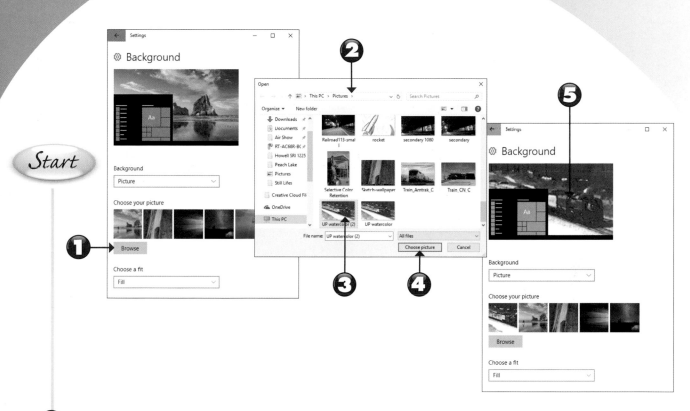

Start

1. Click or tap **Browse** from the Background settings.

2. Navigate to the location of the photo you want to use.

3. Click or tap a picture.

4. Click or tap **Choose picture**.

5. Note the preview of the new selection.

End

TIP

Putting a Slide Show on Your Desktop   Want to show multiple photos? Choose **Slide show** as the background type. You can then navigate to a folder and use its contents. You can also select a picture fit and the frequency for changing photos. ■

CHOOSING A PICTURE FIT

Most of the time, the picture(s) you choose for your background might not be an exact fit. Here's how to use the Choose a Fit menu to select the best setting for your photo.

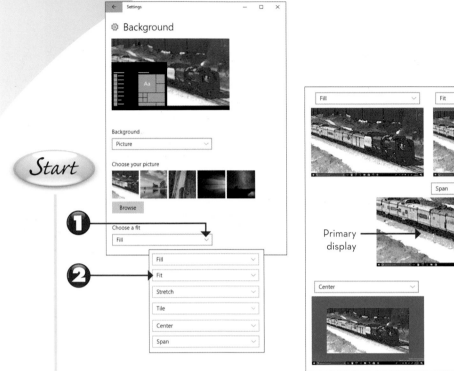

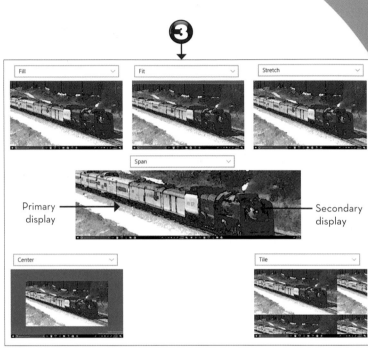

Primary display

Secondary display

Start

1 From the Background settings, click or tap **Choose a fit**.

2 Click or tap to choose a fit option.

3 Here's how the same image looks using different settings on a widescreen display. Depending upon the picture you choose, your results may vary.

Continued

NOTE

Fill Versus Span   Fill does not distort the image and covers the entire desktop, so it's automatically the default. If you use two or more displays and extend the desktop across them, Span covers all desktops with a single image. (The example in step 3 is for two displays with identical resolutions.) ∎

4 This box shows the current fit (Tile).

5 Notice the current background preview.

6 Click or tap to minimize.

7 The Windows desktop uses a personal background.

8 Click or tap to return to the Background settings menu.

End

NOTE

More Background Fit Options When **Fit** is selected, the background will have borders on top/bottom or left/right edges if the image doesn't have the same proportions as the display setting. If the image doesn't have the same proportions as the display setting, selecting **Stretch** distorts the image to fill the desktop. **Tile** repeats an image that is smaller than the desktop to fill it. An image smaller than the desktop will only fill the center of the desktop if you choose **Center**. ■

CHANGING ACCENT COLORS

You can change the accent color used for active apps, dialog boxes, and Start menu tiles with the Colors menu.

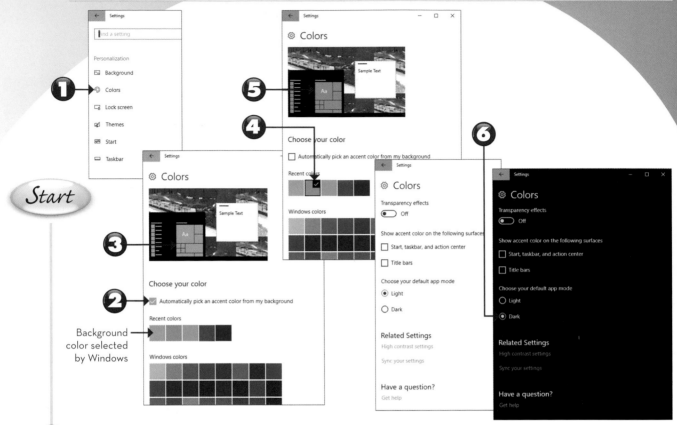

Background color selected by Windows

1 From the Personalization settings, click or tap **Colors**.

2 **Automatically pick an accent color from my background** is the current selection.

3 The preview shows how app windows, tiles, dialog boxes, and other screen elements use the color.

4 Click or tap an accent color.

5 The preview shows how app windows, tiles, dialog boxes, and other screen elements change with the new color selection.

6 Scroll down the Colors settings to view app mode options. Light mode is the default selection; click or tap **Dark** mode to turn white backgrounds to black and reverse black text to white in windows and other screen elements.

End

CHANGING TASKBAR AND START MENU COLORS AND TRANSPARENCY SETTINGS

When you select a color in the Colors settings, you can also use this color in the taskbar and Start menu. Here's how. This example uses the default Light app mode.

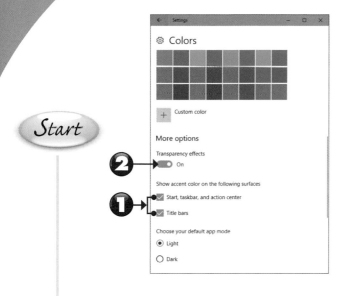

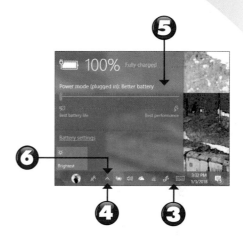

Start

① From the Colors settings, click or tap the empty check boxes for **Start, taskbar, and action center** and **Title bars**.

② Click or press and drag **Transparency effects** to **On**.

③ The taskbar changes to the selected color and displays some transparency.

④ Click or tap **Battery**.

⑤ The battery display changes to the selected color and displays transparency; the desktop background can be seen through the pop-up window.

⑥ Click or tap **Battery** again to close the Battery display.

End

CHANGING START MENU SETTINGS

You can also change the items that appear on the Start menu and its onscreen size. In this lesson, you learn how to make more room for Start menu tiles and how to add folders to the Start menu.

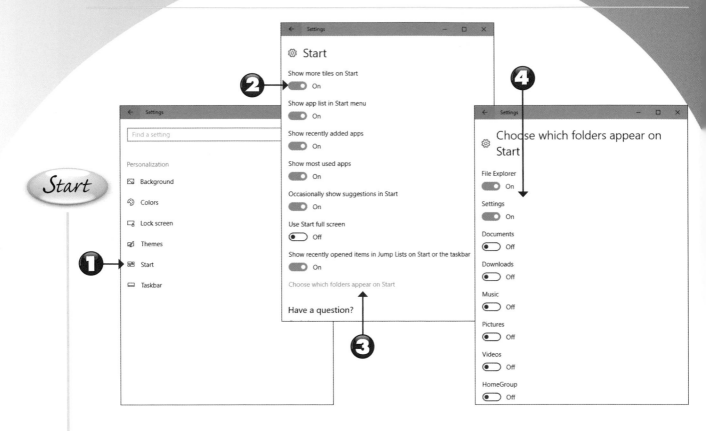

1 From the Personalization settings, click or tap **Start**.

2 Click or press and drag to **On** to show more tiles.

3 Click or tap **Choose which folders appear on Start**.

4 The default Start menu folders (File Explorer and Settings) are already set to the On position.

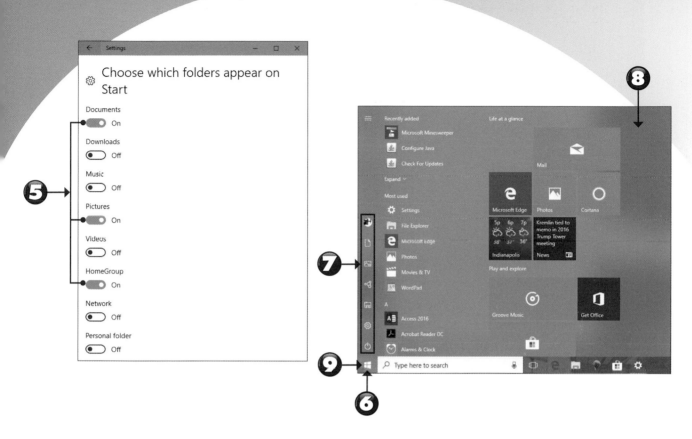

5 To add a folder to the Start menu, click or press and drag to **On**.

6 Click or tap **Start**.

7 In this example, newly added folders display in the menu.

8 Note that more space is added for Start menu tiles.

9 Click or tap **Start** again to close the Start menu.

End

TIP

Using the Additional Start Menu Tile Space   To use the additional space in the Start menu, drag or resize tiles or add programs to the Start menu. To learn more about customizing the Start menu, see Chapter 4. ■

CUSTOMIZING THE TASKBAR

Use the taskbar customization options in Windows 10 FCU to change the appearance of the taskbar. Here's how. For clarity, we changed the color of the taskbar and windows to black.

1 The default taskbar appearance is large taskbar buttons and a large Cortana search window.

2 To customize the taskbar, click or tap **Taskbar** from the Personalization settings.

3 To use small taskbar buttons, click or press and drag to **On**.

4 The taskbar buttons change to the small setting.

5 To use Cortana Search, click the round icon.

Continued

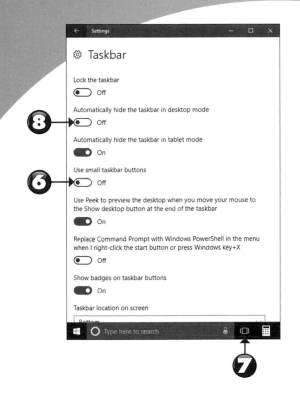

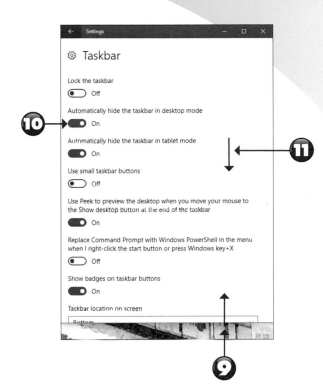

6 To return to the default (large) taskbar buttons, click or press and drag to **Off**.

7 The default taskbar appearance returns.

8 Turn **On** to automatically hide the taskbar in Desktop or Tablet modes.

9 The taskbar disappears until you move your pointing device to the bottom of the screen or touch the bottom of the screen and drag up.

10 Turn **Off** to display the taskbar at all times again.

11 Scroll down the Taskbar settings.

Continued

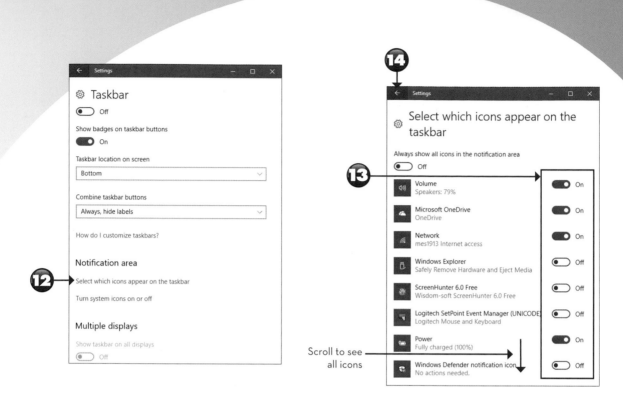

12 Click or tap to select the icons that appear on the taskbar.

13 Select the taskbar icons you want to see with this menu.

14 Click or tap the back arrow to return to the previous settings.

Continued

15 Click or tap to turn on/turn off system icons.

16 Select the system icons you want to see with this menu.

17 Click or tap the back arrow to return to the previous menu. Repeat until the Personalization menu is displayed.

End

NOTE

More Taskbar Options   Lock the taskbar so it can't be dragged to a different side of the screen. Use the **Taskbar location** menu to move the taskbar to the left edge, right edge, or top of the screen. Use the **Combine taskbar buttons** menu to display separate buttons for each instance of an app (Never) or to combine buttons only when the taskbar is full. Use the **Multiple displays** menus to choose whether to display the taskbars on all displays, combine buttons, or specify which display should have taskbar buttons. ■

CUSTOMIZING THE LOCK SCREEN

The Windows lock screen is the first screen you see when you turn on your computer or prepare to log back into it. You can change the picture, change the status messages on it, or change whether that picture is also used when you log in. Here's how.

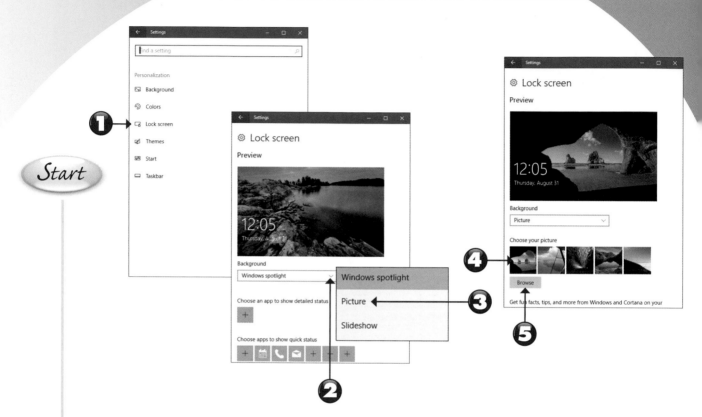

1 From the Personalization settings, click or tap **Lock screen**.

2 Click or tap the **Background** menu.

3 Choose **Picture**.

4 Choose a picture from those displayed to see a preview.

5 Click **Browse** to choose one of your own pictures.

Continued

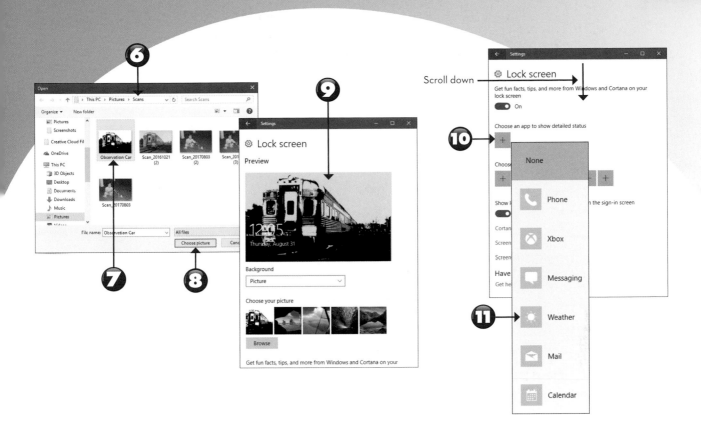

Scroll down

6 Navigate to the picture location.

7 Click or tap the picture.

8 Click or tap **Choose picture**.

9 Preview the new picture.

10 Click or tap to choose an app's details for the Lock screen.

11 Click or tap the app you want.

Continued

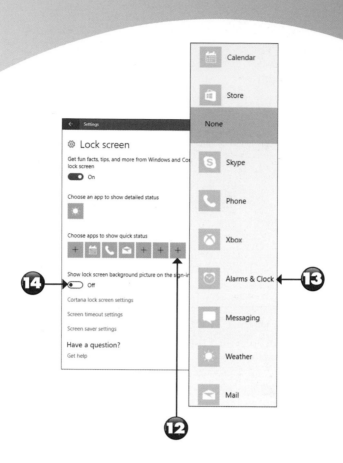

12 Click or tap a + (plus) sign to add an active app's icon to the Lock screen.

13 Click or tap the app you want.

14 To turn off the lock screen background picture, slide this to **Off**.

Continued

15 After you log off, the Lock screen displays the detailed app information below the time.

16 The active apps' icons are displayed to the right of the time.

17 Note the login page after turning off the Lock screen background picture.

End

CUSTOMIZING A THEME

A Windows theme is the collective name for your background, colors, sounds, and mouse cursor settings. In Windows 10 FCU, you can modify and save all four settings from a single location and apply other themes, including those you download.

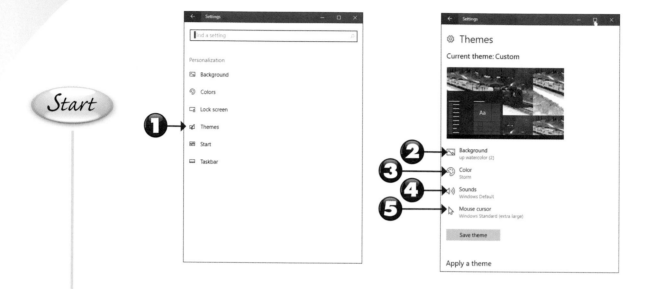

Start

From the Personalization menu, click or tap **Themes**.

Click or tap to change the current background.

Click or tap to change the current color.

Click or tap to change sound settings.

Click or tap to change mouse cursor settings.

Continued

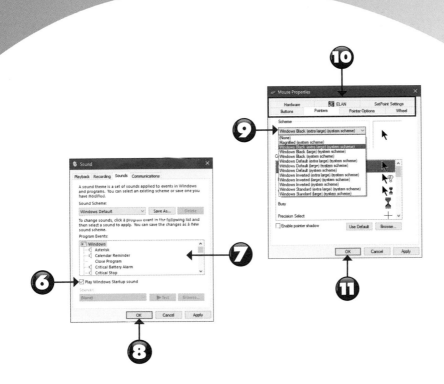

6 From the Sound menu, you can enable Windows Startup sounds.

7 Select program events and assign sounds to them.

8 Click or tap **OK** to return to the Themes menu.

9 Use the Pointers tab in the Mouse Properties menu to change pointer size and color.

10 Change button assignments, touch pad settings, and other options with other tabs.

11 Click or tap **OK** to return to the Themes menu.

Continued

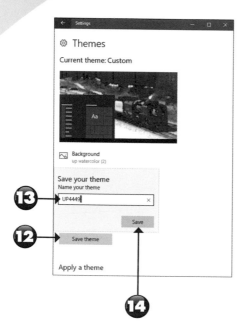

12 After making any changes needed, click or tap **Save theme**.

13 Enter the name of your theme.

14 Click or tap **Save**.

15 View the selected theme.

16 To use a different theme, click or tap it.

End

NOTE

Resetting Your Background Picture Settings   When you save a theme or select a theme, the background picture uses the default Fit setting. After you select a different theme, go back to the Background menu and choose the setting you prefer. ■

ADDING AND MANAGING USERS

Windows 10 Fall Creators Edition provides new and improved ways to log in to your system and keep it secure, whether you are the only user of a device or you share it with others. Windows 10 FCU also includes the new Family options menu, which permits you to set up child accounts that can be monitored and controlled.

Reviewing
your personal
information

Selecting a
user at startup

Additional
users on a
device

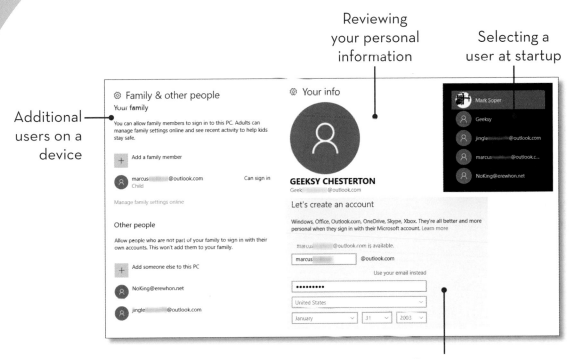

Creating a
Microsoft account

PREPARING TO ADD A USER

A Windows 10 FCU computer always has at least one user account. However, if you share your computer with other users at home or work, each user should have his or her own account. When you use this feature, Windows 10 FCU can provide customized settings for each user, and each user's information can be stored in a separate folder. In this section, you learn how to start the process of selecting the type of user to add from Windows Settings. In later sections, you learn what happens next.

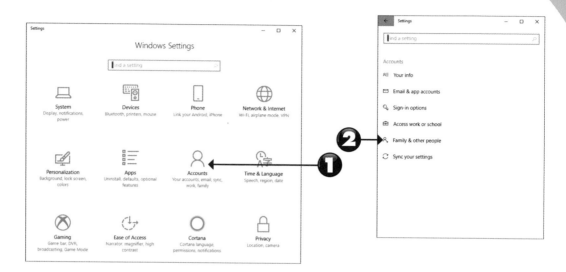

As you follow the exercises in this chapter, you might notice that your computer has a single large window with two sections rather than two separate windows as in this book. We are using small window sizes for apps to help reduce page count.

1 From Windows Settings, click or tap **Accounts**.

2 Click or tap **Family & other people**.

Continued

3 To add an account for a member of your family, click or tap **Add a family member**.

4 To add an account for a co-worker or a friend, click or tap **Add someone else to this PC**.

End

NOTE

Finding Windows Settings To open Windows Settings, click or tap the **Start** menu, and then click or tap **Settings**. To learn more about working with Windows Settings, see Chapter 19, "Managing Windows 10 Fall Creators Update." ■

NOTE

User Types in Windows 10 FCU Use **Add a family member** to add a child's account that can be managed by Windows Defender Security Center's Family options. To continue, see "Adding a Child as a Family Member," p. 484. To add other users, see "Adding Another User Who Has a Windows Account," p. 488 and "Adding a User Who Needs a Microsoft Account," p. 490. To learn more about using Family options, see this book's online content. ■

ADDING A CHILD AS A FAMILY MEMBER

You can add children or adults as users to your Windows 10 FCU device. This example demonstrates adding a child in your household. When you add a child, you can manage his computer and Internet activity with the new Family options built into Windows Defender Security Center. (See online content for details.)

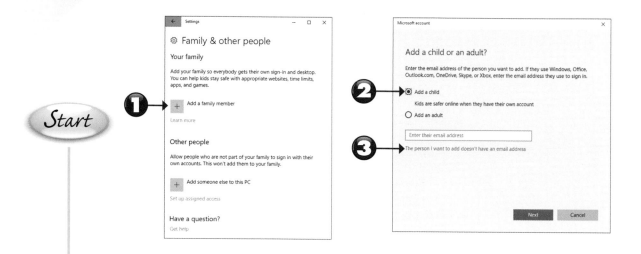

Start

From the Family & other people settings (see the previous task), click or tap **Add a family member**.

Click or tap **Add a child**.

Click or tap this link to create an email address.

Continued

TIP

Adding a Child Who Already Has a Microsoft Account   Add the child's email in the blank provided (after step 2), click or tap **Next**, and click or tap **Confirm**. An invitation is sent to the email address, and after the child confirms the invitation, that account is added to your family members and can be managed by Microsoft Family. ■

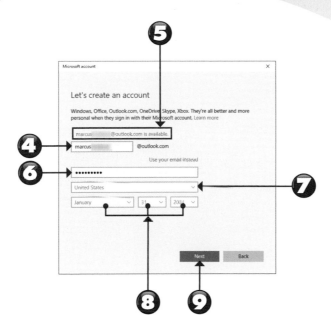

4 Enter an email address. If this address is available, continue; otherwise, try a different address until you find one that is available.

5 The address is available.

6 Enter a password. It must have at least eight characters and at least two of the following: uppercase letter, lowercase letter, symbols, and numbers.

7 Make sure the country is set correctly. If it isn't, open the menu and select your location.

8 Select the correct birthdate (month, day, year).

9 Click or tap **Next** to continue.

Continued

NOTE

Email Addresses and Child Accounts   Microsoft Family now requires that each account it manages has an email address. This example demonstrates creating a Microsoft email address for use by the child account. ◼

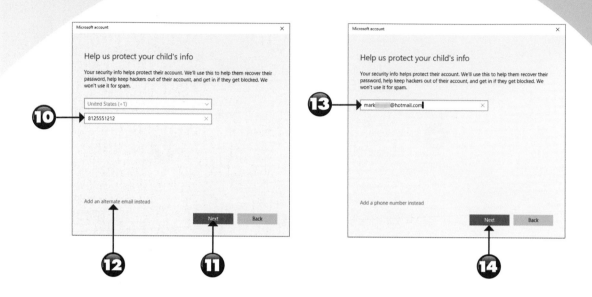

10 To add a phone number for security, click or tap here and enter it.

11 Click or tap **Next** to continue and skip to step 13.

12 To use an alternative email instead, click or tap here.

13 To add an email address for security, click or tap here and enter it.

14 Click or tap **Next**.

Continued

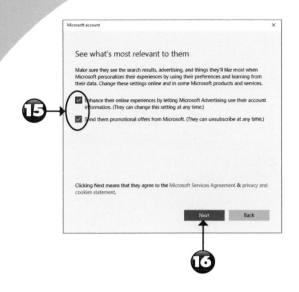

 15 If you don't want your child to receive advertising, clear the check boxes.

16 Click or tap **Next**.

17 Click **Close** to complete the account setup.

End

TIP

Blocking a Child's Account   After you add a child's account to a device, you can block the account from using that device: Click or tap the account name, and click or tap **Block**. You can allow the account at any time. ■

ADDING ANOTHER USER WHO HAS A WINDOWS ACCOUNT

Need to share your Windows 10 FCU device with a co-worker or want to set up an account for a roommate? Here's how to provide other adults with their own accounts on your system if they already have Windows accounts.

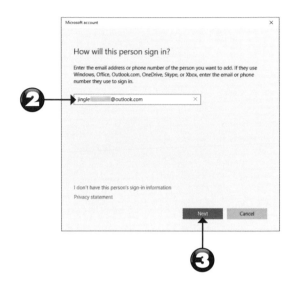

1 From the Family & other people settings, click or tap **Add someone else to this PC**.

2 Enter the email address from the user's Microsoft account.

3 Click or tap **Next**.

Continued

NOTE

Benefits of a Microsoft Account With a Microsoft account, all of a user's online email, photos, files, and settings (favorites, browser history, and so on) are available on any Windows 10 FCU device that person signs in to (as long as those files are stored on OneDrive, that is). A Microsoft account can also be used to purchase or rent apps, TV shows, and movies from the Microsoft Store. ■

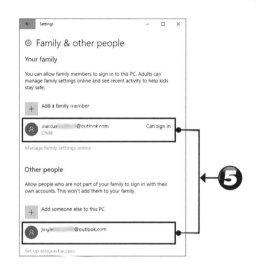

4 Click or tap **Finish**.

5 Users you added are now listed on the Family & other people page in Settings.

End

ADDING A USER WHO NEEDS A MICROSOFT ACCOUNT

As you saw in the previous exercise, there are a lot of good reasons for a user to have a Microsoft account—especially since a Microsoft account is free. Here's how to create one using an existing non-Microsoft email address.

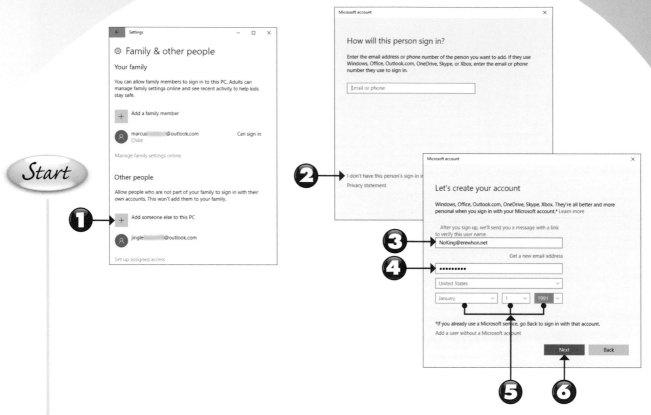

1 From the Family & other people settings, go to the Other people section and click or tap **Add someone else to this PC**.

2 Click or tap **I don't have this person's sign-in information**.

3 Enter the user's current (non-Microsoft) email address.

4 Enter the password that will be used to log into this computer or other Microsoft services.

5 Select the user's birthdate.

6 Click or tap **Next**.

Continued

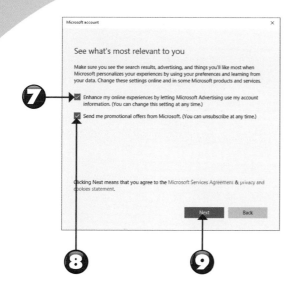

7 To opt out of letting Microsoft Advertising use your account information, clear this check box.

8 To opt out of receiving promotional offers from Microsoft, clear this check box.

9 Click or tap **Next**.

10 The new user is listed in the Other People section of the Family & other people page.

End

SELECTING AN ACCOUNT TO LOG IN TO

After you add one or more additional users, Windows 10 FCU offers you a choice of accounts at startup or whenever the computer is locked. Here's how to choose the account you want.

Start

1 Press any key (such as the spacebar) or swipe up on the screen (if you have a touchscreen).

2 If the account you want is selected, log in as usual.

Continued

3 Click or tap the account you want to log in to.

4 Log in to the selected account.

End

CHANGING AN ACCOUNT TYPE

The first account on a Windows 10 FCU computer is an administrator account. The administrator can add, change, or remove accounts and can install apps and make other changes that affect all users. When you create an additional user account in Windows 10 FCU, it's a standard account. If you want another user's account to be set as administrator of the computer, follow these steps.

1 Make sure you're logged in to your own administrator account, and then open Windows Settings to **Accounts**.

2 Click or tap **Family & other people**.

3 Click or tap the account to change.

4 Click or tap **Change account type**.

Continued

NOTE

Standard, Administrator, and Child Accounts   A standard account needs administrator permission (given through User Account Control) to complete tasks that could change the computer. An administrator account can perform all tasks. A child account is similar to a standard account but can also be monitored by Windows Defender Security Center's Family options. ■

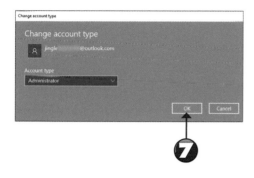

5 Click or tap to open the **Account type** menu.

6 Select **Administrator** as the account type.

7 Click or tap **OK**.

8 The user is now listed as an administrator.

9 Click or tap to return to the Accounts page.

End

NOTE

Why You Might Need Two Administrators When would you want to create more than one administrator account for a computer? There might be times when the original administrator is not available while the computer is in use and systemwide changes need to be made—such as new programs or hardware installations. Be sure that the user you select is trustworthy and not likely to mess around with the computer just for fun. ◼

Chapter 23

PROTECTING YOUR SYSTEM

Computers and storage devices have never been less expensive, but the information you store on them—from documents to photos, video, and music—is priceless. In this chapter, you learn about a variety of easy-to-use features in Windows 10 FCU that are designed to help you protect your computer's contents.

Installing an update with Windows Update

Windows Defender Security Center system status

Backup settings

The Update & Security menu

Preparing to restore a file with File History

Preparing to remove threats with Windows Defender Security Center

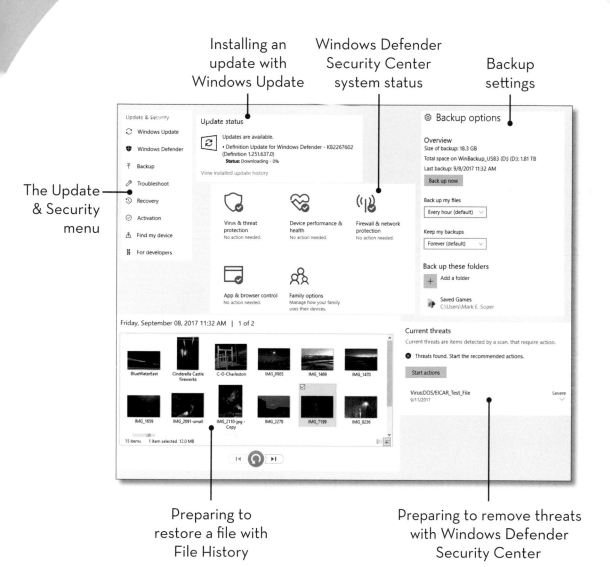

CHECKING FOR WINDOWS UPDATES

Windows Update is your first line of defense against computer problems. It is normally set to automatically download and install updates for Microsoft Windows 10 FCU and for other Microsoft apps such as Office. However, you can check for updates whenever you want using the Windows Update feature in the Settings dialog box. This is a good idea if you hear about a security problem.

Start

Desktop mode

Tablet mode

❶ Click or tap the **Start** button.

❷ Click or tap **Settings**.

❸ Click or tap **Update & Security**.

Continued

NOTE

What Does an Update Do?   Want to know more about an update? Click or tap the **View installed update history** link (step 6), and click or tap the **Successfully installed** link for an update to display its description. The description includes a **More info** link in case you need to learn more. ■

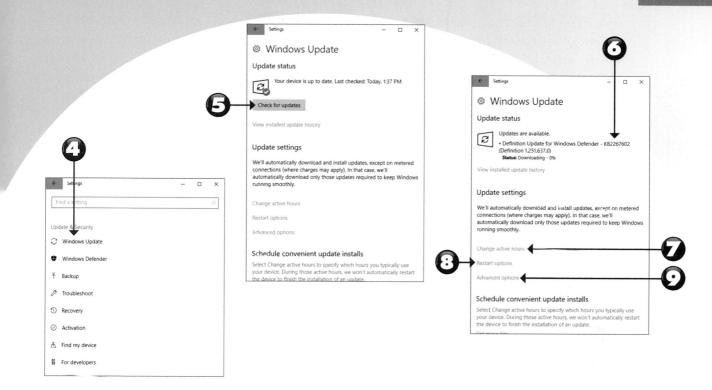

4 Click or tap **Windows Update**.

5 Click or tap **Check for updates**.

6 If there are any updates, they are downloaded and installed automatically.

7 Click or tap to change the hours you use your device so Windows Update will not restart your system when it's in use.

8 Click or tap to specify when to restart your system to finish an update.

9 Click or tap if you want to pause updates or use other computers on your network (Delivery optimization) to help updates go faster.

End

PROTECTING YOUR FILES WITH FILE HISTORY

The information on your device is the one thing you can't replace—*unless* you make backup copies on a separate drive. The File History feature is part of the Backup settings in Settings dialog box. Before starting this task, make sure you have connected a USB hard disk to your computer. (I recommend getting one that's at least twice the size of your system hard disk.)

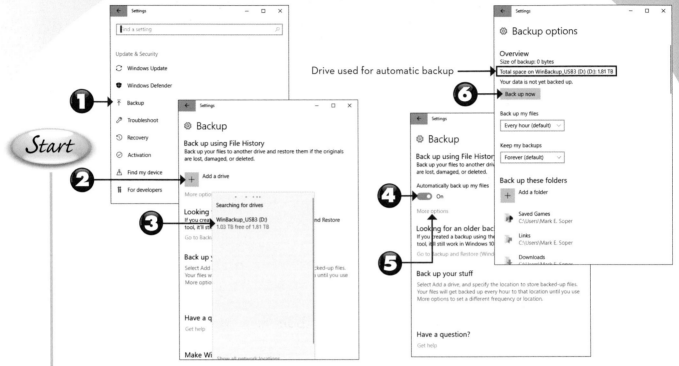

Drive used for automatic backup

Start

① With the Update & Security settings dialog open, click or tap **Backup**.

② If prompted, click **Add a drive**.

③ Click a drive with adequate space.

④ Set **Automatically back up my files** to **On**.

⑤ Click or tap **More options**.

⑥ Click or tap **Back up now**.

Continued

NOTE

Retrieving Backups Made with Windows 7   Windows 10 FCU includes the Windows 7 Backup and Restore, so you can retrieve files from a backup you made with this tool. To learn more about using this tool, see www.que-publishing.com/articles/article.aspx?p=1396503 and www.quepublishing.com/articles/article.aspx?p=1400869. ▪

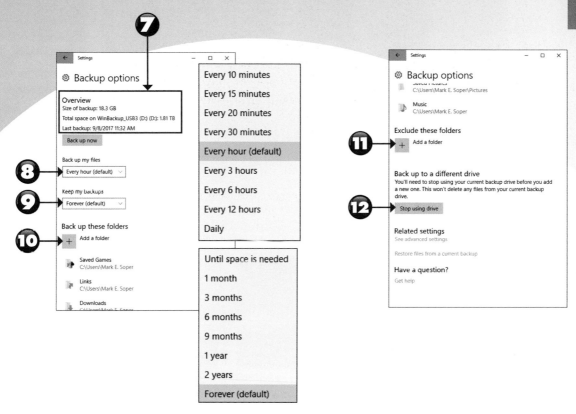

7 After the backup is over, review information about it.

8 Click or tap to change how often File History is run.

9 Click or tap to change how long to keep File History backups.

10 Click or tap to add a folder to the backup.

11 You can exclude a folder from the backup by clicking or tapping **Add a folder** and choosing the folder.

12 If you want to use a different drive for File History, click or tap **Stop using drive**. You can then select a different drive for File History.

End

CAUTION

Backing Up the AppData Folder Although File History backs up all of the current user's visible data folders, hidden folders such as AppData are not backed up by default. To add a hidden folder to your backup, you must first open File Explorer, open the View tab, and make sure the **Hidden items** check box is checked. You can then use **Add a folder** to select AppData for backup. For more information about using File Explorer, see "Using the View Tab" (p. 282) in Chapter 14. ∎

RECOVERING FILES WITH FILE HISTORY

File History creates backups of your files so if a file is erased or damaged, you can get it back. If you haven't yet enabled File History in Windows 10 FCU and run a backup, refer to "Protecting Your Files with File History," earlier in this chapter. Here's how to retrieve a lost file or folder after it's deleted. This exercise demonstrates deleting and retrieving a file.

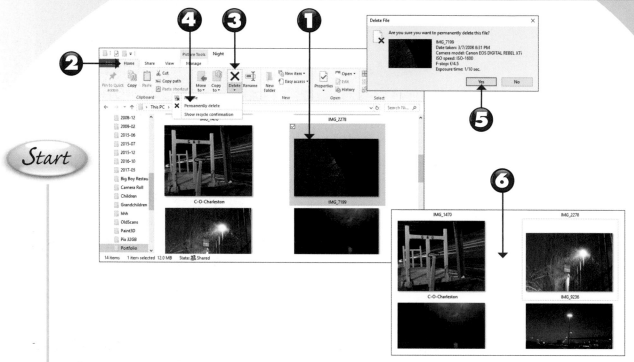

Start

1 After running a backup with File History, open File Explorer and click or tap a photo in your Pictures folder.

2 Click or tap the **Home** tab.

3 Open the **Delete** menu.

4 Click or tap **Permanently delete**.

5 Click or tap **Yes** to delete the file.

6 The file is removed.

Continued

NOTE

Making a File Copy If you're worried about losing your file, make a copy of it before starting this exercise. See Chapter 14 for details. ◼

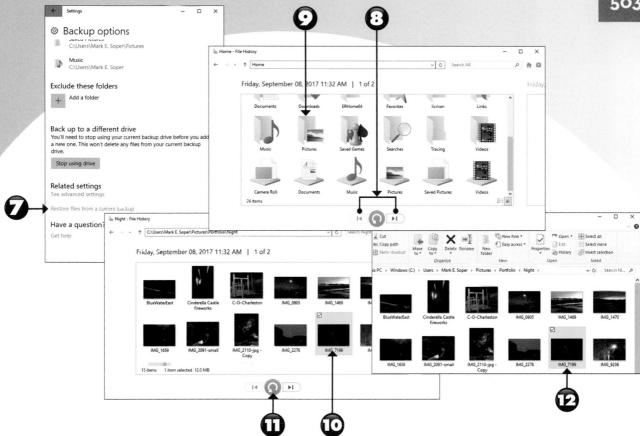

7 From the Backup options in the Settings dialog box, click or tap **Restore files from a current backup**.

8 Click or tap left or right arrows if necessary to locate the backup from which to restore.

9 Click or tap down and scroll through the folders until you reach the folder from which to restore.

10 Click or tap the file (or folder) to restore.

11 Click or tap the green **Restore** button.

12 File Explorer opens. The file or folder (and contents) is returned to its original location.

End

NOTE

Selecting a Version If the left and/or right arrows at the bottom of the File History dialog box can be clicked or tapped, you can select a different version of the folder or file. The most recent version is shown first. ■

TIP

Restoring Multiple Files from a Folder To restore only selected files, click the first file you want to restore, and then use Ctrl+click to select additional files. When you click or tap the **Restore** button, only the files you selected will be restored. ■

USING AND CONFIGURING WINDOWS DEFENDER SECURITY CENTER

In Windows 10 FCU, the Windows Defender app has been completely redesigned to provide a one-stop resource for protecting your computer against malware, viruses, and other types of threats from email, the Web, and downloads. In this task, you learn how to start it from the Update & Security settings dialog box and how to scan for malware.

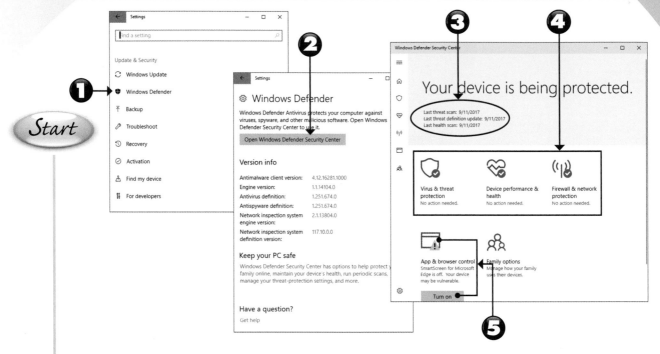

1 Open the Settings dialog box to the Update & Security settings, and click or tap **Windows Defender**.

2 Click **Open Windows Defender Security Center**.

3 View the most recent scan and update information.

4 Enabled protection features are listed here.

5 Here you see a disabled protection feature. Click **Turn on**.

Continued

NOTE

Smart Screen Protection   Smart Screen protection (step 5) protects you from threats when you use the default Microsoft Edge web browser. If it is turned off, you might download potentially dangerous content or access potentially dangerous websites. Keep Smart Screen enabled for best protection while using the Web. ■

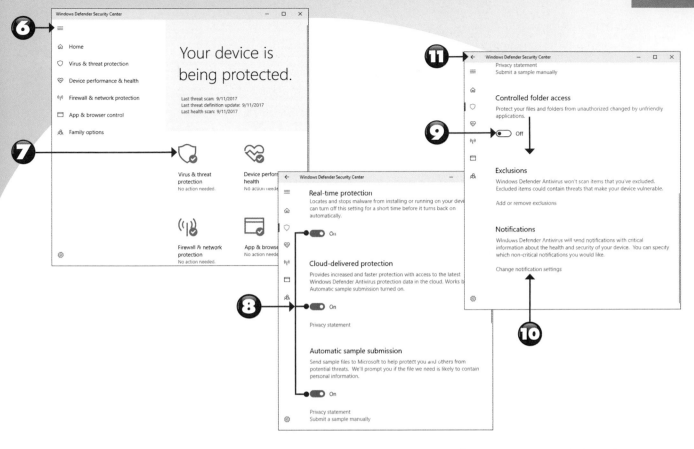

6 Click or tap to expand the menu. You can access features from either the dialog shown in steps 4–5 or from the menu.

7 Click or tap **Virus & threat protection** and **Virus & threat protection settings** to view or change settings.

8 Make sure Real-time protection, Cloud-based protection, and Automatic sample submission are turned **On** for maximum protection.

9 Scroll down or flick up and enable **Controlled folder access** to help protect selected folders from ransomware or other attacks.

10 By default, antivirus and firewall notifications are enabled. Open this menu to turn off selected notifications.

11 Click or tap to return to the previous menu.

End

NOTE

Testing Controlled Folder Access To see how Controlled Folder Access can protect your system, visit https://docs.microsoft.com/en-us/windows/threat-protection/windows-defender-exploit-guard/evaluate-controlled-folder-access and follow the instructions. ■

SCANNING FOR MALWARE WITH WINDOWS DEFENDER

The Windows Defender program included with Windows 10 FCU provides real-time protection against spyware, malware, and viruses. In addition to real-time protection, Defender can scan your system for malware. In this exercise, you learn how to run a scan and what to do with malware after it is discovered.

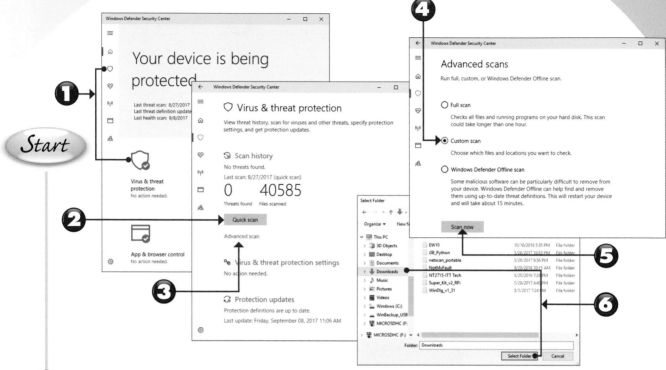

1 From the main menu, click or tap **Virus & threat protection**.

2 Choose **Quick scan** for an immediate scan of the most likely locations for malware infections.

3 Click or tap **Advanced scan** for more scanning options.

4 If you selected Advanced scan, choose the scan type.

5 Click or tap **Scan now**.

6 If you select Advanced scan, choose the folder to scan and click or tap **Select Folder** to start the scan process.

Continued

NOTE

Full and Offline Scans   Use **Full scan** to scan the entire system. Use **Offline scan** to remove malware that cannot be removed when you are connected to the Internet. ∎

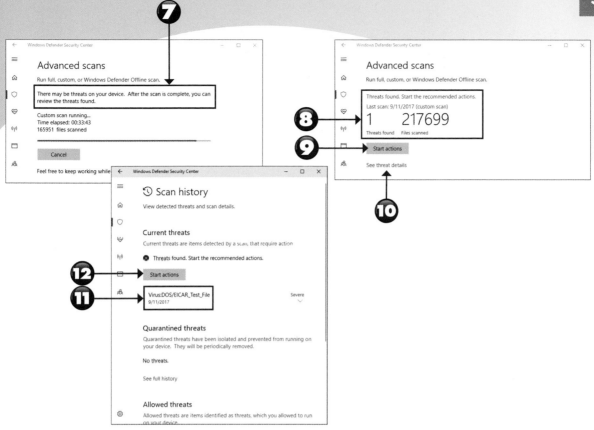

7 If malware is detected, you are notified before the scan is complete.

8 Here you see the results of the scan.

9 To remove threats, click or tap **Start actions**.

10 To see more information, click or tap **See threat details**.

11 Note the threats detected on your system.

12 Click or tap **Start actions** to remove threats.

End

NOTE

Viewing More Information About Threats Click or tap the **See full history** links to learn about quarantined or allowed threats. ▪

Chapter 24

SYSTEM MAINTENANCE AND PERFORMANCE

Windows 10 FCU includes a variety of tools that help solve problems and keep Windows working at peak efficiency. In this chapter, you learn how to use drive error-checking, check battery charge settings, use troubleshooters, view open apps with Task Manager, and fix Windows problems with Refresh.

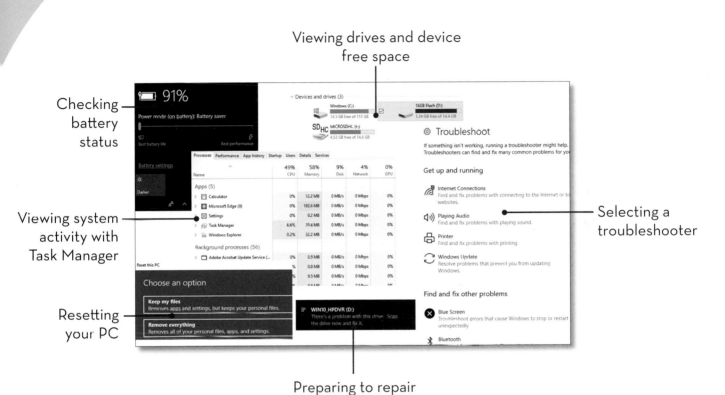

Viewing drives and device
free space

Checking
battery
status

Viewing system
activity with
Task Manager

Resetting
your PC

Selecting a
troubleshooter

Preparing to repair
a drive

CHECKING CHARGE LEVEL

If you use a device that runs on battery power, you can quickly check its charge level from the Windows 10 FCU taskbar. Here's how.

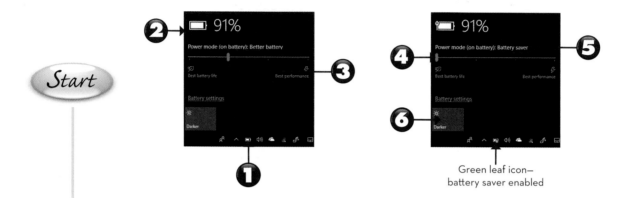

Green leaf icon—
battery saver enabled

Start

1 Click or tap the battery icon in the taskbar. (If it is not visible, click or tap the up-arrow icon.)

2 The battery charge level and power mode are displayed.

3 Use the slider (if present) to adjust the balance between longer battery life (left) and faster performance (right).

4 To turn on battery saver, click and drag the slider all the way to the left.

5 Battery saver is now enabled.

6 Tap the brightness button to move through standard brightness levels.

End

NOTE

Learning More About Battery Saver To learn more about adjusting how apps use battery power, see "Using Battery Saver," in Chapter 19, "Managing Windows 10 Fall Creators Update." ■

SELECTING A POWER SCHEME

With laptops, desktops, and all-in-one devices, you can select a power scheme in Windows 10 FCU that will stretch battery life as far as possible or keep your system running at top speed all the time. Here's how to select the power scheme you want from the Windows taskbar.

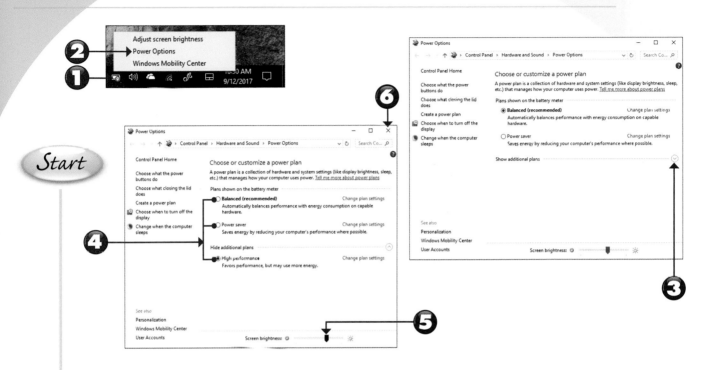

From the taskbar, press and hold or right-click the **power** (battery meter) icon in the notification area. Click or tap the up arrow if necessary to view the icon.

2 Click or tap **Power Options**.

3 The most common power options are shown. To see additional options, click or tap **Show additional plans**.

4 Choose a plan setting from those listed.

5 Click or press and drag to the left to make the built-in screen darker, or to the right to make the screen brighter.

6 Close the dialog box when finished.

End

NOTE

Tablets, Laptops, and Power Schemes   Available power schemes vary by device. For example, Tablets offer only one power scheme: Balanced. Some laptop computers might not offer Power Saver as an option. ■

VIEWING DISK INFORMATION

How much space is left on your drive? What drive letter does your external hard disk use? Use the This PC view in File Explorer for answers to these and other questions about the drives built in to and connected to your computer.

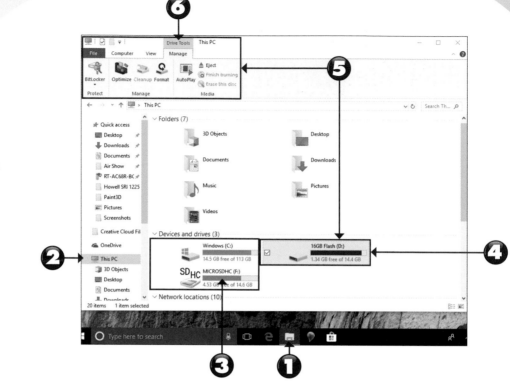

Start

1 From the taskbar (or Start menu or All apps), click or tap **File Explorer**.

2 Click or tap **This PC**.

3 The blue bar indicates how much space is used on the drive.

4 The bar turns red if the drive has less than 10% free space.

5 Click or tap a drive to display the Drive Tools tab.

6 Click or tap the Drive Tools tab to manage your storage devices.

End

NOTE

Using the View Tab If you do not see bars listing drive capacity, click or tap the **View** tab and select **Tiles** from the **Layout** menu. ■

CHECKING DRIVES FOR ERRORS WHEN CONNECTED

As drives are connected to your system, Windows 10 FCU watches for errors. If an error is detected, Notifications displays a message. Here's what to do next.

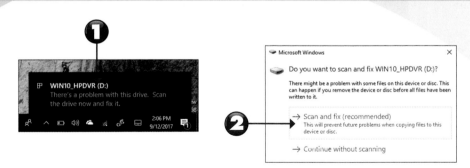

 Start

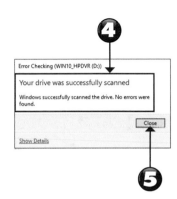

1 This just-inserted flash drive has a problem—click the notification.

2 Click **Scan and fix**.

3 Click **Repair drive**.

4 View the results. On drives with minor errors, you might see a message like this one.

5 Click or tap **Close**.

End

NOTE

Drive Error Causes Removing a drive during a data write or erase process can cause a drive error that could lead to the file being written becoming unreadable. However, if a drive that is properly used and ejected continues to have errors, it might be in danger of complete failure, causing widespread data loss. A hard drive that displays a S.M.A.R.T. error is about to fail. Use the drive vendor's diagnostic software to determine a drive's condition. ■

CHECKING DRIVES FOR ERRORS WITH THIS PC

You can check a drive for errors at any time using This PC. Here's how.

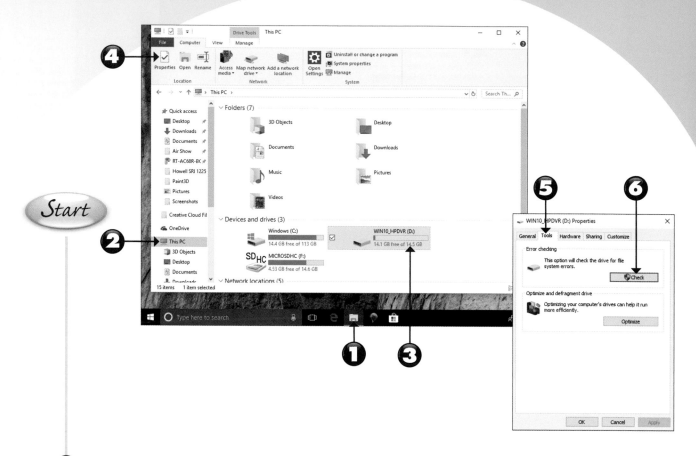

1 Open File Explorer.

2 Click or tap **This PC**.

3 Click or tap the drive you want to check for errors.

4 Click or tap **Properties**.

5 Click or tap **Tools**.

6 Click or tap **Check**.

Continued

7 This drive has errors. Click or tap to repair the errors.

8 The drive has been successfully repaired.

9 Click or tap **Close**.

10 Click or tap **OK**.

End

USING WINDOWS TROUBLESHOOTERS

Windows 10 FCU includes more troubleshooters than ever before to help solve problems with your system. Although some troubleshooters are found in the menus for devices, they are also available with a single search. Here's how to search and use a troubleshooter. In this example, I disconnected from my wireless network before starting the troubleshooter.

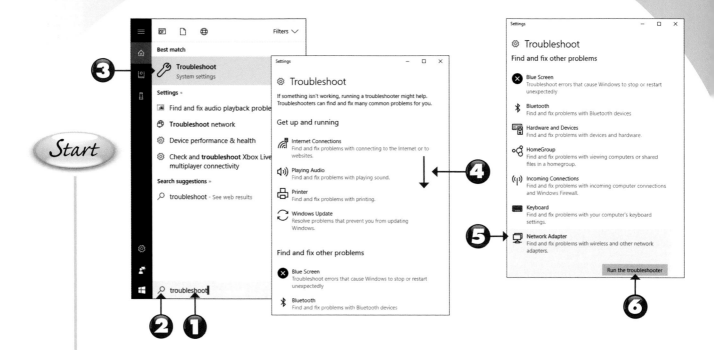

Start

1 Click or tap the Cortana/Search window.

2 Enter part or all of the word **troubleshoot**.

3 Click or tap **Troubleshoot**.

4 Scroll through the list of troubleshooters.

5 Click **Network Adapter**.

6 Click or tap **Run the troubleshooter**.

Continued

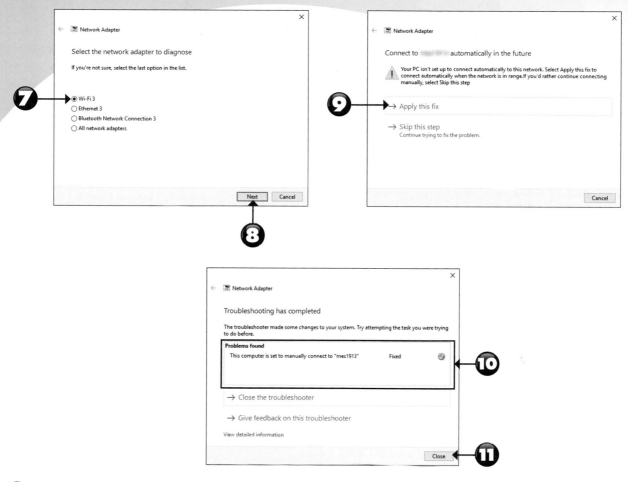

7 If prompted, choose what to diagnose.

8 Click or tap **Next**.

9 Click **Apply this fix** or perform the change recommended.

10 Review the results.

11 Click or tap **Close** to close the window.

End

NOTE

Helping the Repair Process If you need to turn on a device, plug in a cable, or make other changes to your system, you are prompted to do so during the process. ◼

STARTING TASK MANAGER WITH A MOUSE OR TOUCHSCREEN

You can have many programs running at the same time with Windows 10 FCU, even if you see only one program window visible and your taskbar is hidden. However, a running program that is not working properly can cause problems with your system. You can quickly find out what programs and apps are running at a given moment using Windows Task Manager. In this exercise, you learn how to open Task Manager with a mouse or touchscreen.

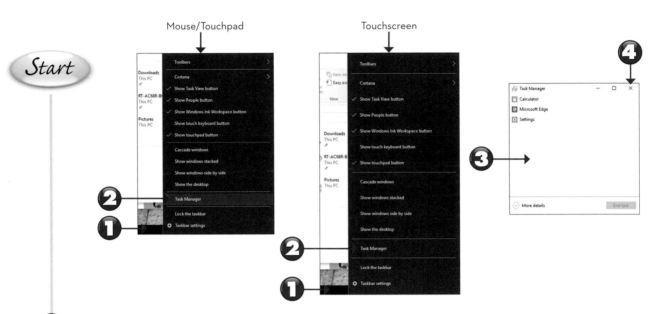

Mouse/Touchpad   Touchscreen

1 With a mouse or touchpad, right-click an empty portion of the taskbar (if visible).

2 Select **Task Manager**.

1 With a touchscreen, press and hold an empty portion of the taskbar (if visible).

2 Select **Task Manager**.

3 Task Manager opens (simple view shown), displaying the currently open apps.

4 Close the window.

STARTING TASK MANAGER FROM THE KEYBOARD

You can easily start Task Manager without taking your hands off the keyboard to view what programs and apps are currently running. This is helpful if your system is configured to hide the taskbar.

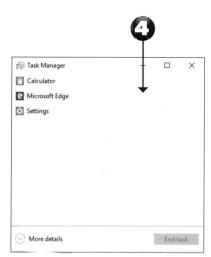

Start

1. Press and hold the **Ctrl** key on your keyboard.

2. Press and hold the **Shift** key.

3. Press the **Esc** key.

4. Task Manager (simple view shown) displays the list of running programs and apps.

End

NOTE

More Ways to Start Task Manager The Task Manager app is known as Task Manager. You can use Windows Search to locate and run it. Task Manager's executable (program) file is called taskmgr.exe, and you can also start it by using the **Run** command. ■

NOTE

Simple and Detailed Views Task Manager might open in detailed view (see next task) instead of simple view. You can switch views by clicking or tapping the **More details/Fewer details** arrow at the bottom of the Task Manager window. ■

VIEWING AND CLOSING RUNNING APPS WITH TASK MANAGER

Task Manager displays active (running) apps. It can also provide a detailed view of services and other activities that are running. In this task, you learn how to change views and how to close a running app.

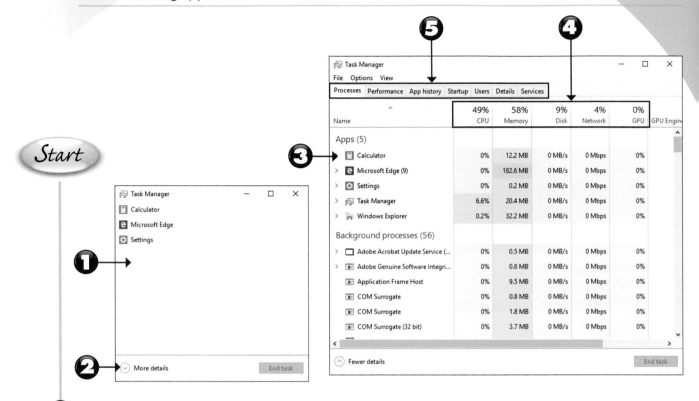

Start

1 With Task Manager open, you can view a list of currently running apps.

2 Click or tap **More details** to switch to detailed view.

3 The Apps section of the Processes tab lists actively running programs.

4 You can view the percentage of CPU, memory, disk activity, network activity, and GPU in use in real time.

5 Click or tap a tab to learn more.

Continued

NOTE

Dealing with a "Not responding" App   If Task Manager indicates that an app is Not responding (simple view), the app has stopped working. Click or tap the app to select it. Then click or tap **End task** to shut it down. ■

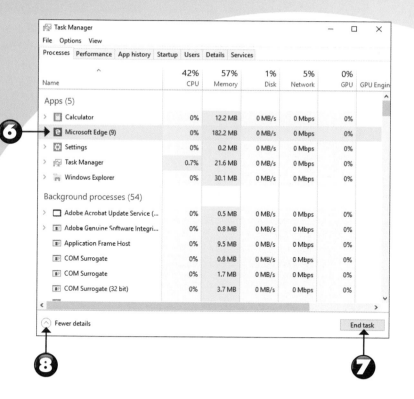

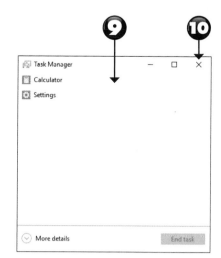

6 From the Processes tab, click or tap an app you want to close.

7 Click or tap **End task**.

8 Click or tap **Fewer details** to return to simple view.

9 Task Manager switches back to simple view, and the app you closed is no longer listed among the open apps.

10 Click or tap to close Task Manager.

End

NOTE

Apps in Detailed View Detailed view also displays apps that are not listed in simple view, such as File Explorer and Task Manager. ■

NOTE

Closing Apps and Tasks In either detailed or simple view, you can close an app or process by clicking/tapping it and then clicking/tapping **End task**. ■

VIEWING TAB DETAILS IN TASK MANAGER

Task Manager can provide a detailed view of services and activities that are running on your machine. In this task, you look at the various tabs at the top of the Task Manager screen.

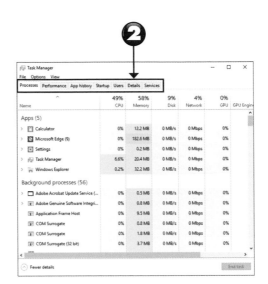

Start

1 With Task Manager open, click or tap **More details** to switch to detailed view.

2 Click or tap a tab to learn more about apps, services, and other details about your computer.

Continued

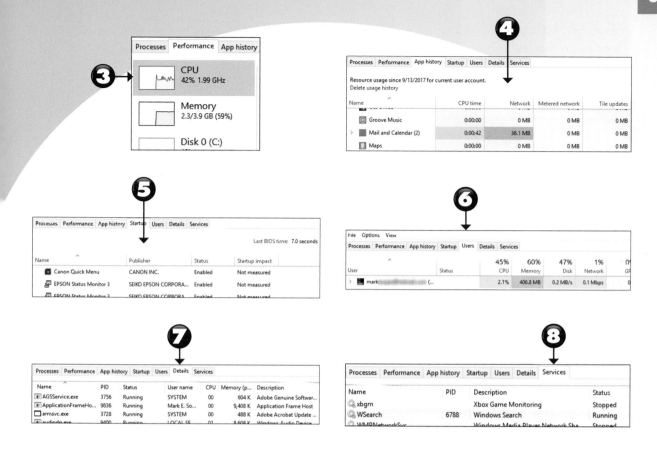

3 The Performance tab shows the performance of system components.

4 The App history tab shows app usage of system resources.

5 The Startup tab shows your startup programs.

6 The Users tab shows the current users of this computer.

7 The Details tab shows apps and process details.

8 The Services tab shows system services.

End

USING RESET

If you're not sure why Windows 10 FCU isn't running correctly, or your system has gradually been running more slowly, the problem could be apps and programs that didn't come from the Microsoft Store. You can use the Reset feature to reinstall Windows 10 FCU for you while retaining your personal files. In this tutorial, you learn how to run Reset with these options.

1 In Desktop mode, click or tap **Start**.

2 In either Desktop or Tablet mode, click or tap **Settings** (gear).

3 Click or tap **Update & Security**.

Continued

NOTE

Refresh and Restore Options Now Included in Reset The Refresh and Restore options included in Windows 8.1 have now been combined as **Reset this PC**. ■

NOTE

Go Back to the Previous Version of Windows 10 This option (not shown in this exercise) is visible for ten days after you upgrade to a major feature release of Windows 10, such as the Fall Creators Update. Use the option if your system runs very poorly after upgrading to Windows 10 FCU. ■

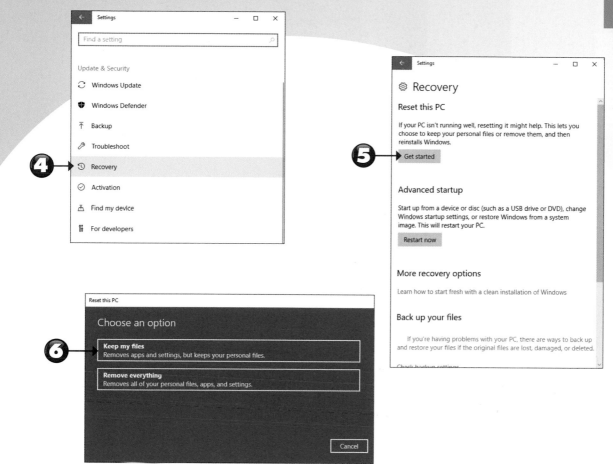

4 Click or tap **Recovery**.

5 Click or tap **Get started** in the Reset this PC section.

6 Click or tap **Keep my files**.

Continued

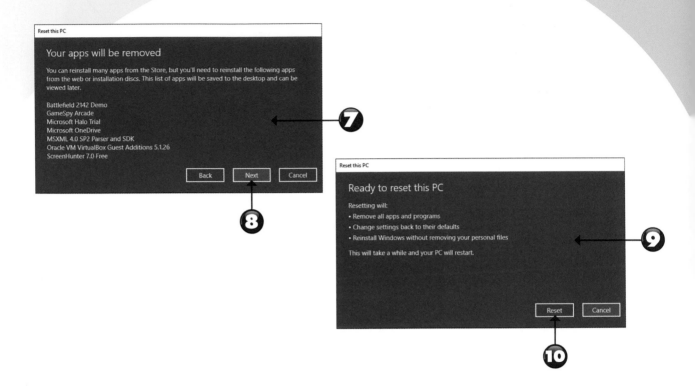

7 A list of apps that will be removed appears; if you want to use them again, you must reinstall them after Reset is finished.

8 Click or tap **Next**.

9 Review what the Reset process does.

10 Click or tap **Reset**. Windows restarts and runs the Reset process.

Continued

NOTE

Reinstalling Apps and Programs   If you need to reinstall some apps, either revisit the Microsoft Store or use the original discs or download files to reinstall programs from other sources. ■

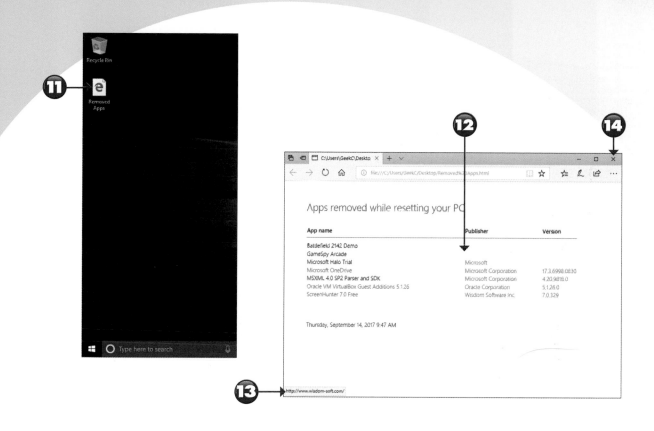

11 After Windows restarts and you log back in to your system, double-click or double-tap **Removed Apps**.

12 Your default browser opens an HTML file containing a list of apps removed during the Reset process.

13 Hover your mouse over a link to see the URL. Click it to go to the app's website for more information.

14 Click or tap to close.

End

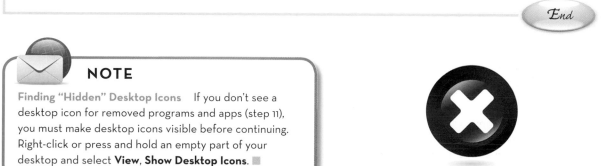

NOTE

Finding "Hidden" Desktop Icons   If you don't see a desktop icon for removed programs and apps (step 11), you must make desktop icons visible before continuing. Right-click or press and hold an empty part of your desktop and select **View, Show Desktop Icons**. ■

Symbols

A

D

G